WARLORD
Tojo
Against the World

Also by Edwin P. Hoyt

Hirohito
Yamamoto
Japan's War
The Militarists: The Rise of Japanese Militarism
  Since World War II
Guadalcanal
The Glory of the Solomons
To the Marianas
Storm Over the Gilberts
The Lonely Ships
The Great Pacific Conflict
The Carrier War
The Battle of Leyte Gulf
Blue Skies and Blood: The Battle of the Coral Sea
Closing the Circle: War in the Pacific: 1945
The Kamikazes

WARLORD

Tojo
Against the World

Edwin P. Hoyt

Scarborough House

Scarborough House
Lanham, MD 20706

FIRST PUBLISHED IN 1993

Library of Congress Cataloging-in-Publication Data

Hoyt, Edwin Palmer.
Warlord : Tojo against the world / Edwin P. Hoyt.
p. cm.
Includes bibliographical references and index.
1. T⁻ojō, Hideki, 1884–1948. 2. Prime ministers—
Japan—Biography. 3. Generals—Japan—Biography.
4. Japan—Politics and government—1912–1945.
DS890.T57H69 1993
952.03'3'092—dc20 92–46439 CIP
[B]

ISBN 0–8128–4017–8

Contents

Illustrations

Tojo: How He Was
An Introduction by Ian Mutsu

Ian Mutsu, president of the International Motion Picture Company of Japan, was born into the Japanese nobility—son of a famous family; his father was a diplomat, and his grandfather was foreign minister at the time of the Sino-Japanese war. His mother was an Englishwoman, and Ian studied at the University of Birmingham in England, so although he was born in Japan and has lived most of his adult life there, he is as much at home at an English dinner party as at a formal Japanese bansankai. When General Hideki Tojo first came to the attention of Japan, Ian Mutsu was a young journalist, working on the Japan Advertiser, *an English-language newspaper, in Tokyo. Later he moved to Domei, the Japanese news agency, where he reformed that company's international service; that is where he was working when Tojo became prime minister of Japan.*

I have not forgotten that day: I was visiting Shanghai on Domei business. The manager of the Shanghai branch and I were dining at a Japanese restaurant with Captain Komata, the naval public information officer attached to the fleet in Shanghai, and Colonel Akiyama, the Army information officer. Someone came to the table to deliver a message to the colonel. Akiyama read it. "The Emperor has asked General Hideki Tojo to form a cabinet," he said. Captain Komata looked blank. Tojo was virtually unknown outside the Army although he had been prime minister Prince Konoye's Army minister in two cabinets.

The colonel smiled broadly.

"Now we will have war," he predicted.

The Emperor actually believed he was appointing a man who could control the Imperial Army, but by that time—October 1941—the Army was out of control. The Marquis Kido is the one who engineered the Tojo appointment. Later he said he had done so on the principle of an old Japanese proverb: *dokuō motte dokuō seisu*—fight poison with poison. The allusion is to the fact that the Imperial Army by 1941 had become toxic to the nation and it seemed likely that only a general could control that army. Because Tojo appeared to be mild-mannered and malleable, his underlying fierce nature was often overlooked. One must examine his background: he came to prominence in the Army through the *Kempeitai*, the Army secret police. He had been sent to Manchuria to bring under control for the Tokyo Army Headquarters authorities the fractious Kwantung Army, after the coup in which that theoretically subordinate command seized Manchuria from its Chinese warlord master.

Tojo had the nickname "*Kamisori*"—razor—which was generally attributed to his possession of what was perceived to be a sharp and cutting mind. But there is another explanation for the sobriquet: a razor cuts swiftly and cleanly, and that is what Tojo's *Kempeitai* did in Manchuria; they brought the Kwantung Army under control by spying, and by threatening. The *Kempeitai* had a reputation throughout Japan as the most vicious sort of secret police agency; those it arrested were routinely tortured during questioning, although they might never be charged with any crime. And from the Manchuria days, the *Kempeitai*, first in Manchuria and then throughout Japan, was loyal to General Tojo, its master as minister of the Army.

One of Tojo's real attributes was loyalty to the Emperor, and that was why those around the Imperial Palace believed his having been chosen might work for the peace that the Emperor wanted. But Tojo had another loyalty, to the Army, and in 1941 the Army was insistent upon war to achieve its ends. Tojo had been a member of the "strike north" faction of the Army, which advocated war against the Soviet Union, but he was quickly convinced that the armed forces must strike south, because of the need for vital resources. Oil was a particular need after the United States cut off petroleum shipments to Japan following the Japanese incursion into Indochina in 1940.

So Tojo was a hypocrite; he accepted the Emperor's mandate, offered with the proviso that Tojo forget the Liaison Conference decision of September 6, 1941, at which the cabinet and military leaders had agreed upon war as the Japanese policy. When Tojo took the mandate he had known that the Army would not settle for less than war. All that happened after Tojo formed his cabinet in mid-October was a charade.

From Tokyo that fall we watched the maneuvers of Admiral Kichisaburo Nomura and diplomat Saburu Kurusu with growing apprehension. At first we did not believe that any Japanese in authority could be so foolish as to seek war with the United States, for it was plain to most Japanese even then that our country could not possibly win such a war. It was a measure of the stupidity of the Army generals that they convinced themselves to believe something totally contrary to all the known facts about America.

Tojo, as Edwin Hoyt documents in this book, committed a continuing series of monumental mistakes during the next two and three-quarter years. He was shortsighted and stupid, but he had presence—almost always transmitted on the radio—that was extremely impressive to the people of Japan at that time. He was eloquent, and he also seemed to be sincere in his beliefs that the Emperor was a god, and that it was Japan's role in the world to lead the people of Asia out of slavery to the white man. He really believed that the Japanese were a race superior to other men. There never has been an invincible race, and such self-delusion as the myth of invincibility is manifestation and proof of Tojo's wrongheadedness.

During his tenure he charged from one blunder to another, many of them self-serving, although he claimed to have no ambition other than to serve his emperor and nation. In fact, however, he schemed to take power, first by removing two important rivals, Field Marshal Count Hisaichi Terauchi and General Akira Muto, and finally by seizing the office of chief of staff of the Army from General Hajime Sugiyama. He bungled there, too.

He wasted many of Japan's slender resources to try to capture Indian territory from the British so he could establish Subhas Chandra Bose's Indian National Government on Indian soil. He believed Bose's claim that millions of Indians would flock to the standard of a Japanese-supported "independent" India.

After Japan's surrender I served as a reporter for the United Press Associations. In that capacity I covered the Tokyo war crimes trials of Tojo, Muto, General Masaharu Homma, and the rest, the only civilian being Koki Hirota, who had the misfortune to get mixed up with the Army. Knowing of many of Tojo's blunders during the war, I was not surprised to see him make others during his trial. His hypocrisy was evident when he denied knowledge of the mistreatment of prisoners of war and civilian internees. Much of the torture and mistreatment was carried out by the *Kempeitai*. The chief of that police force was appointed by War Minister Tojo, and that organization's loyalty was to Tojo, not to the Imperial General Headquarters.

Tojo must have known what his minions were doing but he put on his most innocent face and denied any such knowledge. It was true, as he said, that the Japanese military tradition gave the general in command of a locality almost complete authority over the lives of the inhabitants, but it was not true that the office of the minister of the Army did not know what was going on. During the war, the Allies lodged protests time and again against the mistreatment of prisoners and civilians. A special office was established in the War Ministry to deal with such complaints. But one after another these charges were rejected by the Japanese government. Until the war ended, the domestic fiction of Japanese fair treatment of prisoners was maintained.

I saw one exhibition of Tojo's essential dullness at the trials. There had been some talk of putting Hirohito on trial; the Soviets wanted it and so did some other nations, but General MacArthur made the decision that the Emperor, alive and tractable, would be more valuable to the success of his occupation than a dead Emperor and a vengeful population. Tojo certainly knew all this, but during the trial he in effect testified that the Emperor ultimately had been responsible for the war, because he could have stopped it if he wished.

When this came out in questioning, Prosecutor Joseph B. Keenan was so upset that he asked for a recess, and later brought Tojo back to go over this same ground. In the meantime Tojo had been shown what a disservice he had just committed, and he did his best to undo it.

But insight into the state of affairs recently has emerged from accounts of wartime conversations with the Emperor. If it was true that Hirohito could have stopped the war from breaking out, in his own mind there was good reason not to do so, for he admitted in these conversations that he had been terrified of the Army. He feared that he would be forced to abdicate and that the Imperial system would be destroyed.

We correspondents never were permitted to interview Tojo at the trials but I observed him in the dock day after day. Once, after the verdicts of guilty had been delivered and there was no further news from the trials worth reporting, I made up a story out of whole cloth. I quoted a nameless brain surgeon as saying he was going to apply to get Tojo's brain after the executions to study. I still believe it would not have been a bad idea.

My last "view" of Tojo came early on the morning of December 23, 1948. It was cold and cheerless in the hours before sunrise. My assignment was to drive to Yokohama, find the crematorium to which the bodies of the just executed war criminals had been delivered, and get as much detail as possible. When I arrived outside the crematorium, I saw that the place was alive with American military policemen. Nobody was allowed inside. No one would answer any questions at all. I looked around, and then in the chill predawn light I saw rising from the tall smokestack of the crematorium a column of gray smoke. And that is what I wrote about, as the remains of General Tojo burned.

The ashes, I learned later, were then all mixed together so that no relatives or sycophants could sequester them and claim martyrdom for the executed men. Actually, some of the intermingled ashes were stolen by ultranationalists from the crematorium, and offered to the families involved. But the Americans need not have worried so much about Tojo and martyrdom. He was not the martyr type. He accepted his coming death at the hands of his enemies as Japanese soldiers had done for generations before him, and in his death there was really more dignity than in his public life. Today, in a new Japan, two generations would find it difficult to place Hideki Tojo; that is an indication of how much things have changed in twentieth century Japan.

Ian Mutsu
(Mutsu Yonosuke)
Tokyo, 1991

December 22, 1948

It was the last day. For the other six condemned men all appeals had been exhausted. For General Hideki Tojo there had been no appeal, for he would not permit his attorneys to file one. What was there to appeal? He had lost the war, and for the Japanese warrior the price of failure is death. From the day of the Emperor's acceptance of the Allies' surrender demand he had known what the outcome would be, and in the fashion of his samurai ancestors he was satisfied to die at the hands of his enemies. He expected nothing else.

On Tuesday, December 21 Tojo and the others had been notified that their executions would take place just after midnight on the morning of December 23. He had gone to the notification meeting, handcuffed to a guard, a Buddhist rosary in one hand, wearing the rough U.S. Army fatigues with the big P stenciled on the back.

When the sentence had been read to him, he bent his head to acknowledge that he understood it and said "Okay, Okay" in English.

They asked him if he had any last requests, this man who only months earlier need only say a word and ninety million Japanese would obey. He requested a Japanese meal for all seven of the condemned, and at least a cup of sake. They did not get it. He also asked that something be done for the poor families of those men confined in Sugamo prison. The prison commandant said he had no authority.

On this last day Tojo was visited twice by the Buddhist chaplain, Dr. Shinsho Hanayama, and they talked—the man of peace and the man who had led his nation into a war that had devastated a Japan that before had never known defeat. The General had many things to say and he left a testament, but it was impounded by the victors, and

1

fifteen years later still was kept secret in the American archives. But Dr. Hanayama made notes as they talked and so no matter what the Americans did, Tojo's last thoughts and wishes would be known to the Japanese people.

The General left several poems for Japan; this one expressed his hopes:

> *Saraba nari*
> *koke no shita nite*
> *ware matan*
> *Yamato Shimane ni*
> *Hana kaoru toki.*

> *This is goodbye*
> *But I shall be waiting beneath the moss*
> *Until the flowers in beloved Japan*
> *Bloom once again.*

Then it was 10:30 and time for the chaplain to leave. Tojo waited in his cell. Just before midnight he and three of the other condemned, generals Kenji Doihara, Iwane Matsui and Akira Muto, were led to a small Buddhist chapel. It was not an intimate gathering; each of the condemned was handcuffed to two guards, each manacled so that he could not move his arms. As they entered the chapel a guard told Chaplain Hanayama that he had seven minutes. He handed around sticks of incense, and each man placed his offering on the burner, awkwardly bending his body to reach.

Each prisoner received one sip of wine, not sake. Then, since he still had two of his seven minutes, the chaplain read Buddhist prayers. The four generals then gave cheers for the Emperor and for Japan, they thanked the chaplain for his help, and they began the long march. The steel door clanged open and they left the cellblock. The prison's officer of the day led the procession across the courtyard to the execution chamber, and several armed American officers brought up the rear.

The chaplain turned to go back and minister to the other three men who had been condemned: generals Seishira Itagaki and Heitaro Kimura, as well as Koki Hirota, once premier and foreign minister, the only civilian sentenced to be executed. The four generals then marched up the thirteen steps to the gallows, the nooses were adjusted around their necks and the black hoods placed over their heads. Then the chief executioner gave a signal. It was one minute and thirty seconds into the new day, and there would never again be a rising sun for General Hideki Tojo, the Warlord of Japan.

1

Soldier to Politician

In 1989 the British Broadcasting Corporation created a flurry in the world of public affairs entertainment with a docudrama; it purported to be a documentary movie about the then-dying Emperor Hirohito. The burden was to show that Hirohito was a war criminal who was not indicted for his crimes against humanity because General MacArthur feared that to put the Emperor on trial would be to make a nation of 90 million Japanese intractable and create a crisis occupation that might become unmanageable.

There was nothing new in this rendition except the quite unnecessary use of professional actors to portray scenes from the life of the young Hirohito. For a documentary that was unforgivable, but this was the brief heyday of the unfortunate experiment on both sides of the Atlantic in "re-creation" of fact.

British scholars of matters Japanese protested the airing and one claimed to have found no fewer than 50 errors of fact. A former British ambassador to Japan protested in the *Times* that the film was inexact and unfair.

But all those charges made against the Showa emperor in the docudrama had been made before, most notably by David Bergamini in his book *Japan's Imperial Conspiracy*, in which he piled detail upon detail about events in Japan in the 1930s and 1940s and then awkwardly and unsuccessfully tried to link these facts to the Emperor, chronicling secret meetings and conspiratorial sessions.

Book and docudrama share another significant common factor: they betray a lack of understanding about the way the Japanese system worked up until the second half of the twentieth century. The Showa Emperor, Hirohito, told General MacArthur at the time of their historic meeting a few months after the end of the Pacific war that he assumed full responsibility for the conflict, an announcement that MacArthur chose to ignore. But if Hirohito was not responsible for the war and particularly for the conduct that led to the war crimes trials, then who was? In the trials, which many Japanese still regard as "victor's justice" the burden fell on seven men and most particularly on General Hideki Tojo. He was, after all, prime minister from October 17, 1941, until he was forced out of office in the summer of 1944 following the fall of Saipan and the imminent threat of massive American bombing the capture of that island posed to the Japanese Inner Empire.

But is the story of Japan's war effort as simple as all that? Was General Tojo a dictator in the manner of Hitler and Mussolini? The Rome-Berlin-Tokyo axis certainly had been created to intimidate the United States from interfering in the European war and with Japan's designs for the conquest of Asia.

Editorial cartoonists at first pictured Hitler, Mussolini and Hirohito together. One by C. K. Berryman, cartoonist of the Washington *Evening Star*, showed these three knaves in the "dock of world public opinion," on trial for their crimes against humanity. That was the popular view, but Hirohito was too inoffensive in appearance and too lofty in position to make a compatible third of a trio of villains. So the cartoonists and the public soon adopted Tojo as the symbol of Japanese evil and that is how it remained.

General Tojo was not in fact a dictator when he assumed office as prime minister, but he became one in the end, and personally insisted on holding the posts of prime minister, war minister, minister of armaments, minister of education, and finally chief of the Imperial Japanese Army General Staff, which meant he was the power in the Imperial General Headquarters, which corresponded to Germany's Oberkommando der Wehrmacht. It was in the position of commander of OKW that Hitler ran the German war, and in the Japanese equivalent position that Tojo ran the Japanese war.

Tojo did what all dictators do: he brought in his toadies and he fired or exiled the men who might challenge his authority. This tendency began very early: after General Tomoyuki Yamashita finished his brilliant campaign in Malaya in 1942 with the capture of Singapore and the surrender of a British army three times as large as his own, Tojo immediately shipped Yamashita off to exile in Manchuria, not even allowing him the traditional victor's honor of a personal audience with the Emperor.

But one difference was that until nearly the end General Tojo received and maintained his position because he was first among equals, one of the leading generals of the Imperial Army that seized control of the Japanese government in 1937. His downfall in July 1944 was the product of his excesses; having assumed so many mantles of government, he had also to take the responsibility for their failures. When Japan was faced with the prospect of bombing after the American capture of Saipan, as war minister and Army chief of staff and munitions minister, he could not shift any blame at all.

But in the beginning Prime Minister Tojo was not a dictator. He succeeded Prince Fumimaro Konoye, who had already begun the dismantling of the Japanese political party system and the establishment of a military oligarchy. Nor did Tojo come riding to office on a white charger. He was selected for the prime ministry because the Emperor's advisors realized that they could accept none but a military man, and Hirohito regarded Tojo as one of the most tractable of the generals. But the generals did not hold him in awe. Quite to the contrary, even as Tojo became prime minister in 1941 several of his military colleagues had other choices, notably General Kazushige Ugaki, and expected that Tojo would be only temporarily in the post. The fact that he was able to weather the period of uncertainty was a tribute to his skill as a manipulator and the undoubted professional respect accorded him by his brothers-in-arms.

Tojo was in every sense the professional officer, with all that that traditionally implies, including a serious lack of knowledge about much of the world. He especially lacked understanding of the United States, which he had only passed through on a train, and whose people he found undisciplined, soft, and, he thought, incapable of sustaining a major war effort. But he was familiar with a number of important countries, and was a great admirer of Germany, where he had studied and served as a military attaché. He also had come to appreciate aspects of Prussianism through his officer father's experience. Tojo was an expert on the Soviet Union, and fully expected a major war with Russia, in which Japan would wrench off Siberia and the rest of Sakhalin Island, and settle the question of the Mongolias forever, bringing them under the Japanese roof. He was one of the early main progenitors of the "strike north" faction of the Army, which held for war with the USSR, as opposed to the "strike south" faction, which gained widespread support, including finally his own. He acceded in the realization that the Japanese needs for petroleum, tin, rubber, and other war resources were to be satisfied in the south.

He had come up through one of the military academies, which he

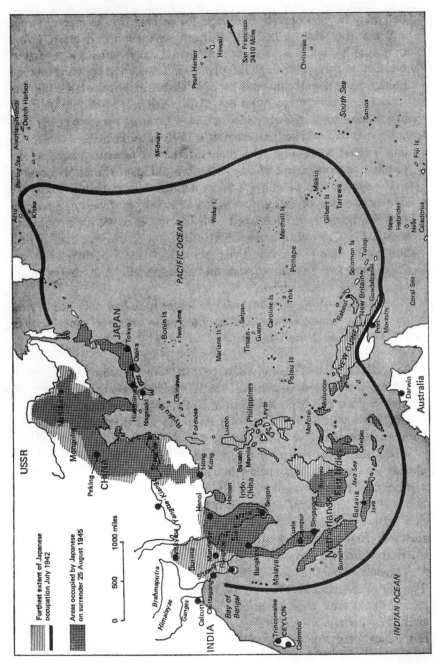

The Pacific

entered in 1902. Three years later he graduated in the middle of his class and then went to Manchuria with the army of occupation in 1906.

His early career was not spectacular. Tojo said himself that he owed his success to constant hard work to keep up with his brilliant young colleagues. He did the work without complaint, and was regarded as one of the most reliable of officers in whatever organization he was serving. Young Tojo had opted for the infantry and had devoted himself to book work and army regulations with such devotion to army life that he became known as *Kamisori*, "the razor," a nickname indicating his shrewdness in military affairs. As with many dictators, Tojo had relatively little war experience. He always became a staff officer because of his penchant for organization. In 1915 he graduated from the Military Staff College in Tokyo, and later was made an instructor at the school.

He was one of a vanishing breed in one sense, the son of a samurai who had successfully converted to the new military system imposed by Emperor Meiji after the "Meiji Restoration" of 1868, when the Japanese Army was reorganized along Prussian lines, with Prussian advisors, just as the Japanese Navy was reorganized along British lines with assistance from the Royal Navy.

Tojo's father had joined the new army and rose within its ranks to serve in the Sino-Japanese War of 1894 and the Russo-Japanese War, ultimately to become a general officer. There was opportunity in the Army for young Japanese of good birth, particularly second and third sons deprived of land by primogeniture, so in the 1920s as the Army came to strength and power many of the high-ranking officers were not from wealthy families. Indeed, wealth and the influence that derived from it were frowned upon within the officer corps, where spartan life and spartan conduct were the rule.

The difference was that even as dictator General Tojo always had the power of the throne above him. Yet he might have challenged the throne. At various times young Army officers had hatched plots to kidnap the Emperor and force him to their will, or to kill him and install his younger brother in his place. Those plots persisted sporadically down to the night before the Emperor announced the Japanese capitulation. But never did one actual plot get to the point of real challenge to the Imperial system, so no one will ever know what might have happened had the Army decided to make that challenge. Certainly it would have been resisted by the Navy and other elements of the Japanese society that remained loyal to the Emperor until the end.

But the Japanese government under Tojo still was an orderly one, however far removed from the Western notion that description might seem to be. Tojo was pushed into resigning by social factors of his era, and he accepted the force majeure and stepped out without any attempt to preserve his power through violence. Such a course would have been impossible, because the limitations on the dictatorial power of the prime minister, while untested, remained the limitations of power imposed by the cabal of Army generals, that loose consortium that held power from 1937 until the Emperor finally defied them in August 1945.

Tojo's rise out of the mold of the ordinary infantry officer began when he was posted to the very important Military Affairs Bureau of the Army as a young officer. He was serving there in 1931 when the Kwantung Army took it upon itself to seize Manchuria. Two years later Tojo was appointed to head the General Affairs Bureau of the War Office, which was really the public relations arm of the War Ministry. As such he became used to handling all sorts of questions about public policy. He also became an adherent of the *Tosei Ha* faction of the Army, a decision that would be extremely important in the development of his career. In the late 1920s the Army had split over political questions into the *Kodo Ha*, or Imperial Way faction, and the *Tosei Ha*, or control faction. The former wanted an army revolution. The latter sought to retain control of the Army in tested hands.

This split came about because of the changing nature of Japanese society. For six hundred years before Commodore Matthew C. Perry's black ships appeared off Japan's shores in the early 1850s, the country had been ruled by a military dictatorship. A succession of shoguns had held actual power, and they were, as the Japanese term says, generals. Japan had been a completely insular kingdom, its only contact with the West coming through a little trade and some missionary work conducted mainly by the Portuguese and Dutch. Its most consequential outside influence was China, from which it secured its writing system and Buddhism and Confucian ethics, and its first literature. But even China was resisted, and when in the thirteenth century Kublai Khan attempted to conquer Japan he was repulsed with the aid of "the divine wind," or Kamikaze, which scattered his invasion fleet in a great storm. So the Japanese fought among themselves, but they had never known a conqueror's boot on their soil, and since they had never had a war, they had never lost one.

But with the coming of the white man in the person of the U.S. Navy's Commodore Perry, all this threatened to change. The men around the young Emperor Meiji saw this and set out to restore the power of the monarchy and bring Japan forward into the nineteenth century. They traveled to Europe and brought back the European contributions they found potentially useful to Japan: a Prussian-style army to replace the samurai tradition of knighthood, and a British-style navy. They also brought a shrewd consciousness that Japan must eat or be eaten, and from the earliest times they embarked on colonial adventure, as they had seen the Europeans do.

By 1894 they were conquering their first colony—Taiwan, renamed Formosa.

In the reestablishment of the monarchy Japan chose what seemed to be a constitutional model. The Meiji regime had a constitution that provided for parliamentary government with a two-house legislature. But the structure was not what it seemed. The rest of the country was governed by Parliament—the Diet—but the armed forces were responsible directly to the Emperor. The one point of meeting was that the Diet controlled the budget for the military. After World War I, when the bloated armies of the world were supposed to be reduced to peacetime standards, the Japanese Army did all it could to retain size and power. First was the occupation of Siberia, which lasted until 1925. Then there were adventures in Shandong Province in China, which kept thousands of men occupied. Then the Kwantung Army, established in 1905 to protect Japanese interests on the Kwantung peninsula of Manchuria, began expanding its activity. In the 1920s the civilians cut back the military budget, and that is when the *Kodo Ha* faction decided it would seize power for the military and do away with civilian politics altogether. They believed that it was the holy mission of the military to ensure that the cause of the Emperor was the highest in the land. Accordingly, *Kodo Ha* officers made Emperor-worship an integral part of their lives. The *Tosei Ha*, on the other hand, believed in law and order, and was receptive to the notion of civilian political control of the nation.

In the 1930s the factionalism grew very intense. The *Kodo Ha* people made several attempts to seize power in behalf of the Army, but were frustrated each time. Their most notable failure occurred in 1932 when the right-wing leader Dr. Shumei Okawa attempted a coup to install General Kazushige Ugaki as prime minister. The plot was stopped when Ugaki refused to have anything to do with it.

But the effort had touched Lieutenant Colonel Tojo; his friend and classmate from military school days, Colonel Tetsuzan Nagata, was involved in the matter. He was a leading member of *Tosei Ha* and also of *Kokuhonsha*, a powerful right-wing society dedicated to Army power. Nagata was involved in the Mukden Incident when the Kwantung Army seized power over Manchuria, and he may have involved his friend Tojo, too; at least, Takehiko Yoshihashi indicates that in his *Conspiracy at Mukden*. If so, Tojo was extremely quiet about his views, and made no attempt to seek leadership in this faction.

The extreme actions came from the other side, the *Kodo Ha*, which engineered the assassination of Baron Takuma Dan, a director of the Mitsui combine, and Prime Minister Inukai, who was trying to settle the conflict with China. *Kodo Ha* wanted to continue using China as a springboard for the development of Army power.

In November 1933, a group of young *Kodo Ha* officers were arrested and charged with plotting more assassinations. General Jinsaburo Mazaki, inspector general of military training, used his influence to get them off, but now-General Tetsuzan Nagata of the control faction managed to get Mazaki relieved of his command. Then a few months later, in August 1935, a young *Kodo Ha* member, Lt. Col. Saburo Aizawa, suddenly appeared in Nagata's office and slashed the general to death with his samurai sword. If there was any remaining doubt in Tojo's mind about the way to go, the murder of his best friend settled it. After this point Tojo was a confirmed member of the *Tosei Ha*, although previously, as noted, he had kept his views very much to himself. This emergence into military politics led Colonel Tojo to a new post. The *Tosei Ha* faction ruled Army Headquarters in Tokyo, but not necessarily the Kwantung Army, which had been a hotbed of *Kodo Ha* and was still very much under that influence. Headquarters wanted to master the wayward Kwantung Army, so it promoted Colonel Tojo to *shosho*, or major general, and sent him up to Manchuria in command of the *Kempeitai*, or military police. The *Kempeitai* was just emerging as a decisive factor in the Army, and now was to be used by the *Tosei Ha* to rein in its *Kodo Ha* opponents.

Tojo went to Mukden and set up in the red brick headquarters of the *Kempeitai*; he soon made it clear that he was in charge of security and that his purview included every aspect of Manchurian life. The Manchurian group, the government and business figures from Japan who really controlled the economy of the puppet-state of Manchukuo, were a veritable cabal. Here, Tojo became intimate with Naoki Hoshino, the supervisor of economic affairs in Manchukuo, a post that fell under the jurisdiction of the Kwantung Army. Also close to the occupation force was Yosuke Matsuoka, the president of the South Manchurian Railway. The principal transportation facility in Manchuria, this enterprise also controlled many related industries, such as coal and iron ore. Other personages important in Manchukuo affairs were Nobosuke Kishi, assistant to Hoshino, and Yoshisuke Aikawa, head of the Manchurian Heavy Industries Development Corporation. They were on very familiar terms, these five, and in the laughing way that the Japanese treat serious subjects they were known as "the two k's and three suke" (*ni ki, san suke*): Hide*ki* Tojo, Nao*ki* Hoshino, Yo*suke* Matsuoka, Nobo*suke* Kishi, and Yoshi*suke* Aikawa. The quintet was generally acknowledged to run affairs in Manchukuo. But in all this, Tojo was the epitome of rectitude. In a situation where corruption was easy (and later Manchukuo's affairs became exceedingly corrupt) Tojo worked by the letter and spirit of the law. The *Kempeitai* regime under his hand was in control, and local commanders had best not try to exceed their authority or the strong fist of General Tojo would slam down on them.

In 1936 Tojo got a shock. A number of officers from his old regiment, the 1st Infantry, who had been moved to Tokyo preparatory to going overseas after the Nagata murder, decided that the time had come for the Army to seize political power and eliminate uncooperative politicians from Japan's public life. They went on a rampage, murdering Makato Saito, the Lord Privy Seal, and the minister of finance, and tried to kill the prime minister, Admiral Keisuke Okada. They did kill his brother-in-law, mistaking him for the prime minister. Admiral Kantaro Suzuki, the grand chamberlain, was severely wounded and left to die, but recovered. They seized control of many government offices that wintry night of February 26, 1936, and the putsch became infamous as the 2-26-36 Incident. When the word reached the Emperor he vowed to put down the rebellion and when faced by reluctance from his generals he threatened to lead the Imperial Guards out himself to fight the 1st Infantry men.

He was so furious he refused to honor in any fashion these men who had "deprived me of my arms and legs" by murdering his faithful courtiers.

After three days, the rebels capitulated in the face of Imperial displeasure.

The ringleaders committed suicide. The Emperor even refused the others the right of public trial. They were tried in secret; 13 were executed, 18 others were imprisoned for long terms, and many others, too, were sent to prison for breaches of discipline. Twenty officers were sent off to Manchuria, where they were treated as heroes by the men of the Kwantung Army—but not by General Tojo. He had stood firm against any efforts of the Kwantung Army to give aid or sympathy to the rebels. Tojo compiled a list of those people who might be sympathetic to the young officers and he had them watched. Gen. Seishiro Itagaki, chief of staff of the Kwantung Army, concurred. The most dangerous types were taken into custody. The crisis that the young officers had sought to extend to Manchuria failed. The failure to enlist the Kwantung Army was one of the major causes of their surrender three days after the rebellion began.

The Army high command had been worried about the behavior of the Kwantung Army, and Tojo gained much credit and favor for his prompt suppression of any signs of sympathy for the rebels. At the end of 1936 he was promoted to *chujo*, lieutenant general. Three months later, in the first weeks of 1937, he succeeded General Itagaki. For the first time the generals in Tokyo were confident that they had the Kwantung Army under control.

The commander in chief of the Kwantung Army doubled as the ambassador to Manchukuo, and thus his duties were more diplomatic than strictly military, so the responsibility for actually running the Kwantung Army rested with the chief of staff.

A few months later the generals had proof that their faith in Hideki Tojo was not misplaced. On June 9, he sent a telegram to the vice chief of the Army general staff in Tokyo and to the vice minister of the Army. As one of the principal advocates of war with the Soviet Union, Tojo communicated his anxiety lest the Japanese army flanks be beset by the increasingly powerful Chiang Kai-shek nationalist government, which was challenging the Japanese buildup in North China, in and around Beijing and Inner Mongolia, where the Japanese had quietly been building up industries and taking control of communications. The Chinese Communists had already challenged the Japanese with guerrilla warfare, and though anti-Japanese sentiment was strong in North China, it had been quelled by the local warlords. The main effort of the Kwantung Army was to establish North China as its very own protectorate, and without all the fanfare and bad publicity Japan had received in the Manchurian Incident. To do so, a China expert, Col. Kenji Doihara, one of the leaders of the Mukden affair, had fomented a ''people's rebellion'' of local warlords against the Chiang Kai-shek government. General Tojo was deep in this conspiracy.

The problem was complicated that spring by the emergence of the Japanese Tianjin Garrison of North China as a political entity, competing with the Kwantung Army. The Tianjin Garrison believed it should have charge of the North China Autonomous Movement. The ensuing quarrel among the Japanese created many problems in Tokyo and led to precipitate action by the Tianjin Garrison. The first step was the transfer of Doihara by Tokyo to the Tianjin Garrison from the Kwantung Army. Subsequently General Tojo superintended another autonomous government next to the Doihara preserve. Tojo sent a Japanese garrison of Kwantung Army troops at Tungchow. And this is the point at which he sent the telegram to Tokyo calling for action.

A month later, the action came, probably sparked by Tojo's telegram and the resulting excitement in Tokyo, wanting to act before their "rival" colleagues, the Kwantung Army and the Tianjin Garrison involved themselves in an open breach. The Tianjin Garrison wanted to act before the Kwantung Army could act. And they did. On July 7, at Lukouchiao (Marco Polo Bridge) Japanese troops and Chinese troops on maneuvers fired at one another. Within three days the Japanese had 20,000 troops in the area with armor and 100 aircraft.

On July 27, local Chinese troops of the Tungchow Garrison rebelled and slew many Japanese, which created an incident the Kwantung Army could not ignore. The Kwantung Army offered a division to the Tianjin Garrison, but this was deemed insufficient in view of the fighting in Tungchow and around Beijing, so General Tojo was sent with two additional brigades to make a flanking movement around behind the Chinese in Chahar Province. General Tojo led a forced march that accomplished the purpose and soon the whole of Inner Mongolia was under Japanese control.

After a few weeks, Tojo had the situation under as much control as he believed necessary, and flew back to Mukden to prepare for the greater conflict the Kwantung Army felt necessary: an invasion of Soviet Russia. During the rest of 1937 he looked for an incident to provoke a confrontation with the USSR but he did not find it. In the spring of 1938 the China Incident had mushroomed into a full-scale war, with the Japanese forced to commit ever more troops and resources on a broadening front in China. Nanking, the capital of Nationalist China, had fallen to the Japanese, but the capture had solved no problems; the Chinese government simply moved farther west, and the Japanese had a much larger area to police and control. The cabinet of Prince Fumimaro Konoye was committed to the China war and to a general mobilization of Japan. Trying to gain support, Konoye reorganized his government and shifted ministries around. General Itagaki, who had been General Tojo's superior in the Kwantung Army, was chosen by the generals as war minister, and he in turn had to choose the efficient book soldier Tojo to be his vice minister of war.

As vice minister, Tojo's principal responsibility was the mobilization upon which Konoye already had decided. But the general did not take his eye off the possibility of a strike against his own priority target: the Soviet Union. But General Itagaki was also getting other advice, especially from vice chief of the Army general staff Gen. Shun Tada, who advocated a quick end to the China Incident before Japan embarked on any more adventures. Tojo believed that it would be quite possible to manage a two-front war if appropriate steps were taken.

In the spring of 1938 the Japanese mounted two new offensives against China, one in the north and the other in the south. The mobilization had increased the size of the Army to 34 divisions, but 20 of these were held in abeyance for the expected attack on the Soviet Union. Even when he was still in Manchukuo in July 1938, Tojo had been one of those urging the foreign office to press claims on disputed lands on the Soviets' Korea and Manchukuo borders. Ambassador Mamoru Shigemitsu made such a demand on the Russians. Their answer was to rush forces to the disputed lands, and on July 13 they were in the Nomonhon area on the Soviet-Manchukuo border. The Japanese army was testing, there and in the Lake Khasan area. But General Tada and others reiterated warnings against getting involved with the USSR, especially now that the China bog was being perceived in some quarters as the quagmire it truly was. A new offensive in the Wuhan area ended with an enormous victory by the Japanese, but somehow the Chinese slipped out of the trap and away to fight again. And the Japanese ended up with more territory to police.

The Kwantung Army was eager to fight the Russians. Its leaders knew they had the support of War Minister Itagaki and Vice Minister Tojo, and so they were not afraid of criticism from elsewhere. They got involved in a fight at Changkufeng—the Japanese 19th Division engaging two Soviet divisions. The Emperor was furious with the whole proposition. "Abominable," he said. "Not one soldier is to be moved again without the express permission of the Throne," he told General Itagaki. And the Konoye cabinet trembled.

Vice Minister Tojo dealt in the political sphere, as distinct from the purely military sphere of the chief of staff and the special army offices. The advice he gave was constantly for preparation for war against the Soviets, but as the months went on and the China Incident remained a mere "incident" only in the Japanese public imagination, the Army knew it was a full-scale and very wearing conflict. Itagaki and Prince

Konoye were getting a lot more advice from outside warning against war with the USSR.

Tojo, however, was very close to the Military Affairs Bureau of the Army, and he gave their views: that Japan would have to reorganize her defense efforts to conduct the two wars simultaneously.

These views had been aired by Tojo several times before various groups. He had talked of the Russian problem to a group of reserve officers in August, and again to another group in September, but one day in late November 1938 he was called upon to address a group of civilian corporate leaders from the munitions industry as part of his duty to mobilize industry behind the Konoye government's policies. On November 28, 1938, he laid out the thinking of the Military Affairs Bureau in this speech.

In the past, said General Tojo, Japan had only tried to keep her strength up with that of the Soviet Union. China, while important, had not demanded her full resources or anything like it, witness the 20 divisions of 34 poised to strike at Russia. But now the armaments industry faced a new and real challenge: they must expand to the point of making it possible to conduct wars on both fronts.

It was now obvious, General Tojo said, from several incidents of past months that the Soviet Union intended to help China enough to keep the Japanese engaged there. They would do so to sap Japan's strength and confidence, and then the Russians would join the Chinese in fighting Japan. The Soviet plot was not only to fight and defeat Japan but to communize China.

Even if Chiang Kai-shek were to be defeated tomorrow, the Communists and the guerrillas they had enlisted would fight on. These forces would not only come to the aid of Russia; they would bring in Britain and France, too. China's resistance would be promoted from abroad.

London was worried because a Japanese victory in China would threaten the British position in China, where they had many investments. The Hong Kong colony also would be placed in jeopardy. Singapore would be at risk, too, and Australia and India would come under the shadow of Japanese success. The Japanese could not trust the British, they were sure, because the British concerns in China were antithetical to those of Japan.

The Americans, too, were showing themselves to be other than neutral, their policy statements notwithstanding. Japan must remain on guard against the United States as well, and she must be capable of fighting a two-front war at any time from now on.

There was nothing new about the views; they represented the

thinking of many senior officers in the Japanese Army. But General Tada had been making public statements of quite another sort, talking about the necessity to limit the military situations and to strive for diplomatic disengagement. On November 29, in America the *New York Times* headlined correspondent Hugh Byas' account of the Tojo speech:

"GENERAL TOJO PREDICTS WAR WITH SOVIET"

and the fat was in the fire.

The Tokyo stock market dropped like a stone with the implied threat of war with Russia. Newspapers began to editorialize, and questions were asked in the Diet. Privately General Itagaki quite agreed with Tojo, but he had been placed, and so had Prime Minister Konoye, in an embarrassing position. Tojo now was quiet. He had been told that it would be best if he resigned his post and got out of the public eye for a while. General Tada, on the other side of the question, was told the same. So Tojo did resign from the ministry in December and was appointed inspector general of the Army air force. General Tada took a military command on the China front.

The issue did not end there. The questions raised in the Diet persisted and War Minister Itagaki felt impelled to respond to them on behalf of the government. General Tojo, said the war minister, had been merely trying to encourage the munitions manufacturers to establish higher performance goals; perhaps he had gone a little too far in his enthusiasm. But in fact, said the war minister, countries such as the USSR were capable of carrying on a two-front war, and Japan should be as well off in her own self-defense interest.

"Which is more important?" asked a member of the parliament, "to prepare for a two-front war against Russia and China or to finish the China Incident?"

"At the moment Japan is concentrating on settling the China Incident," said the war minister, "but we must not lose sight of the need to have the capability of fighting two enemies simultaneously."

The Army, General Itagaki assured the Diet members, would never adopt a truculent policy toward Russia, but would always remain ready to repel attacks on Japanese positions.

So the matter quieted down in the Diet, and most members were convinced that General Tojo had been only indulging in a little hyperbole for the purpose of increasing war production in the munitions industry.

Meanwhile Tojo was out of the fray, and had already begun his duties as inspector general of the Army air forces, in which his major task was to upgrade the quality of aircraft and maintenance. It was the sort of job at which he excelled, calling into play all of his military expertise and his knowledge of how to get things done, still going through the proper military channels. General Nagata had once said that he believed eventually Tojo would become the chief of the Army. Now, having been burned in his first foray into public life, Tojo went back with pleasure to the merely military. If General Nagata's prophecy was to prove correct, then it seemed that General Tojo would come up through the technological operations, and not via the public policy department.

2

Politician-Soldier

To understand why and how General Hideki Tojo reemerged from the obscurity of a highly technical job in military service in the summer of 1940 after more than a year out of political office, one must know what had happened in the relationships between the Imperial Japanese Army and the Japanese government. One could say that Tojo's reappearance was a sign that the Army was in firm control of that government, and it chose one of its most trusted and loyal representatives, a man who had established a reputation for carrying out his duty without a sign of personal ambition.

One must go back, then, to the 2-26-36 incident, in which the Young Lions of General Tojo's old regiment had staged their unsuccessful rebellion. The incident culminated in the final destruction of the *Kodo Ha* faction of the Army, but oddly enough ended in the adoption of the primary *Kodo Ha* principle, Emperor-worship, as a basic Imperial Army tenet, thrust upon Japan.

At the same time, the "fleet forces" triumphed over the "treaty forces" in the Imperial Navy, ending the London Naval Conference of 1934 in failure because the Western powers would not grant Japan parity. Admiral Osami Nagano and the other leaders of the fleet faction came home from London in 1935 and immediately put into effect plans they had drawn months before for the construction of the strongest navy in the Pacific. By the summer of 1936 the building of that armada was under way.

By that same summer, when General Tojo was serving in Manchuria, the Kwantung Army was in complete control of Manchukuo and was moving toward the China war with the enlargement of the Tianjin Garrison and stationing of troops in the Beijing area of North China. The *Tosei Ha* faction of generals in Tokyo was back in control of the

Kwantung Army, largely through the offices of General Tojo, whose loyalty to Tokyo never wavered. The army had increased from 250,000 men to more than 400,000 in the preceding six years. The Army General Affairs office, which Tojo had once run, had now become primarily a censorship bureau through which the press was ever more strictly controlled. New "thought-control" legislation had been pushed through the Diet, and by 1936 rare was the man who dared raise his head and object that the trend of national policy was leading straight for war.

The right-wing theorists were providing the Army with catchphrases and philosophical excuses for Emperor-worship, although the Emperor was objecting to the concept. The phrases Imperial Way and *Hakko-ichiu* had crept into the schools. Imperial Way was Emperor-worship, and youth were being instructed that the greatest act they might take was to lay down their lives for their Emperor. They were also told to expect *Hakko-ichiu*, all the world under one roof, which meant under Japanese control.

One result of the shocking Army rebellion of February had been a melding of the interests of the Japanese foreign office and the Army. Until this time the foreign office had tended to be liberal in outlook, opposed to military adventure, and favorable to international cooperation with Britain and America. Koki Hirota, a member of the nationalistic Black Dragon Society, had been serving as foreign minister for more than two years, and in 1936 Hirota became prime minister, chosen by the Emperor on the recommendation of Prince Saionji as a man who could represent the civil government, get along with the Army, quiet the fears of the business world, and preserve Japan's social structure.

But the Army, having recently gone through its bloodbath, was now firmly under the control of the *Tosei Ha*. And they insisted on two principles that completely altered Japan's government structure. First, the war minister must be an officer on active duty at the moment. He could not be a retired officer, who might not have any loyalty to the Army high command; he must be someone beholden to the Army cabal which would control his future. Second, the Army must have veto power over the members of the cabinet.

Hirota accepted these tenets and they became the new rules for Japan's peculiar form of constitutional government. But the Army tried to exercise its new power, and told Hirota that he could not appoint two cabinet members from the same political party. In this circumstance Hirota said he would not try to form a cabinet but would go to the newspapers and tell them that he could not get Army acceptance. The Army backed down then; they were not yet ready to show their steel fist. So Hirota formed his cabinet. But the principle that the war minister must be an officer on active duty was established, and this marked the end of effective civil government of Japan. All the Army had to do was tell the designated man not to serve and he could not serve. Otherwise he could be promptly retired by the generals and thus made ineligible. Hirota's minister of the Navy was Admiral Nagano, the architect of the enlarging fleet; his war minister was Gen. Hisaichi Terauchi, one of the bastions of the *Tosei Ha*.

Hirota was not an Army man and his was not an Army government. Although he was later tried and executed as a war criminal, that seems to have been one of the miscarriages of justice. Hirota's problem was that he was riding the crest of the Army wave that apparently was unstoppable. The Army was planning a war against the USSR, and the Kwantung Army was independently planning to extend its domain into Mongolia. That is how General Tojo came to be sent to Manchuria in 1936—to bring the Kwantung Army under control. The Hirota government was trying to restore peace to the China scene but without notable success. The Chinese were gathering momentum under Chiang Kai-shek, who was trying to bring the northern warlords to heel. Then in December 1936, while visiting the Suiyuan military front, Chiang Kai-shek was abducted by Gen. Zhang Xui Liang and taken to Xian, where he was forced to agree to cooperate with the Chinese Communists to fight the Japanese. All this made Hirota's attempts to stop the Army juggernaut almost hopeless.

Meanwhile as the Tokyo generals continued their efforts to control the fractious Kwantung Army, they made Tojo chief of staff of that army. Under Tojo, they knew, the Kwantung Army would not embark on any unauthorized adventures. Also the Army and the Navy got together at a series of staff meetings, and worked out a new national policy that called for expansion in China and overseas, and war with the Soviet Union. This was reported to Emperor Hirohito in the summer of 1936 in the fuzziest of terms, as a joint service decision to make Japan a "stabilizing power" in East Asia. It also called for Japan to advance into the South Seas, to develop Japanese influence there. In the process Japan would eliminate the effects of the aggressive policies of the great powers. Anyone reading the memos concerning this matter would not have understood what they meant, but the Army and Navy men knew—they were preparing for war. Specifically, they would prepare to deal with the Soviet Union. This policy, of course, was what Vice War Minister Tojo was referring to in his ill-considered speech to the munitions industry in 1938. Unknown to the outside, it already had been government policy for two years.

The Hirota government took Japan a long way down the military road. The cabinet established a central information agency. It set the wheels in motion for national mobilization of resources. It authorized the enormous naval building program that brought Japan's naval tonnage for 1937 to the highest in history. Also, under the Hirota government the enslavement of Manchukuo was completed. The stage was set for the Rome-Berlin-Tokyo alliance, and the Kwantung Army was given the green light in its plan to detach North China from the Chiang Kai-shek government and set up a separate regime that would be friendly to Japan.

But the more concessions the Hirota cabinet made to the military the more the military demanded. The Seiyukai political party rebelled against the Hirota government and denounced it in one of the rare open confrontations in the Diet between civilian members and the Army. On January 21, 1937, feelings ran high about the secret Army plan to reform the government without political parties—word had just leaked out to the press. The Seiyukai party held a mass meeting condemning the Army and the Hirota government, and called instead for the strengthening of democratic procedures within the Diet.

On January 21, Kunimatsu Hamada, a well-known member of the party, rose in the parliament to make a speech. He had been the president of the lower house, and so he was heard with respect. He restated all his party's arguments and took the Army to task for plotting against the democratic processes.

War Minister General Terauchi was angered by the Hamada remarks and he accused the Dietman of insulting the Army.

"Where does the record show that I have insulted the Army?" demanded Hamada. "If any words of mine have insulted the Army," he added, "I shall apologize to you by committing suicide. If there are no such insults then you should commit suicide."

Hamada's fellow Seiyukai members harbored many grudges against Army arrogance and they broke out cheering. General Terauchi was still more infuriated by this display of independence by the civilian politicians and he demanded that the Diet be temporarily adjourned. The next day the Army replied with a statement threatening all the civilian political parties. Japan must develop, must have living room outside the home islands, and the civilian population needed this room. Only the Army policy would give it to them. The Army would work to abolish the Diet as a political instrument, replacing it with a form of government more suitable to the day.

This chilling open attack on the political institutions of the Constitution was the opening gun in the Army's campaign to seize total power and destroy the political parties altogether.

On January 22, General Terauchi announced that he was resigning because he could not remain in a cabinet in which some members opposed the Army. This was a very real direct threat that if the Army did not get its way, it would make it impossible for any government to govern.

Since Prime Minister Hirota could not assemble a cabinet without a war minister, and the Army would not let any general serve, that was the end of the Hirota cabinet.

Prince Saionji, the principal advisor to Emperor Hirohito, saw how the wind was blowing and assumed that the Army would accept only a general as prime minister. He suggested General Ugaki for the post, and Ugaki accepted. He was one of the most respected of generals. Or he had been.

But General Ugaki in the 1920s had recognized the public need to reduce military expenditures and had approved that civilian policy at a time when the majority of military men were fighting for more money, not less. So he had aroused the antagonism of a certain group who now controlled the Army. And as a retired officer, which Ugaki was, he was not subject to Army discipline. In other words the Army bosses could not control him. The three pivotal figures were generals Isogai, Ishiwara, and Nakajima, whose posts put them in virtual control of the organization.

They sent an emissary to Ugaki asking him to decline the honor, but he ignored their request. And then the Army exerted its full power, the new power, and refused to allow any active-duty officer to join the Ugaki cabinet. Then Ugaki had to report back to the Throne that he could not form a government and that he could not serve.

This was the first time that the active-duty army had rejected one of its own; it represented a major change of philosophy, bringing the military power into the hands of the younger generals.

The Ugaki controversy more or less blinded the military men to what should be done. In a sort of desperation they turned to Gen. Senjuro Hayashi because he was a respected member of the *Tosei Ha* faction, although a man of limited imagination. He managed to put together a cabinet, but it was ostracized by the political parties, and so the military and naval men had to hold more than one cabinet portfolio each to make the government work.

The Hayashi cabinet was a military cabinet through and through. When Hayashi found it impossible to govern with the Diet against him, he ordered new elections. The Army was confident that the Nationalist party, which favored the generals' policies, would emerge triumphant. Instead, the Nationalists polled very badly, winning only fifteen seats although they fielded 72 candidates. The two civilian political parties together had a vast majority of the seats. Never again would be Army trust its fate to the elections. With the fall of Hayashi and the surprising results of the new elections Prince Saionji was at a loss. To whom should he turn next for a suitable candidate? The Emperor did not favor a general, but by this time, threatened with assassination if they did not accept Army dictates, most civilian politicians backed away from cabinet posts. Saionji finally turned to Prince Fumimaro Konoye, a distant relative of the Emperor, who had dabbled in politics for years, although he had no strong policy. Because of this he was acceptable to the Army, and to the civilian side as well. His cabinet was formed in June, 1937, with Koki Hirota as foreign minister. It pledged to resolve the China problem diplomatically.

And what was the China problem, as seen from the Japanese point of view? The Japanese said it was the problem of unreasoning anti-Japanese feeling in China. All Japan wanted, said the right-wing nationalists, was to lead China and the rest of Asia out of the wilderness of Western colonialism and create a Greater East Asia coalition that would stand on its own. It was inherent that this coalition would be built around Japan and Japanese financial interests. But as General Tojo put it, Japan had the industrial resources, and China and other backward Asian countries had the raw materials, resources and markets, and these should be put together. The idea sounds progressive and innocuous enough, but Manchukuo was a practical case in point. The commanding general of the Kwantung Army was actually the dictator of Manchukuo, and it was apparent to all the rest of the world and to China, certainly, that this was the course of cooperation with the Japanese.

For two years the Chinese Communists in North China had been waging guerrilla warfare against Japan, and after his Xian kidnapping Chiang Kai-shek pledged to stop trying to kill off the Communists and to fight Japan as well. This had occurred in December, 1936, as noted, and since that time Chiang had resisted Japanese efforts to expand their influence, particularly in the Beijing area.

June 1937 also was the time when General Tojo of the Kwantung Army sent an urgent telegram to Tokyo suggesting that Japan must put its China house in order so that it could attack the Soviet Union without an enemy at its back. Since Chiang Kai-shek had joined with the Communists, the best course would be a preemptive strike to knock out Chiang, and thus establish a unified China under a government friendly to Japan. Obviously General Tojo did not understand the depth of Chinese national aspirations to independence, but he did understand that as long as the Nationalist government controlled much of China, no settlement with the Chinese could be achieved.

Prime Minister Konoye's government had no chance to work out any sort of arrangement with the Chinese before the Lukouchiao (Marco Polo Bridge) incident occurred. After that, the radical elements in the Kwantung Army and the Tianjin Garrison made accommodation impossible. Two weeks after the first shots were fired, the Konoye cabinet authorized the mobilization of three divisions that the Army claimed were necessary to bring peace. The Tianjin Garrison commander said that negotiations had failed and asked permission to use force—a request which was granted by the Army high command in Tokyo without even consulting Prime Minister Konoye.

On July 26, the Japanese insisted that the Chinese 27th Division withdraw from Beijing; the Chinese refused. The Japanese attacked. The next day, Prime Minister Konoye told the Diet that his government was determined to achieve "a new order" in Asia—one which encompassed a basic readjustment of Sino-Japanese relations. In other words, Japan was now committed to the conquest of China.

Beijing was captured on August 8 and came under Japanese military government. By September, Japan had 160,000 men fighting in China. When the Emperor protested to Gen. Hajime Sugiyama, the Konoye cabinet war minister, Sugiyama promised him that the "China Incident" would be settled within a month. But soon hostilities spread to Shanghai and up the Yangtze River, and Japanese naval forces blockaded the China coast. The whole armed services were to be employed in ever greater numbers. By December the fighting had moved up to Nanking and that month came the capitulation of the Nationalist capital, the flight of the government west, and the "Rape of Nanking."

As noted, General Tojo played a key role in the early stages of the war in China by taking two brigades of the Kwantung Army up into Chahar Province to protect the flank of the Japanese army in Beijing. He conquered Inner Mongolia, and then left his troops up there, to return to Changchun, the new center of the Kwantung Army, and his duties as chief of staff.

With the failure of the attempts to conquer the Chinese Nationalists, Prince Konoye announced a new policy toward China. The Nationalist regime would no longer be considered to be the government of China. A central government would be formed under Wang Ching-wei, a highly-respected member of the Kuomintang and one-time advisor to Sun Yat-sen, who was Chiang Kai-shek's principal competitor for China's leadership. This government would have its own treasury and its own troops, both controlled by Japan.

Meanwhile in 1937 a propaganda storm was unleashed on the Japanese nation. The exploits of brave soldiers on the China front were emblazoned on the front pages—one such story was the adventure of several soldiers in the Shanghai campaign who strapped grenades to their bodies and became "human bombs" to enable their fellow soldiers to break through the Chinese lines. The newspapers were full of inspiring tales of activity on the war front and on the home front. One appeal for subscription for Japanese war bonds followed another, and for the donation of anything the army could use. The public was being brainwashed into support for the China adventure and by the end of the year most did support the venture wholeheartedly, in the mistaken notion that the Japanese were simply trying to make their larger Chinese brother see the light about the need for cooperation of Asian nations.

The Konoye cabinet also established a new Imperial General Headquarters that thereafter would control the activities of the Japanese armed forces in concert, theoretically.

Seeing what an enormous task faced the Army in trying to subjugate China, Prime Minister Konoye lost heart and tried to resign, but was talked out of it. His resignation would destabilize the Japanese government, he was told, so he stayed on.

When the civilian-controlled Diet objected to the enormous expenditures for war, the Army rushed in with pressure for a new mobilization law that would strip the Diet of any power over the military. Eventually the Diet acceded, and the entire nation was mobilized for war as of the date that the law was invoked, May 1938. That spring, too, General Sugiyama, who had lost the confidence of the Emperor over the China prediction, stepped down as war minister. He was replaced by General Itagaki, former chief of staff of the Kwantung Army and one of the architects of the Mukden Incident by which that army seized power in Manchuria. Since Itagaki was formerly a *Kodo*

Ha man and still not entirely trusted by the men who controlled the Army, General Tojo was brought to Tokyo as vice minister, to keep an eye on Itagaki. Since Tojo and Itagaki were old friends, this appointment seemed quite natural, and the Army leaders were content. General Araki, another reformed *Kodo Ha* member, was made minister of education and he introduced new methods. Every morning in all of Japan's schools, the Hinomaru red sun flag was raised, the national anthem was sung, and prayers were offered to the picture of the Emperor, who was declared to be a god. Small boys began drilling with wooden rifles. The militarization of all Japan was under way. The samurai sword became the symbol of authority and the spirit of the Imperial Way, with every soldier and sailor itching to give his life for the Emperor and for Japan.

The coming strike north against the Russians was in the planning stage, and was accentuated by the Japanese provocation of the incident at Lake Khasan that summer. The Emperor reacted strenuously and the Kwantung Army called off the fight, which it was losing anyhow, and began planning to build more strength, which the generals knew would be necessary to fight a two-front war. The perceived need was regarded as so natural by the generals that they spoke of it quite openly.

After Tojo shocked the world with his speech to the munitions men about the coming war with Russia, his resignation had no effect on military planning. The Army continued to prepare for the attack on the Soviet Union, and kept the majority of its divisions free for that war.

The Japanese helped Wang Ching-wei organize his new China government, and Konoye talked about the New Order of Asia, which would be built around Japan, the New China, and Manchukuo.

But nothing seemed to happen as it should and the China war dragged. Unable to solve the problem, Konoye finally resigned and was replaced by Baron Kiichiro Hiranuma, an ultranationalist, who did not succeed either, and was replaced four months later by Gen. Noboyuki Abe, who ended up antagonizing both the Army and the civilians. The Army launched its next program to test the waters of war with the Soviets in June 1939, and got a rude shock. They attacked the Russians in the Nomonhon area, along the Kalkha River that separated the Mongolian Peoples Republic from Manchukuo. The Soviets took the matter very seriously and rushed Marshal Georgi Zhukov to the scene with armor and aircraft. The Emperor was furious and accused the Army of usurping the Imperial prerogative of making war; he demanded that the war be stopped. But it lasted for many weeks and the Japanese learned a sound lesson about taking on the Soviet Union. The Kwantung Army lost 50,000 men to the Soviets' 9000 casualties. The whole Japanese 23rd Division was destroyed in the fighting in August, when the Russians launched a great counteroffensive. The Kwantung Army called for help from Tokyo and the Army chiefs told them sternly to get back on their own side of the border and stay there. The Soviets outgunned them in every way and the chastised Japanese retired finally to begin building up their armor and their antitank and air attack weapons. General Ueda, the commander of the Kwantung Army, was criticized by the Emperor, shipped home, and forcibly retired. Gen. Yoshijiru Umezu then was made commander of the Kwantung Army with orders to bring it firmly and finally under Tokyo control.

By 1939 the official Japanese view was that their nation was fighting in China and quarreling with the rest of the world that did not understand Japan's true intentions. And what were these? Foreign ministry official Yosuke Matsuoka stated the case: Japan was sacrificing herself to preserve China from communism, and China and the rest of Asia from being colonized in the manner of Africa. The Western colonial powers must be driven out of Asia.

Matsuoka said Japan's only friends now were Germany and Italy, and he was pressing for the Tripartite Pact with them, which was obviously aimed at the United States. The objective was to keep America out of the European war as far as Germany was concerned and to keep America from going to war for China as far as Japan was concerned.

Baron Hiranuma's government, which opposed the pact, collapsed in the summer of 1939 when the Germans, whom he had touted as Japan's allies, suddenly signed the Nazi-Soviet Non-Aggression Pact, which would make Germany a Japanese enemy if Tokyo attacked Russia. The Japanese did not understand that Hitler's reason for the accommodation with the Kremlin was to guard his flank against Soviet interference in his war on Poland, which would begin the following month. So the cabinet collapsed, and was replaced by the government of Admiral Mitsumasa Yonai, also opposed to the Tripartite Pact, which was almost a last gasp against Army control. Yonai did not believe in the wisdom of war with the United States and Britain, and he promised to do all he could to avoid it. He was publicly noncommittal about the China war, in which he did not believe either. Since the Japanese Army was then paying lip service to the idea of seeking accommodation with the United States, it could not object to Yonai's attitudes, at least for a time. But in the spring of 1940 the Army let it be known that it wanted the Tripartite Pact and Prince Konoye back as prime minister. They forced the resignation of the Yonai government when War Minister Shunroku Hata told Yonai that if the premier did not resign, Hata would, and that Yonai then would be unable to secure the services of another war minister from the Army.

So Prince Konoye came back into the government, reluctantly. He left the choice of war and navy ministers up to the respective services. Once they had chosen their men, he would appoint a foreign minister-designate, and the four of them would meet and talk policy. If they could agree, then Konoye would appoint the rest of the cabinet and accept the Imperial mandate. His candidate for foreign minister was Yosuke Matsuoka, who had so ably defended Japan to the world in the argument about her intentions in China.

On July 17, 1940, General Tojo was touring the Army air installations in Manchukuo when he was called to Tokyo and told that he would be replaced as inspector general of the Army air force by Gen. Tomoyuke Yamashita and that he had been chosen to be war minister. In fact, he was the only candidate. The Big Three, the men who ran the Army, had been consulted by Gen. Kengo Noda, the chief of Army personnel. The Big Three were Gen. Shunroku Hata, just then war minister; Prince Kan-in, the chief of the Army General Staff; and Otozo Yamada, inspector of military training. They had agreed unanimously that Tojo could be trusted to present the Army point of view at all times and that he was the most suitable candidate. Because General Tojo was the man he was, he did not complain or make any remarks. He had been chosen not because he was unique, but because all the other candidates for this role had been eliminated. Both generals Terauchi and Sugiyama had made enemies. General Umezu, who also was considered, had a job to do with the Kwantung Army, and General Hata, who then held the post of minister of war, felt that he had held it long enough.

The next day Tojo met with Konoye, Navy Minister–designate Kengo Yoshida, and Matsuoka. The prime minister said that the settlement of the China issue was the most important matter, and they all agreed with him. They also agreed that Japan must improve her defenses and remain armed and on guard against all comers. The Tripartite Pact should be signed, although the Emperor had serious reservations about it.

One big change that came to Japan in 1940 was a shift in attitude. The Army, having been chastened in Siberia, now decided that its future lay in the south, not the north. The expansion of Japan would be into the European colonies: French Indochina, Malaya, and the Dutch East Indies. By mid-1940 the way was open in Indochina, for the French were defeated by Germany in the European war and had no strength to defend the Asian outposts of her empire. The way was also open in the Dutch East Indies, for the Netherlands was under German occupation, and the colonial government in Java was not very strong. The Japanese Imperial Army was getting ready to move.

And so in July 1940, General Tojo became one of the leaders and policymakers for Japan, at a time when the policies being made were about to revolutionize Japan and pave the road to world war.

3

War Minister

General Tojo was extremely effective as war minister in the Konoye cabinet because he believed completely in the three basic tenets of the second Konoye administration: the establishment of a controlled economy, the elimination of civilian political parties, and the alliance with Germany. The first idea was Konoye's own, the second was the Army's, and the third was really Tojo's. Since his days as military attaché in Berlin he had had a strong affinity for the Germans and considerable antipathy for the British and especially for the Americans, whom he considered to be meanderers.

Prime Minister Konoye set the tone in the first two weeks of the new cabinet with a radio speech to the country warning that "no nation has ever progressed by looking for the good life." So the Japanese people were on notice that the pursuit of power was the purpose of the Konoye cabinet and that they could expect an enforced frugality on the civilian front. The pursuit of power was certainly the aim of the Imperial Army, the extension of sovereignty and the growth of the armed forces.

General Tojo believed in all these ideas, so he was indeed the ideal figure to be war minister.

By the composition of the Konoye cabinet and the relative power assumed by the members, one could say that the cabinet was a Kwantung Army cabinet. First was War Minister Tojo; second was Naoki Hoshino, chief of the cabinet planning board; and third was Yosuke Matsuoka, foreign minister. These three had run affairs in Manchuria in days gone by. Now they were to impose a planned economy on Japan along lines drafted by Hoshino—more than a planned economy, a regimented life style in which the efforts of every citizen would be devoted to the perceived common good. The military forces would be built to be second to none; the educational system would reflect the national policy; in the name of the Emperor the lives of every man, woman, and child would be devoted to the betterment of the nation. The birth rate would be increased, and Japan would be a nation of a hundred million people with a single aim.

On July 27, 1940, at the request of the Army, Prime Minister Konoye called a Liaison Conference that involved his cabinet and representatives of the armed services. The agenda was presented by the Army, and had been drafted by a group of those young officers, none of them higher in rank than lieutenant colonel, to whom it was Army practice to give the responsibility (and power) to prepare major plans. This conference was to consider "The Main Principles of Japan's Policy for Treating with the Current Situation of World Development."

The main items under consideration were the ending of the China war and the securing of natural resources in the south. The first would be achieved by maintaining unrelenting pressure on Chiang Kai-shek, including pressure on third countries to refrain from giving aid to China. Japan's world position would be enhanced by strengthening the ties with Germany and Italy and coming to an agreement with the USSR. France, which had just surrendered to Germany, would be pressed to provide transit through Indochina for Japanese troops moving into China, the use of Indochina airfields as well, and to supply rice, rubber, and other resources that Japan needed from the colony. The United States could be expected to be difficult, but Japan would try to placate her with words while maintaining a stern posture with deeds. As soon as the China issue was settled, Japan would move south, invading Malaya and the Dutch East Indies. Until the China issue was settled, however, she would make few military moves elsewhere, but prepare all the time for war, particularly against the United States.

This plan was not a spur-of-the-moment concoction. The first draft had been prepared nearly a month before in Army headquarters, passed to the Navy for adjustment, and subjected to many discussions. Many Navy officers opposed it. The ease with which it was presented and accepted by the liaison committee indicated the basic attitude of Prince Konoye and the other members of the cabinet: Japan was committed to a course of empire-building; it would be attained by negotiations from strength and by force if necessary. The key to everything was the conquest of China and the employment of its resources thereafter.

Much later, during the war crimes trials in Tokyo, Chief Prosecutor

Joseph B. Keenan would try to show that Tojo and the Army were scheming all the time to seize power from the civilians. But that was not exactly the case. Prince Konoye, who was anything but a military man, quite agreed with the necessity of Army leadership. As a businessman was to say at the time of Tojo's execution, it was too bad that he and the other six defendants sentenced to death had to die for what were really the crimes of the whole nation. "We were all in it together," he said. And so they were. Also, more than half a century after the fact it is easy to forget the impact that Nazi and Fascist single-party rule had on many countries. The Japanese were enormously impressed by Hitler's accomplishment of taking a supine Germany ridden with war debt, and creating a powerful state out of it.

What is not even yet perceived in the West about Japan is the yearning for consensus that overpowers logic. The Japanese suffered and suffer from a deep feeling of inferiority to the West that colored and colors still their responses to international behavior. Japan in many ways by 1940 was a modern state, but in the Japanese heart it was not much changed from the days of the shoguns.

Within the first week after this new Konoye cabinet had taken office, Japan was on the road to war. First was the cabinet's final approval (signed Sept. 27, 1940) after many months of Japan's signature to the Tripartite Alliance. The matter had been raised in three previous cabinets and always the forces of moderation had managed to table the issue. In the Hiranuma cabinet it had been raised more than 70 times, and on each occasion Admiral Yonai had objected. But now there was no Yonai to object, and all the other cabinet members approved. The second big issue that was resolved in those first days was the establishment of the Imperial Rule Assistance Association and the virtual dissolution of the independent political parties that had been part of the Japanese scene since the Meiji Restoration. Parties were deemed a negative factor in the drive to create a new Japan, a nation whose citizens, theoretically, were all dedicated to the same ends. Parties then would be replaced by a single political entity. Prince Konoye was very enthusiastic about this plan. The Imperial Rule Assistance Association would be formed in October and all the political parties would "voluntarily" disband; the association would take their place, with branch offices in every prefecture. In fact no one dared publicly disagree; no one dared suggest that the system was less than perfect; no one dared doubt, and let it show. Were he to do so he would be arrested and perhaps prosecuted under what amounted to thought-control laws.

Early in September the cabinet voted to accept a plan offered by Foreign Minister Matsuoka to strengthen the alliance with Germany and Italy, with the understanding that Japan was to be the paramount power in Asia. Ultimately, Matsuoka said, Japan wanted to see the Dutch East Indies and Indochina become independent within an association led by Japan. This was the beginning of the idea of the Greater East Asia Co-prosperity Sphere, although it was not yet called by so formal a name.

The Army, the Navy, and the foreign ministry reached agreement on the plan to sign the military alliance with Germany and Italy. Marquis Kido, who represented the views of the Palace and also of Prince Saionji, the aging advisor to the Emperor, did not like the idea; he felt it would lead to war with America. But Konoye had been convinced by Foreign Minister Matsuoka, who was the resident expert on America since he had gone to school at the University of Oregon. Matsuoka had advised him that the reaction of the Americans would be to avoid getting involved in war. They would do so particularly since the European war was then raging, and the Axis powers were winning. The proponents of the alliance declared that if Japan did not join the Axis she ran the danger of being attacked by the United States at any time. "The conclusion of a tripartite alliance would force the United States to act more prudently in carrying out her plans against Japan," Matsuoka said.

On September 19 the prime minister convened the Liaison Conference to discuss the treaty. Several members of the cabinet hoped that a formal pact would not be necessary, just a statement of principle, but Foreign Minister Matsuoka held out for a treaty. Matsuoka, again in the role of expert on American matters, predicted that the presence of many Italian-Americans and German-Americans was going to exert influence on the U.S. to stay out of the war and that the treaty would strengthen the influence of those groups.

The other big question discussed was the chance of securing an alignment or alliance with the Soviet Union. How soon the military men forgot. The way Matsuoka was talking, and the generals agreeing, the Nomonhon incident, in which Japan had lost 50,000 men, might never have happened. Tojo, one of the first to advocate the "strike north" theory, now acceded to all that was said. He, too, could see how Japan must turn south for resources, and he, too, knew how strong the Soviet armies could be. There would be no more Nomonhons, no more mistakes in choosing the time and the place and the enemy.

That same afternoon of September 19, with everyone in agreement, the prime minister called the Imperial Conference, the purpose of which was to acquaint His Majesty with the matters under consideration and the decisions that had been reached. The Imperial Conference was an institution begun when the Meiji Emperor was alive. Then it really was an Imperial Conference at which many decisions were made. But over the years, particularly in the Taisho period, 1912–1926, the function of the conference had changed. The Taisho Emperor had not been able to carry the burdens of state, and the government had functioned in spite of, not because of, him. His great joy was in drinking and in carousing with his women, the Imperial concubines. He had so many that when Crown Prince Hirohito was twelve years old the Emperor sent one to the Crown Prince with instruction to teach him how to be a man. Hirohito was much more interested in bugs, and sent her back.

Before he was eighteen years old Hirohito had taken the reins of government as regent, but because he was so young the Imperial Conference had deteriorated to a level it never again surpassed. The Emperor no longer participated in the discussions, but listened. If he had something to say, he would convey it privately through an advisor or the prime minister, but he did not interfere openly in the affairs of state.

Now at the Imperial Conference agreement was reached on the matter of the treaty with Germany and Italy, but the Navy, having second thoughts about its approval of the war policy, asked that the government stop showing so much hostility to the United States. But no one really believed. The nation's leaders were determined to conquer China, determined to ally themselves with Germany and only hopeful that somehow the Americans could be threatened enough not to go to war. People around Prince Konoye who were knowledgeable about the United States warned that America was like a sleeping tiger, apparently indolent, but underneath holding enormous economic power. That tiger should be left alone, they told the Japanese government. But so insular were the men of the cabinet, and so shortsighted, and so much in the hands of the *chuken shoko*, the young officers who were allowed to have their way in planning—young officers who had little understanding of the possible consequences of their acts—that there was no thought of slowing down and ascertaining what Japan's real needs might be and what her real potentialities were. They should have learned from Nomonhon that if the Soviet Union could deal a serious blow, challenging American productive power could put Japan in serious trouble. But nobody in authority in Tokyo was thinking that way in the fall of 1940. They still regarded America as a bumbling nation, a big overgrown boy that had no idea of what to do with his own strength. In reality, the Japanese government was not thinking about America or American intervention at all. Time had proved already that America was unwilling or slow to act. It had not acted in the matter of Manchukuo, although much public concern was expressed.

And so, on September 26, 1940, the Tripartite Pact was signed, and Japan sealed her own fate, thus declaring herself to be an enemy of the United States. Secretary of State Cordell Hull called it the "joining of the bandit nations." Early in September 1940, the Japanese were negotiating with the French for the right to move troops through Indochina. On the scene, however, the Japanese of the South China Expeditionary Force were behaving in the manner already common to Japanese forces overseas. They took matters into their own hands; one battalion of Japanese troops violated the Indochina border and staged some raids on French forces. When the Emperor was informed of this activity he called in War Minister Tojo and told him he did not approve. Meanwhile Japanese planes had dropped bombs on Haiphong, the port of Hanoi, and Japanese troops had fought with French forces in the Red River area.

This was too much for the Emperor and too much for Tojo. He started court martial proceedings against offending officers and relieved the commanding general of the South China Expeditionary Force. He also transferred and punished some of the officers responsible in Tokyo's Army headquarters. It was embarrassing to have the Emperor ask questions that could not be answered.

Tojo advocated one more chance for Chiang Kai-shek to come to terms with the Japanese, but Chiang ignored the invitation. Thus the Japanese efforts gained a sort of legitimacy in their own eyes. Tokyo made a deal with Wang Ching-wei's new China government; it gave the Japanese the right to keep troops on Chinese soil.

In the spring of 1940 the Japanese were negotiating with the Dutch for East Indies oil; they wanted one-seventh of the oil produced there, which amounted to about 20 percent of Japan's annual needs. But by that autumn they had raised the figure of Japan's requirements to five times what they had been receiving from the Indies, or about 60 percent of Japan's needs. The change came because of the stiffening of American attitudes toward Japan and the probability that imports from America would be cut off. Since Japanese policy under the new wave was to negotiate for what they wanted and if negotiations failed then to use force, the Japanese army was getting ready for a foreign war. Troops were training for tropical combat, and reconnaissance flights were being made over Malaya and the Philippines.

At the same time, the Japanese were trying to arrange a four-power pact with the USSR and their Axis allies; they knew nothing of Hitler's plans to attack the Soviets. The Japanese hoped with the four-power pact to frighten the United States into a continued state of neutrality. But Matsuoka learned the truth when he went to Germany and discovered the tensions there. He did secure a Neutrality Pact with the USSR, which at least assured the Japanese that if they did go to war with the United States and Britain they would not have to worry about their northern flank.

The Army was eager to plan for the move south, and in June several conferences were held to accelerate that planning. On June 22, acting on his own, Foreign Minister Matsuoka had an audience with the Emperor in which he tried to convince Hirohito that Japan should join in the German attack on Russia but the Emperor did not like the idea. Neither did Prince Konoye nor anyone else important in the cabinet. The Army's interest was now in the south. It had by this time become apparent in Tokyo that the Germans were not consulting the Japanese on points of global strategy, so the Konoye government turned away from the European alliance and decided to make their plans altogether on their own, a view in which General Tojo fully concurred. He had pointed out to his colleagues that the Germans had not consulted with Japan about their intentions regarding Russia.

Matsuoka still wanted to attack the Soviets, but no one else in the cabinet agreed. General Sugiyama, the chief of staff of the Army, put it very succinctly: "As long as we are employing a vast army in China, at present we cannot do what you suggest. . . ." And the vast army was going to become greater and extend through southeast Asia in the not distant future. So the Matsuoka plan, a dream that once had also been Tojo's, had to be abandoned in the Japanese realization even in the spring of 1941 that their resources were limited. The dream would persist, and the Kwantung Army would remain strong in the north for another three years, but no overt move would be made now.

In July the cabinet addressed itself to the Greater East Asia Co-prosperity Sphere, and announced that building a new Asia was their serious policy. To do this, the cabinet decided, Japan would not decline (*Jisezu* is that Japanese word) a war with Britain or the United States if either stood in the way of settling the China issue or tried to block Japan's movement south to secure the natural resources she needed.

The Americans had been watching (and listening to secret Japanese messages through the Magic interceptions and code-breaking), and on July 26, 1941 they froze Japanese assets in the United States and suddenly imposed a thorough economic blockade. This move was followed by similar action by Britain, the rest of the British Empire, and the Dutch East Indies. Japan suddenly felt totally isolated and ringed in by the ABCD powers (America, Britain, China, and the Dutch). General Tojo believed that the Americans were provoking Japan to the point of war.

All during the spring of 1941 Foreign Minister Matsuoka had been acting as gadfly, demanding an attack on Russia, demanding an attack on Singapore, demanding, demanding. The generals in the Imperial General Headquarters were thoroughly sick of him and so were most of the cabinet members. Navy Minister Oikawa said he thought Matsuoka was out of his mind.

In May, Prime Minister Konoye had called a special meeting with General Tojo and Admiral Oikawa to see what attitude they should adopt to Matsuoka. They agreed that he needed watching, and that they must be careful because Matsuoka did not seem to care how much he antagonized the United States. He said he wanted to carry out a policy of firmness regarding America. What Matsuoka did, in fact, was adopt such a belligerent stance that he persuaded the Americans that the Japanese really wanted war, when that was not quite the case. They were willing to run the risk of war with the West to achieve control of resources they could call their own, but they would have preferred not to fight, at least not until the "China Incident" was settled. Matsuoka's behavior undermined the efforts of the others in the Konoye cabinet to achieve some sort of understanding with the United States. By May 1941, relations between Matsuoka and the others in the cabinet hit a new low point, since the foreign minister was behaving as belligerently as the least self-disciplined young staff officer.

Matsuoka worked on his own and at a critical juncture rejected a proposal made by the United States in negotiations aimed at improving relations. Moreover, he did so in such an insulting way that it damaged Japanese-American relations still further. By July 16, Matsuoka had caused so much trouble in the government with his rushing back and forth that Konoye had decided on a cabinet resignation for the purpose of getting rid of Matsuoka. That night of July 16, Konoye submitted the resignation of the whole cabinet, but the elder statesmen (*jushin*, the retired prime ministers association) decided that Konoye should continue to serve, and the next day he was asked to form another cabinet. So the third Konoye cabinet came into being, with one major change: Yosuke Matsuoka was out and Vice Admiral Teijiro Toyoda took over the foreign ministry. The trend to the military was certainly obvious: seven of the fourteen ministers were generals or admirals. But this was much less shocking to the Japanese than it would have been in a Western society because since the days of the Emperor Meiji the military had always played a major role in the government of Japan. General Tojo, who was regarded as the mainstay of the Konoye cabinet, of course remained.

And from this point, the course of events moved unevenly, with Konoye and his cabinet members largely looking for ways to improve relations with America, without sacrificing their own position.

A few weeks after the political demise of Yosuke Matsuoka, in order to retrieve some of the goodwill the foreign minister had cost Japan, Konoye invited American Ambassador Joseph C. Grew to a very private dinner at the house of Baron Ito, one of the prince's intimates. All the family servants were dismissed for the night, each man was accompanied by only one aide, and the two parties drove to the Ito house in limousines from which the identifying tags and insignia had been removed. They were served by the daughter of the house. Every care was taken to see that news of the meeting did not reach the *Kempeitai*, who had virtually become the Thought Police, and whose presence by now was ubiquitous in Japan. At this dinner Konoye proposed that he go to Washington to meet President Roosevelt for face to face negotiations. Ambassador Grew approved.

General Tojo knew about the dinner, and he approved of the plan. Tojo really wanted to avoid war at this point, if possible. The pressure for action was coming from Imperial General Headquarters where the young staff officers exercised authority far beyond their ability and judgment.

Both Konoye and General Tojo, for their disparate reasons, wanted to avoid conflict with America just now. But under pressure from the young officers, they must have some indications from America of room for maneuver.

4

The ABCD of Paranoia

Tojo was a militarist, pure and simple. He had no yearning for personal power, in the manner of a Hitler or a Mussolini or even a Chiang Kai-shek or Mao Zedong. He was a member of a select group, the senior officers of the Japanese military clique at a time when that clique seized power in Japan. His motivation, and theirs, was to extend the Japanese Empire and promote the welfare of Japan. Tojo always said, and there is no reason to disbelieve him, that the Japanese militarists also felt that what they were doing was in the interest of Asia and Asians, to bring them out from under the yoke of colonialism. It is easy to riposte: "And yes, to bring them under the yoke of Japanese colonialism," but the Japanese did not take that view.

To understand General Tojo and the other militarists who had seized power by 1937, one must first understand the nature of the Japanese society of that day. It was not so far removed from the society of the past as one might imagine. Although the militarists wore uniforms that looked much like those of the Germans, and their military and naval forces had all the trappings of modernity, beneath the modernity beat the hearts of warriors who were essentially samurai in their attitudes.

The Japanese warriors—the samurai—had always lived to die. Their maxim was to expect death every day and to comport themselves in a fashion to be ready for it. That was also the way in which the Japanese soldiers lived in this new army, and it explains why the Japanese had the attitude they did toward dying in battle and taking or being taken prisoner. There was no place in the Japanese military code for prisoners. If you won, you were victorious. If you lost, you were dead. It was as simple and as cruel as that, and the Japanese fully expected the same sort of cruelty to be visited on them that they inflicted on others. That was the personal aspect of the Japanese soldier's creed.

Even more fundamental was the situation of Japan in the 1930s, and to understand that one must know what Japan was and how she got that way.

First, Japan was isolated, even after the Meiji Restoration. The Japanese had taken an ambivalent attitude toward Westerners: in a way they felt inferior to them, because of the Westerners' power and knowledge about a world that was all new to the Japanese but obviously was a superior world of machinery and growth. The Japanese were dragged into that world in 1853 by Commodore Perry, who threatened to use force to get his way if the Japanese would not negotiate. And from that first encounter derived the Japanese decision to yield to the West—seemingly—to learn from the West, to take what was best from the West. They would join the West in its colonial enterprises, and become little Eastern Westerners on the surface, rather than be enslaved as had the Indians, Annamites, Indonesians, Filipinos and, in a sense, the Chinese.

Hideki Tojo had grown up with all that tradition. His father was one of the first of the samurai to convert to the new Western-style military, and his father had risen through the ranks to become a general. As noted, his father had been a soldier in the time of the Sino-Japanese war and at the time of the Russo-Japanese war. He had seen the fruits of the first of those conflicts (Manchuria) wrenched away from Japan by cabal of Western powers. He had seen Japan victorious (and so had young lieutenant Tojo) in the Russo-Japanese war, and had seen the fruits of that war wrenched away by American President Theodore Roosevelt, who prevented the payment of a cash indemnity that the Japanese military sorely needed, and let the Russians off with the loss of their Manchuria rights and their interests in Korea.

Another aspect of the Japanese that set them apart was a homogeneity of culture and language; it made them quite different from the Chinese, Filipinos, Indians, and Indochinese peoples. All the Japanese spoke that same tongue and observed the same festivals, and by and large shared the same religion. They had a single emperor who was the object of reverence if not devotion and worship. Because they had one of the most difficult languages in the world, they were also culturally isolated, though much of their literature came from China. Their roots, Chinese and Korean, had been twisted and turned so that by the twentieth century they were a singular people. Hideki Tojo was a product of all these forces.

One of the factors that induced a paranoia among the Japanese was the attitude of the Americans, who in the last quarter of the nineteenth century had turned passionately anti-Oriental. The basic reason was economic; the European-descended American laborers from the east coast who travelled west encountered the Chinese and Japanese who would work harder and cheaper than they. The early period of the young American labor movement was the heyday of anti-Orientalism. The attitude culminated in the Chinese Exclusion acts, which were as racially biased as any laws in the world, and the Japanese-American Gentlemen's Agreement, which effectively prevented Japanese emigrating to the United States on reasonable terms. These acts of prejudice and even of violence stemmed from the broad base of the American people, the working class, rather than the intelligentsia and the upper middle class, who were never anti-Oriental.

These attitudes begot a combination of paranoia and arrogance on the part of the Japanese. At home they were one sort of people, when abroad another. In China, when they achieved a position of power, they abused it shamefully; they seemed never to regard the Chinese as human. And in such cities as Shanghai, when they seized parts of the International Settlement in the early 1930s, they behaved brutally. Outside his own country the Japanese tended to become a monster; the Japanese even have a proverb for it.

Muri ga toreba
Dori hikkomu

Where might is master, justice is servant.

During the period before World War I the Japanese stepped out a bit in their international relations. They signed a treaty of commerce with the United States and they signed an alliance with Britain that would serve them well when they joined in the fight against Imperial Germany. Again in World War I, the Japanese had triumphed and conquered Germany's China colony of Kiaochao, which included the city of Jingdao and the railroad that ran to Jinan in Shandong Province, and they had occupied Shandong.

After the war, the Japanese expected to be made full allied partners, but instead they were treated shabbily at Versailles by the Western victors. They considered themselves to be the leading nation of Asia, and that they were, but the fact only aroused the resentment of the Western colonial powers and of the United States. America claimed a special interest in China dating back to before the Boxer Rebellion and demanded an "open door" to all foreign trade with China.

When the Japanese invaded Manchuria, the Americans and British preached, but they did not act. When Japan extended her activity in Shanghai and elsewhere in China, the Westerners again raised their voices but did not act. But by the late 1930s the Americans, the British, and the Dutch perceived the Japanese as their enemies. Japan by this time was embarked on the course of suppression in China that demanded that she have enormous supplies of natural resources, and most of the necessary items came from the East. In February 1939, with Japan's occupation of China's Hainan Island, and the Spratly Islands, halfway between Indochina and Borneo, the Americans, British, and Dutch began to react. One of the first such steps was the American movement of much of its fleet from the Atlantic coast to the Pacific, and ultimately into Hawaii. This was obviously done to threaten Japan. At the same time, because of the war in Europe, the United States instituted export controls on strategic materials needed for its own defense. This was natural enough and the Japanese had done the same, but in Japan this American tightening was regarded as an unfriendly act.

The *Panay* incident of 1937 had left an unpleasant source of friction between the United States and Japan, although the Japanese apologized profusely in the person of Admiral Yamamoto, who really meant it—he considered the bombing and strafing of the American gunboat *Panay* on the Yangtze River a serious mistake. But little by little and basically because of news reports and newsreels showing the horror, destruction and cruelty of the Japanese in China, the American mind was being closed to Japan.

Watching the Americans in the summer of 1940, General Tojo had the feeling that they were moving toward entry into the European war, and he was quite right. President Roosevelt by that time was doing all he could short of war to shore up the British defenses. In 1940 Congress gave the administration as a diplomatic weapon the National Defense Act by which the administration could halt the shipment of oil and steel and other strategic material. This could have been invoked against Japan but it was not; Washington was really sincerely trying to get Japan to cease its adventuring. But the real problem was that America saw that China could not exist without aid, and so she gave that aid, all the while insisting as the price of amity that the Japanese halt their aggression in China. The Japanese absolutely refused to stop; they were engaged in what they regarded as part of a holy war to bring Asia together. It was their view that Chiang Kai-shek was the culprit for refusing their overtures and continuing to resist their big-brotherly approach. By 1940 the American and Japanese views were irreconcilable and all that happened thereafter was talk, but no basic change in the position of either side. From the Japanese point of view, to give up the China effort was to undo all that they were trying to do to bring Asia out from under the European boot and to lose the chance to get the economic resources they needed. The imposition of new Japanese power in Asia, which the Japanese denied was colonially inspired, had its particularly ugly aspects. The Army and to a lesser extent the Navy showed themselves as singularly arrogant and unattractive in Shanghai and other areas where they had control. American diplomats were slapped, and Americans and Europeans were pushed off the sidewalks into the streets by Japanese soldiers and sailors. In groups the Japanese servicemen were a fearsome lot capable of all sorts of violence, but when alone they were almost always well-behaved. It was as if the violence and bad behavior was some sort of national syndrome to show a superiority that in their hearts most Japanese did not feel.

In the summer of 1940 matters began to approach crisis stage. The Japanese were insisting that the British close the Burma Road. They were pressing the Pétain government of surrendered Vichy France for use of airfields and troop transit rights in Indochina. They were demanding that the Dutch East Indies continue to supply oil and other materials, and they were demanding that the British evacuate their troops from Shanghai.

In 1940 the Japanese paranoia grew and began to show in the increase of unfriendly acts against the European and American interests in the Far East. This year the Japanese attitude brought unfriendly response. Starting in 1932 the Japanese had invaded Shanghai and roughly handled foreigners who got in their way, to say nothing of the Chinese. In 1937 they had begun to wage the China war, they came to Shanghai again, they blockaded and bombarded and seized property and pushed the foreigners around. These foreigners were used to the ways of extraterritoriality. They were colonials. They did not like being pushed around by little yellow men. But more important than personal preference were humiliations wreaked on the Western people by the Japanese, who were openly showing their feeling that the colonial powers should get out of Asia. Back in Tokyo what the Japanese in government could not seem to fathom was the fact that action begets reaction. If the Japanese in Shanghai slapped American diplomats and threatened the British, if they forced men and women in Tianjin to disrobe and revelled in their shame, then there was going to be a reaction. But the Japanese in Tokyo said they had no control over local forces, and left it at that, having no conception of public relations or their effects of their people's acts. That is why they were always genuinely surprised to find that foreigners hated them.

Japan was pursuing a single-minded policy, dedicated to the unification of Asia under the leadership of Japan. In February 1939 she annexed Hainan island, which was Chinese territory, and the world knew that the reason was to have a base for attack on south China. It was harder to explain her annexation of the Spratly islands some 650 miles southeast of Hainan which were halfway to Borneo.

The result of this activity and the continued fighting and movement inland in China, and the outbreak of war in Europe caused the U.S. to take a long look at trade and defense policies and to restrict to all comers a number of raw materials that were important to its American defense industry. The Japanese objected, paying no attention that they had done exactly that as soon as they got involved in China. What was remarkable about the Japanese attitude all along the road to war was their ability to maintain one set of standards for themselves and another set for the "have" nations, who were supposed to give the Japanese what they wanted with nothing in return.

Early in the year 1940 the Japanese began negotiating with the Dutch East Indies seeking a preferred position as oil customer. Noting the continued Japanese movement in China, the Americans moved their fleet from the east coast to the west coast, a pointed reminder to Japan. The act was regarded by the Japanese as the precursor to a war buildup but it had no effect on their planning. They were willing to run enormous risks to achieve their objective of a United Asia, and they did not stray from the path.

In the spring, concerned lest the Japanese seize the Dutch East Indies now that Holland had been overrun, the Americans made the warning more pointed by moving the fleet to Pearl Harbor. There, as General Tojo put it, "lay the American fleet, a gun pointed at our heads."

In June the Japanese made a treaty with Thailand. Almost at the moment that France was defeated by the Germans, the Japanese began demanding the right to use airbases and move troops through Northern Indochina for the China war. On July 27, 1940 the Japanese cabinet and the military men reaffirmed their earlier agreement: they wanted first to end the China incident, and now that the United States was cracking down on shipments of oil they needed a secure source of petroleum. There were two places to get it: Northern Sakhalin and the Dutch East Indies. They did not get very far by negotiations with the

Russians. So they put their full efforts in the south, prepared to seize the Indies by force if they could not have their way by negotiations.

On September 22, 1940, they concluded an agreement with the French about the bases in Indochina. It was, of course, an agreement reached at the point of a gun. What were the French to do? Exhausted by the European war, how could they defend Indochina against the Japanese? They had to give in to keep the Japanese from simply seizing the country.

The Japanese, for their part, guaranteed French sovereignty over Indochina, but they did not mean it. In Tokyo's master plan was a section that called for ultimate "independence"—for Indochina, Malaya, and the Dutch East Indies. It would, of course, be *Hakko-ichiu* independence (under the Japanese roof).

As noted, Japanese troops misbehaved in the occupation of Indochina, and at the Emperor's demand, General Tojo moved against those responsible, but that had no real effect on the basic problem of Japanese army control, which had always left to local commanders the responsibility and authority to deal with the local situation as they saw fit. The excesses would occur again and again.

Late in December 1940 Japan took a hand in a territorial dispute between Thailand and Indochina over land around the town of Battambang, which had been ceded under pressure by Thailand to the French some years earlier and which the previous owners now wanted back. The Japanese mediated and decided in favor of Thailand, which was quite understandable since Thailand was falling into the Japanese orbit. The French did not like the process, but in May 1941 a treaty was signed giving the disputed territory back to the Bangkok government.

In planning to move south quickly the Army was anticipating the combined resistance of the Dutch and the British. If Tokyo wished to strike at the East Indies, it could expect war with Britain. Therefore the Japanese must also strike Malaya, for resources and to protect their flank. They must have bases in southern Indochina too, and in Thailand. Besides this, Japan needed the rice of Indochina and Thailand for her war economy.

What was Japan to do about the East Indies oil? The Army said the country should take it, either by negotiation or by force. The cabinet, and this included General Tojo, said "go slow." So there was no real policy, but the Imperial General Headquarters staff continued to press, looking for a German offensive against Britain in the spring of 1941— an offensive that might open up Japan's chances to seize British possessions in Asia. Therefore Imperial Headquarters wanted bases in

Thailand and Indochina, and wanted them immediately. General Tojo did not much like the idea. He was committed to the Emperor to keeping the Army under control, and if Japan had bases in southern Indochina he could anticipate more incidents of the sort that had been so embarrassing the year before.

By the spring of 1941 the young staff officers of the Imperial General Headquarters were fairly self-satisfied. They had gone a long way in implementing "The Main Principles of Japan's Policy for Coping with the Situation in Accordance with World Developments." They had allied themselves with what appeared to be the winning side in the European war, and if that trend continued they could expect to share in the looting that would accompany the breakup of the British Empire. They had taken several steps to bring the China Incident to an end, including, as noted, pressing the British to close the Burma Road, thus cutting off China's access to the world, since northern Indochina was now a Japanese base. What remained was to secure the resources of the Dutch East Indies, but the Dutch were stalling. The Japanese negotiators at Batavia made the same requests, week after week, and always got equivocal replies. The Japanese requests had burgeoned until in 1941 they were asking for 40 percent of the oil produced in the Indies, which would provide 60 percent of Japan's needs.

The June 22, 1941 German invasion of Russia came as a terrible shock to the Japanese Army. It posed a whole raft of new problems involving the possibility of German victory over both the Soviets and Britain, and the nightmare of dealing with Germany over the pieces of the British Empire.

A few days after the German attack on Russia, the Yamashita military mission returned from Germany with a report that suggested the Japanese should first unify their military services under a command like the Oberkommando der Wehrmacht and then join Germany in her war against Russia. But alarmed by the prospect, and very busy with the "strike south" movement, General Tojo led the Army in pigeon-holing the Yamashita report. Yamashita, whom Tojo saw as a rival for power within the military establishment, was shipped off to Manchuria to set up a new army headquarters, and ostensibly prepare for the attack on the Soviets. But in fact, the whole idea of attacking Russia had been so overstated by Foreign Minister Matsuoka, who had been pressed time and again by the Germans, that with his departure from the cabinet that scheme was foreclosed as well. As General Tojo maintained, Japan must act from self-interest alone. As far as the Germans were concerned, they had not consulted their ally Japan before they decided to attack the Russians, so Japan had no responsibility to consult the Germans or to worry about their interests. In the back of the generals' minds was the suspicion that it was best to play the two European behemoths off against each other, Russia against Germany, now that the Tripartite Alliance threatened to become a burden rather than an asset.

In mid-June the Japanese had broken off as useless the negotiations with the Dutch in the East Indies. Then they immediately began demanding from the French the right to move into southern Indochina with bases. Imperial General Headquarters was confident that such a move would not provoke any particularly strong action by the United States, because experience indicated that the United States was inclined to stop at mere protest.

On June 21 the Americans had submitted proposals for settlement of their differences with Japan, but Secretary of State Cordell Hull had also submitted an oral statement objecting to the activities of "certain Japanese leaders" in relation to the Tripartite Pact. He was pointing a finger at the then foreign minister, Matsuoka.

As for the proposal, Foreign Ministry spokesman Yoshie Saito summed up the Japanese government's general reaction and attitude to the whole matter:

The present world, divided into those who are for the maintenance of the status quo and those who are for its destruction, the democracies and the totalitarian states, is in the midst of a war. Hull's reply is for the status quo and for democracy. It is obvious that America sent it after consultation with Britain and China. Thus I think that the countries that are for the status quo are getting together to put pressure on Japan. On the matter of Sino-Japanese negotiations the United States hopes to make us negotiate on the basis of conditions existing prior to the China Incident. . . . This proposal does not recognize the stationing of troops in China to maintain peace and order; it seeks the unconditional withdrawal of all troops. The stationing of troops to maintain peace and order is a most important element in our national policy. If we withdraw our troops unconditionally, the Chinese Communists, the Nationalists, the Nanking government and the warlords would fight causing great disorder. . . .

Japan aims at complete cooperation between Japan and China. By contrast the United States is advocating nondiscriminatory treatment. This makes it impossible to establish a New Order in East Asia. Britain and the United States have continued to aid Chiang until the present time; and they are planning to obtain an advantage position in China in the future. When an overall peace comes to China the influence of American dollars, which are backed by 80 percent of the world's gold supply, will spread all over China. Working from today's special position, America's intention is to bring about peace between Japan and China by means of an agreement between Japan and the United States and then to let Japan and China negotiate directly within the limits thus set. This procedure will transfer leadership in the Far East to the United States. It will interfere with the implementation of an independent policy by our Empire. It will give the United States the right to have a say in the China Problem.

Matsuoka, who was still foreign minister at the time, had put Saito up to making the statement; he declared the American proposals unacceptable. He did so without offering any counterproposals and without telling Prime Minister Konoye. But officials of the foreign office refused to transmit the Matsuoka refusal without Japanese counterproposals. Matsuoka, by this time, had annoyed Konoye so often and had so bothered General Tojo and Navy Minister Oikawa with his activity that Konoye finally decided that Matsuoka had to go. Thus the cabinet was dissolved on July 16, and Matsuoka was out. Matsuoka's removal should have made dealing with America easier. However, through interception of Japanese diplomatic messages and through code-breaking, by the first week in July the Americans knew what was happening in Japan. On July 18 President Roosevelt discussed the Far East situation with his cabinet and concluded that the time had come at last to take a really strong action against the Japanese. The plan would involve the freezing of all Japanese assets in the United States and the absolute cut-off of oil to Japan. Ambassador Kichisaburo Nomura in Washington heard of the coming action and on July 23 warned Tokyo to hold up on the Indochina move unless the cabinet was prepared for an American response just short of a breach of diplomatic relations. On July 24, President Roosevelt personally met with Admiral Nomura and told him that he would attempt to secure a guarantee of the neutralization of French Indochina. Also on July 24, when the third Konoye cabinet had been formed, a meeting was held to reaffirm the cabinet policies. For some reason Nomura had failed to send this information through to the Japanese government. At that meeting, Navy Chief of Staff Nagano summed up the problem Japan faced.

"As for war with the United States, although there is now a chance of achieving victory, the chances will diminish as time goes on. By the latter half of next year it will already be difficult for us to cope with the United States, after that the situation will become increasingly worse. The United States probably will prolong the matter until her defenses have been built up and then try to settle it. Accordingly as time goes by the Empire will be put at a disadvantage. If we could settle things without war, there would be nothing better. But if we conclude that the conflict cannot ultimately be avoided, then I would like you to understand that as time goes by we will be in a disadvantageous position. Moreover, if we occupy the Philippines, it will be, from the Navy's point of view, easier to carry on the war." These words of warning, advocating a preemptive strike, came from Admiral Isoroku Yamamoto, the commander of the Combined Fleet, who had always opposed war with the United States. But now, in the knowledge that Imperial Headquarters was moving toward war, he was doing his best to win it for Japan in the only way he saw it could be won—by a lightning stroke that would cripple the American fleet and bring the Americans to the peace table.

But since the Roosevelt message of efforts to try to neutralize French Indochina had been delayed in transit, the juggernaut had taken over and Japanese troops had set sail for Nha Trang and other ports in southern Indochina. On July 25 the Americans finally acted: they made the cuts, and froze Japan's assets. Britain, her empire, and the Dutch East Indies followed suit. Now Japan had no oil supply at all. Obviously this was an intolerable situation and could be resolved in one of only three ways: the securing of oil from the USSR, backing down to the U.S. demand that Japan remove her troops from Indochina and China, or war. The Soviets, now under attack from Germany, were no longer a potential oil supplier. It was unthinkable that the Japanese militarists would abandon their national policy of "freeing Asia from the Western yoke," and so, with full understanding of the possible consequences, war was perceived as the only option.

To the Japanese, the Western economic blockade was a sort of war, and the culmination of all they feared—the unification of the colonial powers. To the threatening Europeans the Japanese added America, in the perceived move to encircle and suppress the Japanese aim. That is precisely how General Tojo felt. He said that Japan was exercising the justifiable right of self-defense when she went to war. She was not prepared, he said, but there was no alternative but to take a tough stand against this encirclement.

Tojo and the other generals were certain that it was only a matter of time before the Western powers attacked them militarily, not just with economic strictures. They cited the presence of the U.S. fleet at Pearl

Harbor, the increase in expenditure for America's armed forces, the establishment of a new base of operations at the 13th Naval District in Alaska, the huge increase planned in the U.S. fleet, and the evacuation of American women and children from East Asia. All these were seen in Tokyo as preparation for aggressive war.

5

The Decline and Fall of Prince Konoye

Early on September 6, 1941, Prime Minister Konoye called at the Imperial palace to acquaint the Emperor with the latest developments in the tense situation between the United States and Japan. The Emperor observed that the Konoye cabinet policy seemed to put more emphasis on war than it did on diplomacy, and the Emperor was quite right, because the military men had already decided on war. It was apparent in the plan called "The Essentials for Carrying Out the Emperor's Policies," which had been adopted by the Liaison Conference on September 3. The wording of the policy even referred to the United States and Britain as "the enemy," and the last ten days of October had been set by the military as the target date for completing war preparations. Navy Chief of Staff Nagano had predicted a long war, and suggested the necessity of achieving quick territorial gains and then protecting them. They could hope for a miracle, which would be either the Americans bringing their fleet to the western Pacific and having it destroyed, or a German victory in Europe that would wreck the British Empire. Other than that they were going into war blindfolded. Could they win? Asked directly, no general or admiral would predict victory. But, they said, each month the situation would deteriorate. So, if there was to be war, the sooner the better.

The Army chief of staff, General Sugiyama, did not address himself to the problems of conducting a war, but to starting one. If diplomacy did not work by October 10, then it had to be war, he said, because the Army was again talking about attacking Russia in the north, to secure Sakhalin oil primarily. And to act in the north they had to win a quick victory in the south.

Army and Navy chiefs agreed that war should come if diplomacy failed, but the cabinet officers, General Tojo included, held out for a bit more time for diplomacy.

"In the event that there is no prospect of our demands being met by the first ten days of October, we will immediately decide to commence hostilities against the United States, Britain, and the Netherlands."

Tojo had asked General Sugiyama if the Army intended to build up military supplies in Indochina in the next few weeks, and Sugiyama replied that they would. Then everyone would know their intentions, Tojo observed.

"That can't be helped. We can't conceal everything," explained Sugiyama.

When the Emperor heard about all this from Prime Minister Konoye, he insisted that the Army and Navy chiefs of staff be brought in to explain this warlike stance when they were supposed to be talking diplomacy. They were summoned to the Palace.

The Emperor addressed Sugiyama. "In the event of war with the United States, how long will it take the Army to win?"

"Operations in the South Pacific will be concluded in three months," said Sugiyama.

"When the China Incident broke out, you were war minister," the Emperor reminded Sugiyama. "You said that operations in China would end in one month. That was four years ago. The China Incident still has not been concluded. . . ."

"The interior of China is huge," fidgeted Sugiyama.

The Emperor's face turned red with anger.

"If the interior of China is huge, isn't the Pacific Ocean even bigger? How can you be sure that war will end in three months?"

There was silence.

"Does the Imperial Headquarters intend to put the emphasis on military or diplomatic measures?" the Emperor then asked.

Navy Chief of Staff Nagano hastened to reply. "Diplomacy, of course," he said.

The Emperor was totally dissatisfied with this turn of events, which clearly contradicted Nagano's answer. An Imperial Conference was scheduled for later in the day. The Emperor never spoke in these conferences, that was the custom that had characterized the meetings since the days of the Taisho Emperor, but today Hirohito told his close advisor the Marquis Kido, Lord Keeper of the Privy Seal, that he wanted to speak instead of giving questions to Kido to ask for him.

Kido knew that this breach of custom would upset the military, and so he persuaded the Emperor to let President Hara of the Privy Council ask the questions.

"That is all very well," said the Emperor, "but the fact that a time limit has been put upon the time for decision and the fact that the military will now prepare for war tips the balance in favor of war."

So this vital Imperial Conference was convened at 10 a.m. on September 6, and the Emperor held his tongue and let Privy Council President Hara do the questioning.

First, the Emperor's attention was called to the minimum demands and maximum concessions that his government was willing to make for Britain and the United States. The demands:

The U.S. and Britain must not interfere in China. Britain, which had reopened the Burma Road, must close it permanently. Britain and the U.S. must stop giving any aid to China. The U.S. and Britain must not take any action that threatened the Japanese Empire. They could not make treaties with Thailand, the Dutch East Indies, China, or the USSR. They were not to increase their military presence in the Far East; they must not interfere with the Japanese in Indochina; they must give the Japanese what they needed in the way of goods and supplies, and restore all trade with Japan.

As for concessions the Japanese were willing to make: Japan would not advance in the Far East, except in China, which meant she would not attack Malaya or the Dutch East Indies. The Japanese would not attack Russia unless Russia violated the Soviet-Japan Neutrality Pact. They would withdraw their forces from Indochina after the settlement of the China question. Japan would guarantee the neutrality of the Philippines.

From the Japanese point of view, this seemed eminently fair. They were not willing to return to the status quo ante—the situation that existed before the Japanese takeover of Manchuria.

Of course the demands of Britain and the U.S. were precisely that, that the Japanese give up Manchuria and withdraw their troops from China and Indochina. The Japanese knew the Allied attitude, and thus the Japanese military men had very little hope of the diplomacy succeeding.

This statement was accompanied by several set speeches, including those from the prime minister and the two military chiefs of staff. General Tojo and Navy Minister Oikawa did not speak. The gist of the presentations was that although there was enormous danger attached to the possibility of war, Japan was being hemmed in from all sides by the Western powers, and that if she waited, her chances of survival would grow slimmer every year.

There would never be a better time for war than this autumn of 1941, said the Japanese military, even though the outlook for such a war was very cloudy. Such a war, said the cabinet and Imperial Headquarters in a combined statement, would become a war of endurance, and very long.

It is very difficult to predict the termination of war and it would be well nigh impossible to expect the surrender of the United States. However we cannot exclude the possibility that the war may end because of a great change in American public opinion, which may result from such factors as the remarkable success of our military operations in the south or the surrender of Great Britain. At any rate, we should be able to establish an invincible position by building up a strategically advantageous position through the occupation of important areas in the south; by creating an economy that will be self-sufficient in the long run, through the development of rich resources in the southern region, as well as through the economic power of the east Asian continent, and by linking Asia and Europe in destroying the Anglo-American coalition through our cooperation with Germany and Italy. Meanwhile we may hope that we will be able to influence the trend of affairs and bring the war to an end.

After all the statements had been made and all the questions asked by Hara, the Emperor read a poem, one composed by his grandfather, the Meiji Emperor.

> All the seas in every quarter are
> as brothers to one another.
> Why, then, do the winds and waves of strife
> rage so turbulently throughout the world?

The conferees were silent, knowing that this poem registered the Emperor's censure of their preoccupation with war, rather than diplomacy, and they promised that every effort would be made to achieve their ends without military action.

In the Atlantic came events in September that affected the Pacific. The Americans had been escorting British convoys, protecting them against German submarines. In the second week of September the destroyer U.S.S. *Greer* was attacked by a U-boat. Japan was very much concerned lest the Germans now invoke the Tripartite Alliance and force Japan into war with the United States. But in President

Roosevelt's fireside chat with the American people on September 11 he did not mention the Pacific, much to the relief of the Japanese.

But the diplomacy between Japan and the United States was not advancing, for both sides had assumed strong positions. The Japanese wanted to keep troops in China against the Communist threat. They wanted the Chiang Kai-shek government to merge with the Nanking government. They wanted recognition of Manchukuo.

The Americans demanded that Japan and Chiang settle their differences, and that American business in China not be discriminated against; neither would they concede that America would make no agreements restricting its aid to nations under aggression. The two viewpoints were not reconciled in the exchanges of messages in the next few weeks. For example, Ambassador Nomura in Washington knew that the Americans would look dimly on the Japanese keeping troops in China after a settlement, so he proposed that the Japanese withdraw the troops two years after settlement. But the Japanese Army general staff objected and now began to throw roadblocks in the way of meaningful negotiation. The Army did not trust Nomura to represent its views, and Nomura knew that to represent the Army faithfully was to bring on war. Prince Konoye made a real effort to break the deadlock. At his dinner with Ambassador Grew he suggested that he go to Washington to meet with President Roosevelt, a suggestion that Grew endorsed heartily but that was greeted suspiciously by the professional diplomats in Washington as some sort of Japanese ploy.

On September 20 the Army rejected a statement prepared by the foreign office. It was obvious that the Army was running the government. Tojo, always the practical man, told the liaison conference on September 20 that time was running out. And it was. Everything that the Army did was geared to war, such as a new law to restrict travel inside Japan. Foreign Minister Toyoda objected to it as a highly suspect act. Tojo replied that it was necessary to protect military secrets, but this was nonsense, because foreigners were already so well watched that they could scarcely move in Japan.

October 15 was the deadline finally agreed upon for negotiations with the U.S. When the Army insisted on this, Prince Konoye was so shocked that he withdrew to his home in Kamakura; he would not come to Tokyo and threatened to resign. And what of the Konoye-Roosevelt meeting? The Americans were stalling, because they did not want to show apparent approval of the Japanese position. The Japanese wanted the meeting; the American Secretary of State, Cordell Hull,

did not. It was that simple. Admiral Nomura told Secretary of State
Hull that if the meeting did not take place the Konoye cabinet probably
would fall, and be succeeded by a much tougher, Army-oriented
cabinet.

But on October 2, the Army was directing the negotiations by
objecting to almost anything the foreign office proposed that seemed
in the least conciliatory. It was quite apparent that the young officers
running affairs in Imperial Headquarters were determined on war. And
why not? War meant enlargement of the armed services and more
chances of advancement to general, more opportunities for adventure
and heroic exploits. The Japanese Army was filled with young dream-
ers who were anxious to lead troops into battle, flourishing their
samurai swords like knights of old, and hewing down the enemy. The
Japanese of this period had a highly idealized, "samurized," view of
conflict.

On October 4, for all practical purposes, the American government
rejected the possibility of a meeting between the "two heads of
state"—Roosevelt and Konoye. Perhaps one reason was that the
Americans were not quite sure who was the head of state, the prime
minister, as stated in the Japanese Constitution, or the emperor. It was
a question that the Americans had not resolved, because the Japanese
had not resolved it.

But by this rejection, as Ambassador Nomura quickly understood,
the Americans had put the negotiations into deadlock. The Japanese
Army would not yield. The Americans would neither yield nor let
Konoye come and try to exercise whatever personal magic with Roosevelt to save the situation. By this time the Army said there was no
purpose in conducting further negotiations; most of its most influential
officers wanted to get on with the war. And by this time Tojo concurred, although Navy Minister Oikawa did not. Koshiro Oikawa
admitted that he did not like the prospect because he had no confidence
that Japan could win a prolonged war with the United States. But now
virtually no one was listening—certainly not Tojo, who had been
infected by the enthusiasm for war over at Imperial General Headquarters.

On October 12, with the Army clock set for October 15, Prime
Minister Konoye called a meeting with his foreign, war, and navy
ministers at his house in the Ogikubo section of Tokyo. He tried to
persuade General Tojo that there was still hope for negotiations with
the Americans, but Tojo had been listening to his Army comrades who
said all hope was gone.

At this meeting, Oikawa was noncommittal, and Tojo reflected the Army view that the time for negotiation had run out without any progress. Could the prime minister guarantee that delay would result in an agreement with the United States that would be satisfactory to Japan?

Of course Prince Konoye could make no such guarantees, and his position had been undermined by the refusal of Roosevelt to meet with him personally. So Tojo remained unconvinced, and refused to do anything to change the timetable of the Army zealots.

The next day, October 13, Tojo reiterated his stand in the cabinet meeting. October 15 had been the day decided upon and it was nearly on them. If the prime minister wished to repudiate the date of October 15, then all the cabinet should resign as having failed the Emperor, and let a new cabinet make a new try.

Otherwise, let the cabinet agree to break off the negotiations on October 15 and go to war.

"You know," said Tojo, "at some point in man's lifetime he may find it necessary to jump with his eyes closed from the veranda of Kiyomizu-dera into the gulch below." This classical allusion to a samurai tale was Tojo's way of saying that he and the other generals believed it time to take the great adventure.

Prince Konoye replied wryly that the idea of jumping thus might occur to him as an individual but he was not a samurai. He was, however, the prime minister, responsible for a 2600-year-old national entity and a hundred million people. To Konoye jumping hardly seemed a proper response.

But that was the response of the Army, which was now reimbued, courtesy of General Sadao Araki, with the samurai spirit. They operated on the premise that working against great odds was a normal aspiration, and that fighting spirit transcended all. And thus was Japan's commitment to war forged in such conversations between the politicians and the military.

The statement by Tojo brought the matter to a head. Prime Minister Konoye felt that the Army was being ridiculous. Nobody could guarantee them a victory but they seemed bent on war. His own view was that if war was necessary, that was one thing, but if one was to go to war one must feel certain of victory. He was not a samurai of the new school, nor imbued with its new thought—that of necessity right injects might, and that if the Japanese were right in their holy crusade to save the other Asians from the white man, their efforts would be crowned with success if only they persevered and had the spirit of sacrifice.

At this point Prince Konoye said he had no course but resignation, which meant also the resignation of the entire cabinet. He and Tojo discussed the possibilities for the future, and they agreed between themselves that Prince Higashikuni was the best man for the job of prime minister in this difficult situation. Toshihiko Higashikuni was a cousin of the Emperor's and a high-ranking Army officer who had served as chief of staff.

But the Marquis Kido, the *éminence grise* behind the Emperor in these days, did not favor this move. He said that Higashikuni did not have the political experience to lead a cabinet. What he really thought was that it was too dangerous for the Emperor and the Emperor-system to have a relative of the Emperor making decisions about war and peace. What if Japan lost the war? Then, Koichi Kido reasoned, the enemy victor would have a real reason to come after the Emperor and claim that Hirohito had led the nation into war, using his relatives. No, it could not be that way.

If not Higashikuni, then who?

On the night of October 15, Prince Konoye called on the Marquis Kido at the Palace and held a long discussion. They considered possibilities. One was Navy Minister Oikawa. Another was General Tojo, who was recommended by Konoye and the Marquis Kido. On the next day, October 17, the senior statesmen assembled at the Palace. They included seven former prime ministers. Konoye was not there because he was running a fever and had stayed home in bed. Several names were mentioned, including Prince Higashikuni, but the Marquis Kido gave his objections to that choice. When asked his own choice, he said it would be Tojo. He alone could control the Army, Kido believed, and just now the young officers were growing extremely restless; the Tokyo press was filled with pro-war propaganda obviously gained from Army sources.

If Tojo were chosen, Kido said, and this indicated that he had discussed the situation with the Emperor, Tojo would be commanded by the Emperor to forget about the September 6 decision that the question of war or peace would be settled on October 15, and to re-examine the situation from the beginning.

Several other names were mentioned, including that of General Ugaki, but finally the choice came down to Tojo, and the senior statesmen agreed on him.

General Tojo knew nothing of this and that afternoon was at his official war minister's residence, cleaning out his personal possessions and getting ready to move back to his Tokyo house, when the Grand Chamberlain of the Palace arrived and told him that the Emperor wanted to see him at once.

Tojo assumed that the Emperor would want to question him about the cabinet resignation of the day before, so he got together his papers and headed for the Palace, where he arrived just after four o'clock in the afternoon. He was immediately taken to the Emperor, who wasted no time. As soon as Tojo came into the room Hirohito said: "We direct you to form a cabinet and to abide by the provisions of the Constitution. We believe that an exceedingly grave situation confronts the nation. Bear in mind at this time that cooperation between the Army and the Navy should be closer than ever before. It is Our intention to summon also the navy minister and speak to him in this same vein."

Tojo was completely surprised, and asked for a short time to consider. He withdrew to the adjacent waiting room. Meanwhile the Emperor was receiving Admiral Oikawa and saying the same thing he had said to Tojo about service cooperation and the crisis that Japan faced. After Oikawa's audience ended the Admiral went into the waiting room with Tojo and the Marquis Kido came in and told them that the Emperor thought it very important that the cabinet rethink the situation that existed at home and abroad without reference to that binding September 6 Imperial Conference decision. Tojo had been arguing that it would be impossible to reverse the decision of September 6 because it had been made in the presence of the Emperor. But now the Emperor had ordered them to consider reversing the decision; Hirohito's instructions came to be known as his "clean slate" message.

It was this statement that made Tojo decide to accept the prime ministry. He felt that matters had gone so far that Japan either must prepare for war, or must make some supreme effort to find a road to peace. He would start with a blank sheet of paper.

Tojo began to consider how he would constitute his cabinet, and so thinking he left the palace and hastened to the Meiji Shrine to pray for guidance. He continued on to the Togo War Memorial, and then to the Yasukuni shrine. As he made this pilgrimage he decided upon his cabinet, which would be appointed quickly; the selection of the navy minister would be left to the Navy, of course.

He chose Naoki Hoshino, that old friend from Manchurian days, as chief cabinet secretary, and this was the first appointment. He needed a detail man and he knew that Hoshino was just that. That same evening Hoshino began his duties, making telephone calls to the men Tojo had chosen for his cabinet.

So Japan was to have a new government, and the Emperor hoped one that would lead the way out of the threat of war that engulfed Japan.

6

The Rise of Tojo

Prime Minister-designate Lieutenant General Hideki Tojo moved swiftly to select his cabinet and demanded answers virtually on the spot from the people he chose. Two refused to be rushed, however, and insisted upon a discussion first. They were Okinori Kaya, minister of finance, and Shigenori Togo, who was slated to be foreign minister. They wanted to be sure that Tojo was going to try to solve problems by diplomacy and not with a samurai sword. So they came to meet Tojo and were satisfied that he was going to negotiate with the Americans.

When the cabinet was constituted it contained three of the *ni ki, san suke* group: Tojo, Hoshino, and Nobosuke Kishi, who was to be in charge of commerce and industry. There were no members of the *Zaibatsu*, Japan's coalition of economic cartels, and only five military men, two fewer than in the last Konoye cabinet.

On the afternoon of October 18 the investiture of the cabinet was held, at which time it was also announced that Tojo had just been promoted by the Army to be a full general. So here he was at the pinnacle: a full general, prime minister, and minister of war of the Japanese government.

In his study of the coming of the war to Japan, Robert J. C. Butow captured the essence of Japan in the fall of 1941:

The Japan of which General Tojo became premier was operated by remote control. It was a country in which puppet politics had reached a high state of development, to the detriment of the national welfare. The ranking members of the military services were the robots of their subordinates— the so called *chuken shoko*, the nucleus group which was active "at the center" and which was largely composed of field grade officers. They, in

65

turn, were influenced by younger elements within the services at large
and by ultranationalists outside military ranks. The civilian members of
the cabinet were the robots of the military, especially the nucleus group,
working through the service ministers and the chiefs of the army and
navy general staffs. The Emperor himself, through no fault of his own,
was the robot of the government—of the cabinet and supreme command,
the prisoner of the circumstances into which he was born—an unfortunate
individual who wanted very much to be free to pursue the life of a man,
yet who knew that he must act like a god and so remain an unapproacha-
ble mystery to one and all. Finally, the nation—the one hundred million
dedicated souls, the sum and substance of Japan, from whom the blood
and toil and tears and sweat of Churchill's phrase were wrung—the nation
was the robot of the throne.

And in this period, the key to Japan's behavior lay in the young
officers. Many years after the war Shin Itonaga, a retired captain of
the Self-Defense Force, made a special study of the history of the
Pacific War. He had been one of those young officers. He believes that
one of the principal Western analysts' problems in understanding the
Japan of the period has been their failure to give enough emphasis to
the role played by the *chuken shoko*, who literally made the plans for
the military and then bullied their superiors into accepting them.
Captain Itonaga's analysis in every way agrees with that of author
Butow.

In the autumn of 1941, the Tojo appointment was regarded at home
and abroad as a signal that the Army was in control of the Japanese
government. *Yomiuri Shimbun*, one of the largest Japanese dailies,
said editorially at the time that in Tojo's decisiveness was an induce-
ment to the nation to rise and administer a great shock to the anti-Axis
powers. *Yomiuri*, by then, was thoroughly inculcated with supernation-
alism. Americans such as Ambassador Grew tried to hope that in Tojo
there was resilience. He had, actually, been one of the five members
of the Konoye cabinet who had supported the rethinking of relations
with the U.S., in opposition to Foreign Minister Matsuoka. Cynics,
like the Chinese Nationalists, saw in the Tojo emergence the final
Japanese admission that the Army was in charge. And they were
correct, for Tojo had come to office largely because he was the man
most acceptable to the generals, and he had been accepted by the
Emperor in the forlorn hope that Tojo could control his brothers in
uniform. In fact, if he had tried, he would soon enough have been
forced out by the Army cabal that now was itching for action. The
reality of the situation in Japan in the fall of 1941 was stated by the

young officers in a document prepared to answer questions that might be asked by the Emperor about the October decision to make war or have peace. In essence the document said that if the United States would accept Japan's Greater East Asia Co-prosperity Sphere, there could be peace. Otherwise there must be war.

After the formation of the Tojo cabinet the representatives of the military high commands and the government met nearly every day, as ordered by the Emperor, to resurvey the Imperial Conference decision of September 6. But the papers from which they worked were prepared by the same young officers who had prepared the original batch, so it was obvious that the conclusions were not going to change. This was all the more likely because the Army and Navy chiefs of staff were not formally ordered, as the government ministers had been, to take a new look. So the war preparations continued apace.

What the cabinet wanted was information, and that is what they did not get from the military. It was known that the supply of oil from the U.S. had been cut off. What was not known was how much oil reserve Japan had, and the military jealously guarded that secret from the ministers, who also could not get other statistical information about military matters. "Top Secret" was the answer given them, until in exasperation Foreign Minister Togo complained, "I was astonished at our lack of the statistical data required for a study of this sort, but even more, keenly felt the absurdity of our having to base our deliberations on assumptions since the high command refused to divulge figures on the numbers of our force strength, or any facts relating to operations."

In fact, many of the questions asked by the conferees were answered by the military men, using that same aide memoire that had guided them on September 6, so the deliberations were really a sham. For example, the Army was building up strength in Manchuria for possible action against the Russians, but when asked if the buildup was adequate to win, Chief of Staff Sugiyama replied that with good luck and clever strategy they might win. This was hardly a scientific attitude toward war. And as far as the Navy was concerned, the young officers had completed a staff study concluding that shipbuilding capacity would be 400,000 tons the first year and 600,000 tons the second. Navy Minister Shimada, an old hand at figures, said, "Young people are too optimistic. There is the problem of repairing warships, too, so ship construction probably will be 200,000 to 300,000 tons, about half."

The discussions continued again on October 30, but nothing really new was said or decided. It was apparent that war was going to be a risky course, but the Army and Navy were forging ahead with their plans for hostilities and it was agreed now that November 30 would be the absolute deadline for the decision to take action or not. But in their minds and particularly in General Tojo's there was no doubt about what they must do, failing the miracle of an American agreement to all their demands. To give in to the Americans would reduce Japan to the status of a third-rate power, to economic dependence on the West, and would signal an end to the dream of a united and independent Asia. So at the end of that meeting Prime Minister Tojo summed up. What they must consider now were the following alternatives:

1. Avoid war and undergo great hardships.
2. Decide on war immediately and settle matters by combat.
3. Decide on war but carry on war preparations and diplomacy together, remembering that they wanted the diplomacy to succeed, as did the Emperor.

Foreign Minister Togo embraced that last option, but the Navy minister was vague and Finance Minister Kaya asked many questions, but got only rote answers from the book of the young officers.

As requested by the government, and reluctantly accepted by the driving generals and admirals who wanted to get on with the matter, there was no conference on October 31. But on November 1 the conferees met again. Before this session Tojo had held several private meetings.

The premier, too, supported the third position, to negotiate and prepare simultaneously. The Army general staff said it was all a waste of time: they should prepare for war and get on with it. But everyone else, including the Navy, preferred the third alternative. Tojo held private sessions with General Sugiyama, the chief of staff of the Army, but was unable to sidetrack the generals from their determination. So the meeting began with the Army, less General Tojo, on one side and everyone else on the other.

At this meeting the Navy requested something new: enormous supplies of steel for ship construction. Everyone agreed, although no one knew where the steel was going to come from. There was, as has been suggested, an Alice in Wonderland quality to these meetings from the outset. No one except the Army knew the statistical facts, and they weren't sharing them. Accordingly no one else really knew what he was talking about. The Army was willing to place its trust in the

Imperial Way. Virtue would provide victory in the end, assured the generals.

On November 1, Foreign Minister Togo and Finance Minister Kaya both tried to get the war decision postponed, but were shouted down by the militarists. These two ministers were so angry they would not assent, and so the decision for war was made by majority vote, not the usual consensus. Only later, out of respect for Tojo, did the two dissenting ministers give him their pledge to support the decision.

The Liaison Conference adopted a proposal that the war begin on December 1 and that diplomacy would continue until the end of November. By the time this decision was reached the conference had lasted seventeen hours and all concerned were exhausted.

A few hours after the long conference Tojo went to the Palace to acquaint the Emperor with the details of their deliberations. The Emperor said he could see how it was necessary to decide on war and to make preparations for war, but he repeated his request that every effort be made to break the deadlock with the United States through diplomatic negotiations.

And when Tojo returned to the war ministry after the audience he told his subordinates there that he was praying to the gods that somehow Japan could make a diplomatic agreement with the United States that would avoid hostilities. For some reason not readily ascertainable, given the attitudes of the Army and Navy staffs, Tojo still assessed the chance for peace at 50 percent, or in his bleaker periods at 30 percent. That was quite in contrast to the other generals, who assessed the chance for peace through negotiation at zero.

On November 5, the Imperial Conference met to ratify the decisions made at the Liaison Conference. The ministers made their statements and the president of the Privy Council asked questions. The Emperor was silent as precedent demanded, but everyone knew that the chances for peace were not very great. Admiral Yamamoto, chief of the Combined Fleet, had already approved Secret Operations Order No. 1, which called for war to be declared on X-Day. And since Admiral Yamamoto was one of the most fervent opponents of war against the United States, what could anyone expect now?

One important matter that was established in this meeting was the manner and extent of military operations at the beginning of the war. General Sugiyama detailed the plan:

"Targets of this operation are military and air bases in Guam, Hong Kong, British Malaya, Burma, British Borneo, Dutch Borneo, Sumatra, Celebes, the Bismarck Islands, and small islands southwest of the

Bismarck Archipelago.'' (The last included Guadalcanal, which would be the turning point of the war.) Sugiyama then went into questions of the numerical strength of the enemy opposing Japanese forces.

"The Army," he said, "will carry out operations under these conditions in cooperation with the Navy, and its major efforts will be made in the Philippines and Malaya. The operation is planned to start in Malaya and the Philippines simultaneously and then move southward toward the Netherlands East Indies.

"In this way it is estimated that it will take 50 days to complete the operations in the Philippines, 100 days in Malaya, and 50 days in the Netherlands East Indies and that the entire operation will be completed within five months after the opening of the war.''

The question of the American fleet was raised by Privy Council President Hara. Navy Chief of Staff Nagano replied vaguely that 40 percent of the American fleet was in the Atlantic and 60 percent in the Pacific, and spoke vaguely again about the possibility of the American and British fleets combining for operations. Not a word was said about Admiral Yamamoto's secret fleet order for the attack on Pearl Harbor. The Army knew nothing about the plan, nor did Prime Minister Tojo.

Finally Tojo summarized the reasons that he still had hope for a diplomatic settlement of the American issues, although President Hara had just finished asserting that "a war against the United States and Great Britain is inevitable if Japan is to survive.''

The prime minister said of America:

"They will learn how determined Japan is from our troop deployments which we will carry out on the basis of the present proposal. The United States has from the beginning believed that Japan would give up because of economic pressure; but if they recognize that Japan is determined then that is the time we should resort to diplomatic measures. I believe this is the only way that is left for us. This is the present proposal. This is the last measure we can take that is in line with what President Hara has called 'going by diplomacy'; I cannot think of any other way out of the present situation.''

Privy Council President Hara then warned of one of his major worries: that the struggle between Japan and the Western world might become a racial war. He observed that the Americans, British, and Germans all looked on the Japanese as "a second class race." Tojo agreed that there was danger here, and said that if war came, "I intend to take measures to prevent a racial war once war is started. . . . As to what our moral basis for going to war should be, there is some merit in making it clear that Great Britain and the United States constitute a strong threat to Japan's self-preservation. Also if we are fair in governing the occupied areas, attitudes toward us will probably relax. America may be enraged for a while, but later she will come to understand why we did what we did. In any case I will be careful to avoid the war's becoming a racial war."

Following the Imperial Conference of November 5, most of the internal discussions in Japan were concerned with the manner of conducting the war that everyone now expected. On November 15 the Liaison Conference approved another document drawn up by the young officers and submitted by the Imperial Headquarters.

"Our Empire will engage in a quick war, and will destroy American and British bases in eastern Asia and in the Southwest Pacific region. At the same time that it secures a strategically powerful position, it will control those areas producing vital materials, as well as important transportation routes, and thereby prepare for a protracted period of self-sufficiency. At the appropriate time, we will endeavor by various means to lure the main fleet of the United States and destroy it."

Now came a matter that would loom large in the future, particularly at the end of the war. The young officers of the Army and Navy had prepared a policy document calling for *military* government of Southeast Asia. Foreign Minister Togo objected to this plan at the Liaison Conference on November 20, 1941, and called for civil government, recognizing what had happened under military occupation in Shanghai, Tianjin, and Nanking, where the troops had run amok. But General Sugiyama countered:

"Our experience in the China Incident has shown that often in the administration of occupied areas there is fragmentation of leadership that leads to undesirable consequences. We are suffering from its harmful effect even now. In view of this I would like to have sufficient attention paid in our discussions to the problem of creating a unified administration in the South."

The Army, obviously, did not want any interference. Such places as the Foreign Legation quarter in Peking would be taken under Japanese control, but because neutrals and allied Axis nationals—Germans and Italians—were also involved, the Army would not exercise control. But the wave of the future was indicated in the plan for the occupation of Thailand, which was an essential move before the attack on Malaya:

"Just before we occupy the country we will demand the following and secure Thailand's immediate agreement; (even if Thailand accepts our demands, our troops will enter the country as planned; however,

efforts will be made to preclude armed clashes between Japan and
Thailand): (1) that the transit of Japanese troops and the use of facilities
be allowed and other aid also be provided, (2) that immediate steps be
taken to prevent clashes between Japanese and Thai troops in connection with the transit of Japanese troops, (3) that a mutual defense pact
be signed if Thailand wishes it. . . . We will promise to respect the
sovereignty and territorial integrity of Thailand, in order to facilitate
our negotiations. Depending on Thailand's attitude, she may be secretly told that in the future she might be given a part of Burma, or
perhaps Malaya.''

So the young Japanese officers, not yet having started their war,
were already carving up the map and rearranging empires.

Of course no mention was made of the atrocities committed by the
occupying forces in China. Foreign Minister Togo seemed to be aware
of them, but they were never a matter for public discussion in Japan;
the Army would not permit it. With very little discussion the foreign
minister's proposal for civil government was tabled, and it was apparent to all concerned that the military would insist on running the show
in the occupied areas as it saw fit. General Tojo, despite his promise to
take care to observe "fairness" in the governing of occupied areas,
did not raise the issue or support the foreign minister when he did raise
it.

On November 17 the Diet met in 77th Extraordinary Session and
Tojo made a major speech. It was deemed important enough to be
broadcast to the nation (and to the foreign listeners)—the first such
speech broadcast in Japan. Tojo announced that third powers were
expected not to obstruct Japan in reaching a conclusion of the China
Incident. He also said that Japan was determined not to let the
European war spread to Asia.

Foreign observers were not quite sure what the speech meant except
that it was a clear warning to the United States not to continue to
obstruct Japan's attempt to conquer China. Foreign Minister Togo
added to the warning, telling Japan (and America) that the negotiations
in Washington had to be fruitful by November 29, or thereafter the
situation would develop "automatically."

The speeches were received with ovations; there was no mistaking
how the Japanese Diet members felt, and generally how the Japanese
people felt, in favor of war against the Westerners to drive them once
and for all from Asian shores. The propaganda barrages for years had
brought the nation to this point of view. *New York Times* correspondent
Otto Tolischus cabled his newspaper an account of the events that day,

including a fiery speech by a Diet member named Toshio Shimada, Tolischus' reaction: "In so far as Diet members speak at all, they are so belligerent that the government appears moderate by comparison."

And so were the patriotic societies belligerent: 19 of them had just petitioned Prime Minister Tojo to start the war with the West.

On November 20, 1941 the Imperial Japanese Army issued its war orders for the attacks against Malaya and the Philippines.

By November 22, the young officers had decided what sort of occupation the Japanese would undertake. It would be a military government and its principal aim would be to milk the resources of the area for the Emperor's forces. As to the treatment of enemy aliens who would be captured in these lands, "The treatment of Americans, British, and Dutch will be such as to get them to cooperate with the military government; those who do not so cooperate will be evacuated or dealt with in other appropriate ways."

As for the native populations, the treatment "will be guided in such a way that they will increase their confidence in the Imperial forces. Premature attempts to encourage independence movements among them will be avoided."

The negotiations continued in Washington, but they did not get very far. On November 22, Secretary of State Hull met the Japanese ambassadors, Nomura and Kurita, to talk about the relaxation of the freeze on Japanese assets and trade, and said that the U.S. and Britain and the Dutch thought it was possible if the Japanese government could assert control over the armed forces, "as related to the policy of force and conquest."

The negotiations centered around a Japanese proposal called Proposition B, which the Americans could not possibly accept. It would have placed the United States in the position of condoning all Japan's aggressions in China while agreeing to supply Japan all the oil she needed. The U.S. was also to agree not to obstruct the restoration of peace in China—in other words, to keep hands off.

On November 26, Secretary Hull handed Ambassador Nomura a note called "Outline of Proposed Basis for Agreement Between the United States and Japan"; it took the parties back to their original positions. It was simply a reiteration of the strong American requirements. Japan would have to withdraw all troops from China and Indochina, abandon her extraterritorial rights in China, and comply with all the other measures the Americans had originally demanded. The Japanese regarded this as an ultimatum that made no concessions and confirmed that the negotiations were accomplishing nothing. But the Hull note had no "or otherwise" clause. There was no threat of American action if the terms were not complied with. All the threat of action was on the other side. The Japanese, having worked themselves into a national frenzy, now saw no movement toward their position by the Americans, and therefore they wanted war.

At 6 p.m. on November 26 the naval task force that would attack Pearl Harbor had sailed from Kitokappu Bay in the Kurile Islands. No one had even thought of stopping them. The Hull "ultimatum" had settled the issue of war or peace. There was no way agreement could be reached.

Reports of the Hull reply had come to Tokyo a few hours before the Liaison Conference of November 27. The military men took the position that negotiations had now ended and their entire attention was focused on that war they were about to unleash. This meant there would have to be another Imperial Conference, to ratify the war's beginning.

The Emperor had asked Prime Minister Tojo if all the former prime ministers were in favor of the war. Hirohito wanted them to take part in the Imperial Conference, but Tojo objected to this as a breach of protocol: the former prime ministers, after all, were not vested with power, and so should not be intimately involved in the decision-making process. The Emperor, as usual shackled by his position, let the prime minister have his way. But on that day, November 29, the former prime ministers of the *jushin* gathered at the Imperial Palace to listen to the cabinet members explain what was going on. The proceedings went on until 1 p.m., when they broke for lunch, the Emperor attending. After lunch the Emperor spent an hour in his study listening to the views of the former premiers. Not one of them opposed the war. The Emperor said only, "A very difficult period, isn't it?", which was approximately what Tojo had said when Tojo asked if anyone had any bright ideas he would like to hear them. Prince Konoye congratulated Tojo on his efforts, and said it looked as though nothing would do any good, but couldn't they delay?

Admiral Yonai suggested there must be something they could do rather than risk all. Two former prime ministers, generals Senjuro Hayashi and Nobuyuki Abe, said they felt the government had done all it could and that war was inevitable.

For weeks the military men had been talking about war, but on November 29 at the Liaison Conference, for the first time Foreign Minister Togo learned that the Zero Hour was December 8, Tokyo time. Even now, theoretically, there was time for the meetings in Washington to produce agreement with the Americans, but everyone in the decision-making process had now about given up hope of that in view of Secretary Hull's uncompromising statement.

In Tokyo on this day, November 29, it was apparent that war was coming and the military men made it quite plain that the only reason for continuing the talks in Washington was to keep the Americans from preparing for war.

Foreign Minister Togo: Can't we tell our representatives in Washington that our minds are made up? We have told the naval attaché, haven't we?

Admiral Nagano: We have not told the naval attaché.

Togo: We can't continue to keep our diplomats in the dark, can we?

Someone (not identified): Our diplomats will have to be sacrificed. What we want is to carry on diplomacy in such a way that until the very last minute the United States will continue to think about the problem. We will ask questions and our real plans will be kept secret.

Togo: The situation is critical. I think there is no possibility of a settlement. I will tell our representatives to exert efforts in diplomacy so that the United States will continue to consider the problem and we will continue to ask questions.

Someone, probably Tojo: On this occasion the entire population will have to be like Oishi Kuranosuke.

(Oishi Kuranosuke is one of the characters in "The Story of the 47 Ronin," who set out to avenge the death of their feudal lord. In order to deceive their enemies, Oishi posed as a dissolute samurai.)

So now, everyone in high authority in Japan was to make the pretense of continuing to negotiate for peace, when actually for the next nine days they were preparing for war and knew when it was going to occur: they were now waiting for the Navy to strike Pearl Harbor. Yet Tojo apparently had still a little hope that by enough saber-rattling the Japanese might frighten the U.S. into acceding to their demand. Now came a strange occurrence that could only have happened in Japan. On November 30 the *New York Times* reported that the Japanese prime minister had made a speech saying it was Japan's intent to purge the Orient of the British and Americans.

Ambassador Grew, when he heard about the speech, became very depressed. He regarded such a threat as nonsensical and based upon a misguided Japanese impression that pressure on the U.S. would bring positive results. In fact, Tojo had made no such speech, but had authorized the Asia Development League to write a speech for his approval. They had written these provocative words, and though Tojo had neither seen the words nor uttered them, the "speech" had been released by the association to the press on November 29. It created trouble in Washington and Tokyo, but by this time there really was not much that could have changed matters on the diplomatic front. The Japanese military were bent on war, and the sincere Japanese diplomats in Washington, who were trying very hard to prevent it were indeed being sacrificed. Everything that happened in those first seven days of December had to be characterized as *shibai o yaru*, or putting on a play.

At two o'clock on the afternoon of December 1 the cabinet and the military men and others who attended the Imperial Conferences assembled in the Palace. Prime Minister Tojo opened the proceedings saying that the Army and Navy had been making plans for war while the government had been trying to negotiate peace with the Americans. But it was impossible to negotiate with the Americans; Secretary Hull's new statement went further afield than any had gone before. It was uncompromising and added new strictures, demanded the complete and unconditional withdrawal of Japanese troops from China, withdrawal of the recognition of the Nanking government that Japan had helped set up, and the abandonment of the Tripartite Pact.

"This," said Tojo "not only belittled the dignity of our Empire and made it impossible for us to harvest the fruits of the China Incident, but also threatened the very existence of our Empire. It became apparent that we could not achieve our goals by means of diplomacy."

So there was no alternative. It must be war.

Then came an incident that proved how completely the control of Japan had gone into the hands of the young staff officers who had been subverting authority for so long. In the last hours of peace, President Roosevelt had decided to make a last-ditch effort and had sent a message by triple priority to Emperor Hirohito showing general good will and a willingness to try to compromise the Japanese-American differences. But, although the Japanese government and Ambassador Grew were informed that such a message was coming, it did not appear. The clock ticked away, and then the attack on Pearl Harbor began right on schedule, but no message from President Roosevelt arrived in Japan. And so the war began.

Only after the war was it discovered what had happened.

An obscure civil servant named Tateki Shirao was in charge of the Tokyo censorship office of the Ministry of Communications. On November 29—after the decision for war had been made and ratified by the Imperial Conference, an equally obscure young Lt. Col. Morio Tomura from the Army general staff had approached Army officer Shirao and asked him on behalf of the general staff to hold up all foreign messages for five hours. It was to be done as a "precaution," said the lieutenant colonel. A precaution against what he did not explain. Without thinking more about the matter Shirao had issued such orders to his subordinates and had told no one else about it. Later the lieutenant colonel amended his request to make the delay five hours on one day and ten hours on the next. So when the Roosevelt message to the Emperor came to Tokyo, it sat in the telegraph office for ten hours without moving, and the Emperor did not receive it until after the Pearl Harbor attack.

Would it have made any difference?

Ambassador Nomura thought so. Much later, after he had been repatriated to Japan, he asked Prime Minister Tojo what had happened to the message from Roosevelt to the Emperor, of which the ambassador had been aware all along. Tojo did not know what had happened, but he did by that time know the contents of the message, which was most conciliatory. What would have happened if the Emperor had received the message before the Pearl Harbor attack? Nomura asked.

"Very simple," replied Tojo. "We could never have gone to war."

But war came, and in a way the manner of its coming was quite in keeping with the spirit of Japan. The young officers controlled Japan, and here was one more bit of the evidence.

7

Easy Victories

Before five o'clock on the morning of December 8, 1941, Tokyo time, Prime Minister General Tojo was informed about the success of the Pearl Harbor attack. That morning the Imperial Rescript announcing the war ("It has been truly unavoidable and far from Our wishes," the Emperor said) was issued. From that day on, on the 8th day of every month, every newspaper in Japan reprinted the Imperial Rescript, first as a happy reminder of the day, and later as a grim reminder. In a broadcast to the people of Japan, Prime Minister Tojo declared that they must prepare for a long war to "construct a glorious tomorrow" for the empire as "builders of Greater East Asia." He called on the people to stand fast, and he pledged his faithful assistance to the Throne. This theme of hardship and suffering for the nation was one that Tojo would sound frequently, for he was very much aware of the difficulties that his country faced in prosecuting this war. Of course he announced great pleasure in the success of the Pearl Harbor attack, as well as the success of initial operations in the Philippines, which had caught the Americans by surprise and wiped out virtually all their air power within the first few days. Within the first forty-eight hours it was also clear that events were going very well in Malaya.

In Malaya, the Japanese plan called for elimination of British air power immediately, and on December 8 the air battle began. Independently, the landings of Japanese troops of the 25th Army began that morning at Khota Baru and Singora on the eastern shores of the Malay peninsula.

That day Tojo plunged into the process of leading a government at war, which meant endless meetings and consultations.

The first few days of the war found the Japanese people agog at the manifestations of their own power. The results of the Pearl Harbor attack—the destruction of the American battle fleet—was proof to them that their navy was the finest in the world. In the homeland, stories of Japanese heroism were common; the China war had been under way for four years, but now new datelines appeared in the newspapers: "with the army in the Philippines," "with the army in Malaya." Two days after the Pearl Harbor attack came another triumph: the sinking, off the coast of Malaya, of the battleship HMS *Prince of Wales* and the renowned battle cruiser *Repulse* by Japanese land-based naval planes flying from Indochina bases. It was victory upon victory, because the destruction of these major elements of the British Far East Fleet made it easy for the bulk of the Japanese 25th Army to land. The ground forces then began the drive on Singapore.

The 23rd Army moved against Hong Kong from the Canton area, and captured Kowloon, the city across from Hong Kong on the China side, on December 12. Two days later the Japanese began a general assault on the British Crown Colony. Prime Minister Tojo bore the heaviest responsibilities. Not only was he prime minister, and thus responsible to the Diet and to the Emperor, and bound to keep both informed about the war, but he was also minister of war and minister for home affairs. In the latter capacity he was very busy; this post controlled the National Police and the thought-control apparatus of Japan, and even before war had been declared Tojo had been working on new measures for Japan's internal security. First, he was working on the Communists.

Already Communists and others who had shown either anti-military tendencies or sympathy for the Soviet Union or America were being rounded up or kept under observation. So were Koreans.

Next on the list to be watched were the nationalistic organizations like the Cherry Blossom and Black Dragon societies.

Tojo was concerned about the supernationalist organizations of the right that had caused so much trouble in Japan for so long. Some of these people were going to be subject to "preventative detention." Protection particularly had to be provided for all those leaders who had belonged to the "treaty faction" of the Navy before the war— loyal Japanese who had disagreed with the thesis that war was inevitable. Now that the Army had its war it was inclined to be forgiving to those in its ranks who had had another point of view, so long as they supported the war now, and almost everyone did. In the Navy, two of the most outspoken opponents of the war policy had been admirals Yonai and Yamamoto. Yamamoto was safe enough aboard the Combined Fleet flagship *Nagato* (later *Yamato*) but Admiral Yonai needed protection from hotheads who had vowed to kill him for his views.

Tojo's third problem was to control rumors. That meant tighter restrictions on public meetings, on the press, and on all other printed matter. The neighborhood associations would prove ideal for this purpose. Everyone automatically belonged to a neighborhood association, further divided into blocks. This would be the unit that would conduct air raid protection, fire-fighting, and other close-to-home organized civilian efforts demanded by the war. Neighbor watching neighbor, and all under the watchful eye of the local police box, was part of the answer to the internal security requirement.

His fourth concern was control of foreigners. American-born ethnic Japanese, or Nisei, would have to be watched, as well as the children of Japanese families from other countries who had been caught by the war in Japan. All Europeans and other foreign residents of Japan were suspect. If there was the slightest reason, they would be arrested and detained.

The fifth aim of the Home Office was the control of the civil population's ordinary crimes. With so many men in armed service the police would have to be more and more vigilant. Arrest and trial procedures would have to be simplified, which meant putting more onus on the suspects. The quality of civil justice would have to be lowered; there was no time for endless appeal and argument.

Sixth, the police and firemen would have to take more responsibility for dealing with emergencies, from fires to crowd control. Their authority would have to be broadened.

Seventh was the control of public attitudes. The people had to be kept calm, and no rabblerousing could be permitted. The Ministry of Home Affairs was setting up several new sections to deal with the daily lives of citizens and to guide them in the proper direction for promotion of the war effort.

One such was a section to promote the wearing of Japanese-style clothing and the elimination of European fashions. Photographers patrolled the smart districts like the Ginza, taking pictures of women in Paris or California dresses. It did not take long. Within a month Western fashions had all but disappeared from the streets of Japan. Another section, working with the Ministry of Education, was concerned with the elimination of Americanisms and Briticisms from the Japanese language.

This was a losing battle because the Japanese had borrowed so much from everyone, but the baseball terms were among the first changed.

Geographical name changes became common. It was all *Dai Nippon*, now, Great Japan, and the whole area was to be known not as *Kyokuto* (Far East) but *Dai To A* (Greater East Asia). Soon the term Greater East Asia Co-prosperity Sphere would be on the lips of the politicians and military as they attacked and won new possessions, and then began to exploit them for the greater glory of Japan.

The classified advertising columns of the newspapers, particularly the foreign-language press, reflected the changes as well. Western-style clothing, Western furniture, Western anything was either hidden or gotten rid of in a flurry of effort to be more Japanese.

Prime Minister Tojo launched a new war bond drive on December 15, the day that the Diet opened in special session to deal with some of the new laws he needed for national control.

On December 16, the Kawaguchi Detachment of the Imperial Japanese Army invaded Borneo. This unit was spearheaded by three highly-trained shock battalions under the command of Maj. Gen. Kiyotake Kawaguchi. The first landings were made near Miri. Japanese forces were moving rapidly in the Philippines, and every day Prime Minister Tojo was briefed on the progress of the war. On December 18 he spoke to the Diet about the Borneo invasion and other matters. He bragged that·the Japanese on Borneo had found 70 of the 150 oil wells in working condition although the enemy had sabotaged some of the others. The oil problem of Japan was solved, he announced. The Japanese could expect to get 500,000 barrels of oil from these fields in the next year.

Tojo accused the Americans of war crimes. In Davao, he said, on Mindanao Island the Americans had tortured ten Japanese citizens to death and machine gunned 38 others.

On December 19, Tojo attended a meeting and luncheon of more than 30 industrial leaders, and spoke of the need for ever more effort. It seemed a long, long time since that speech to the munitions industry cost Deputy War Minister Tojo his job. Now these men of the *Zaibatsu,* the big industrial combines, were preparing to move into new fields to exploit the victories of Japan and further the cause of the Greater East Asia Co-prosperity Sphere. On Saturday December 20 he met with Minister of Industry Kishi and spent the rest of the day with Chief Cabinet Secretary Hoshino on official reports. December 21 was a quiet day for the Prime Minister, who spent most of it relaxing at the official residence. But the next day it was government business again, beginning with a visit to the Imperial Palace and report to the Throne at 10 o'clock. He brought the Emperor up to date on the war results, and the Emperor showed particular interest in resources and related matters, such as the oil prospects in Borneo. There was a luncheon banquet for Prince Kotohito of the royal family who was celebrating his 77th birthday; after that it was back to work, this time in his hat as minister of home affairs. That day he devoted the hours from two p.m. to four p.m. to Home Office business. He held several meetings, with assistants and a longer meeting with the minister of education to discuss the curriculum in the schools that trained teachers and in the state schools. For a half hour just after five o'clock in the afternoon he was briefed by one of the officers from the Imperial General Staff on the progress of the war, and at six p.m. he held a news conference for reporters. The big news was the successful landings of the Japanese expeditionary force on Luzon Island at Lingayen Gulf.

Tuesday, December 23, was the day for the regular weekly cabinet meeting, and all members were present. Prime Minister Tojo had three matters to discuss. Now that Japan was moving south, it was more important that steps be taken immediately to send more people, military and civilian, to establish the Greater East Asia Co-prosperity Sphere in those places that had been occupied. The other two items on the prime ministerial agenda concerned censorship. He was not at all pleased that the report of the torture and killing of Japanese in Mindanao had come to Japan through the newspapers. This was not the way to handle such matters (and there was some doubt now if the report from Davao was true). If it proved to be untrue it could be very embarrassing with neutral nations. Also, the prime minister noted, Director Kogane of the fuel program had made a serious error by talking too much to the newspapers, and thus vital war information about the fuel supplies that could be expected from Borneo probably would fall into enemy hands through neutral sources. For that reason, Tojo said, he was going to have to tighten newspaper censorship through the Ministry of Home Affairs.

If anyone objected to this new program of regimentation, no one said so.

On December 25 the Japanese Army captured Hong Kong, and 11,000 British troops surrendered. Thus began the first of the mass captures of enemy forces that the Japanese were not equipped to handle, either emotionally or physically. The Japanese soldier had been taught that he who surrenders to the enemy is a coward and not worth consideration. This attitude colored the Japanese treatment of prisoners from the very first. Equally important, the Japanese Army medical and supply services always operated on a shoestring, and so had little to spare for the prisoners of war. This issue was to grow in importance very rapidly.

On December 27 Tojo spent much of the day hearing reports on Japan's resources—coal, iron, and aluminum—all essentials for the war effort. Three days later he had another formal report on the progress of the war—very satisfactory—and details of the first great victories, Pearl Harbor and Hong Kong. In Malaya, Ipoh fell on December 28, as the Japanese continued the drive toward Singapore.

Elated, Tojo traveled to the shrine at Ise and the shrine at Atsuta to pray to the gods and thank them for these Japanese victories. At the end of December, without consulting the prime minister/war minister, the Army decided to advance its timetables. Victory was so easy that Japanese forces cut through the enemy like a knife through cheese. General Terauchi, the commander of the Southern Army, recommended to Imperial General Headquarters that the attack on the Dutch East Indies be moved up a month, and it was done.

Over the New Year holiday, Tojo left the official house of the prime minister in Tokyo and moved to his private house. And then, partial modernist as he was, took a flying trip to Kobe, rather than travel down by train.

On January 2, 1942 Tojo was informed that the Japanese troops under General Homma in the Philippines had captured Manila.

The matter of Japan's allies, Germany and Italy, was very much on Tojo's mind. He did not have much faith in them, for Hitler had never hinted at the attack on Russia before it came, and Tojo had learned that Hitler had been planning it for many months. But what was Japan's response to the German and Italian request for more action against points of mutual interest? It was not time to attack Soviet Russia next. What about India and the Moslem world of the Arabs? The German ambassador and the Italian ambassador paid a joint call on the prime minister on January 3. Their purpose was to suggest an attack on the British in India, and also the turning of the Moslem world to the interests of the Axis. Tojo listened, and the ambassadors pressed him for a commitment to act.

The prime minister said he was aware of the situation of India, where the Congress or Nationalist party had been fighting for independence for many years. Perhaps something could be done with India. As for the Moslem world, it was a completely unknown quantity in Japan and this would require research before the Japanese government would be willing to commit itself to a program of action to further the mutual aims of the Axis partners. This was all part of a larger issue that must be solved quickly. So fast had the Japanese advanced southward that it soon would be time to set new goals or lose the momentum of the war. Hong Kong had fallen on Christmas Day to the Japanese. They were driving ahead in the Philippines, where on Christmas Gen. Douglas MacArthur had evacuated Manila and made it an "open city" to prevent its bombing by the Japanese, and had moved his army headquarters to the Bataan Peninsula. Tokyo could expect a swift victory in the Philippines, the Army boasted. On January 2 when the Japanese troops marched into undefended Manila, General Count Hisaichi Terauchi concluded that Lt. Gen. Masaharu Homma was far ahead of schedule and did not need General Abe's 48th Division. So without consulting Homma, he ordered the division to take part in the moved-up assault on Java in the Dutch East Indies. Someone at Imperial Headquarters raised the issue that this decision might slow down Homma, but the high command did not care. It was more important to assure the success of the southern operations against the Dutch East Indies oil fields than it was to capture the Philippines quickly. Soon the 48th Division was shipped out.

The Japanese were victorious everywhere. On January 11, Maj. Gen. Shizuo Sakaguchi's detachment of three battalions seized the island of Tarakan on the east coast of Borneo, and on January 24 they took Balikpapan. That was followed by a move to Ambon Island on January 31 and Makassar in the Celebes and Banjermasin in South Borneo on February 9.

But the sweeter victory came in Malaya, where the unnerved British army collapsed early in February. By the 8th of that month the Japanese had landed on Singapore Island, and threatened the naval base.

On February 11, Tojo worked with his secretaries to put together the manuscript for his speech to the Diet on this victory. The information department of the cabinet was given the responsibility for making and broadcasting an English translation of the victory message. And on February 12, Tojo had the pleasant task of reporting to Emperor Hirohito on the collapse of the British forces and the capture of Singapore. It was premature, but the real victory came on February 15, when the entire city of Singapore fell into Japanese hands, and 100,000 British Empire soldiers became prisoners of war. The next day Tojo brought several Army officers from the Malaya campaign to the Diet with him and had them open the session with an account of the victory and the fall of Singapore. After the meeting the premier visited the Yasukuni shrine, the resting place of the souls of the departed heroes of Japanese wars, to pay homage to the dead and give thanks for the victory.

The next day, February 18, Tojo received the Italian ambassador and accepted his congratulations on the victory. The other Axis powers were very pleased, for they had wanted the Japanese to move against Britain.

It was not yet apparent in Tokyo, but there was trouble brewing in the Philippines for the Imperial Army. General MacArthur had evacuated Manila but had moved his American and Philippine forces to the rugged peninsula of Bataan whose hills were ideally suited for defense. General Homma's troops now began to slow down. Homma had planned to make use of his 48th and 16th divisions to converge on the Americans in Central Luzon and surround them. But Lt. Gen. Susumu Morioka's 16th Division had lost the 33rd Infantry Regiment in the fighting after the main landings, and the 48th Division had lost its 2nd Formosan Regiment. Then after the capture of Manila, as noted, General Terauchi had decided it was practically all over with the Americans and had moved the 48th Division to the Dutch East Indies. Meanwhile 15,000 American and Filipino troops who had been cut off by the Japanese fought their way through the lines and joined their comrades on Bataan, swelling the number of soldiers to 80,000 (and 26,000 civilians). So the Americans on Bataan outnumbered the opposing Japanese more than four to one. Homma's 14th Army had been cut drastically, but under the initial plan Homma had a total of just fifty days in which to complete operations in the Philippines. After the Americans had slipped through his fingers into Bataan, it was a different war.

Only by mid-January had General Homma managed to capture his first defense point on the west coast of Bataan, the town of Moron. By January 22 he had forced General MacArthur to abandon his first Bataan defense line and pull back. The Japanese attempted to outflank the Americans but failed, and by mid-February, with his original time allotment already expired, Homma found himself locked in a battle of attrition with the Americans. In fact the American strength was such that had MacArthur received the assistance from land and sea that he originally expected, the Philippines might not have fallen at all and the Japanese might have suffered their first defeat there.

But instead, MacArthur and his men got nothing but a few planeloads and then submarine loads of ammunition and medical supplies.

In Washington the Philippines had been written off by the Roosevelt administration when the decision was made to prosecute the war against Hitler first, and to try only to hold in the Pacific for the time being.

Still the "Battling Bastards of Bataan," as the American soldiers proudly termed themselves, put a serious crimp in the Japanese time-table for the Philippines, an embarrassing problem to the Imperial General Headquarters and the government information agency which were trumpeting to the world the superiority of the Japanese soldier and sailor. The quick victories in Malaya and Hong Kong had made the entire nation triumphant. Only the holdout of the Americans in the Philippines marred the picture. Almost every day that winter and spring, the Tokyo newspapers predicted immediate victory at Bataan.

Because of the speedup of plans by Imperial General Headquarters, the end of January saw the Japanese forces firmly in place on both sides of the South China Sea, in the Makassar Strait, and on the Molucca Sea. They were moving on Java and Sumatra weeks ahead of the original schedule. Soon after securing air supremacy, Japanese paratroops seized Palembang in southern Sumatra on February 14, and the 38th Division followed up and captured the whole city area.

In Tokyo Prime Minister Tojo was impressed by the successes and observed at the dining table in the official residence on February 18 that the Army deserved kudos for its excellent organization in the Dutch East Indies, which was a compliment to the leadership and command of Lt. Gen. Haruyoshi Hyakutake, who was in charge there. In that same conversation Tojo remarked on the brave struggle being waged by the Dutch, British, and American troops in the area.

"They have fought very bravely and suffered many casualties," he said. "They deserve to be treated very kindly."

By mid-February the Japanese were closing in on the Allied forces in the Dutch East Indies. The American Asiatic Fleet had moved down there from the Philippines to make a common defense with elements of the British Far East Fleet and the Dutch naval forces. On February 27, the Japanese wiped out the Allied fleet at the Battle of the Java Sea, and on March 1 the last American warship was sunk off Batavia. That day the Japanese landed in northwestern Java. Batavia fell on March 5 and Soerabaya on March 7. Some 93,000 Dutch troops and about 5,000 British, Australian and American troops surrendered on March 9. By mid-March the Indies were in Japanese hands, and General Hyakutaki now faced a serious and unaccustomed problem: as had happened in Malaya and Singapore, the swift victories reaped an enormous number of prisoners of war and enemy civilians who were now under the control of Japan and who must be dealt with. We already know that dealing with the captives was a problem Japan was ill-prepared to face.

8

The Limits of Power

The cartoonists and political writers of the Western world never could agree on whether to focus on Emperor Hirohito or Prime Minister General Tojo as the personification of Japan's villainy. It was simple enough to equate Hitler with German and Mussolini with Italian dictatorship, and these designations were essentially correct. But the case of Japan was quite different, and the villain the commentators wanted was harder to identify. In fact the villain was a system rather than an individual: the cabal of generals who ran the Army were the masters, and not until 1943 did Tojo make an attempt to increase the power of the prime ministry.

Tojo had two bases of power, neither of them absolute. First of all he was a general officer and a member, although not a leader, of the junta. He was trusted by the three most important generals: Count Hisaichi Terauchi, the senior field commander, who would run the war in the Pacific; Akira Muto, chief of the Military Affairs Bureau, which actually controlled the Army; and General Gen Sugiyama, the principal architect of the China war and the leading figure in the Imperial General Headquarters. Tojo's position within the Army depended on his absolute loyalty to the ruling clique and his support of the decisions made by them.

Tojo's other source of power derived from the Emperor's innate distrust of the Army and his fear that the generals might try to unseat him. Tojo, the Emperor believed, was the one man who could control and limit them. Hirohito had had proof of that strength in the fall of 1940. Then War Minister Tojo sacked the commanding general of the undisciplined Japanese forces in South China at Guangzhou, doing so without a whimper from Imperial General Headquarters.

Yet once war was declared, the conduct of military operations was in the hands of the commanders, and as prime minister Tojo had so little power over day-to-day events in the field that he was not always kept informed of them until well after the fact. In a sense, Tojo as war minister (a portfolio he kept with full Army approval) had far more influence in these matters than Tojo as prime minister. For the long run it was a different matter; as the prime minister, Tojo controlled the Japanese budget, and thus he exerted a major influence on the long-range conduct of the war, from the beginning.

Tojo set out in early 1942 to increase his power, with the unstated support of the Emperor and the Imperial family, and the civilian elements in the cabinet.

The whirlwind of victories had first stunned Japan and then created a national euphoria and sense of power. The apparent great victory at Pearl Harbor, the Christmas fall of Hong Kong, the lightning campaign in February in Malaya, the overwhelming of the Allies in the Java Sea, and the capture of the Dutch East Indies had brought many new problems. The Emperor had asked General Sugiyama if the fall of Singapore might not be an excellent juncture at which to offer the British a peace. The war had changed greatly in recent months. The Soviets had not been defeated by Hitler in the summer of 1941 but now had rebounded and were holding their own.

Still, Sugiyama and Tojo both looked forward to the day that they would be able to strike north and wrest from the Soviet Union control of Siberia and Mongolia. They also were dedicated to winning a victory in China. At this moment the two men had common goals.

Within the Army there were heated disagreements over the new course recent events might require. On March 7, Tojo and the cabinet held a liaison conference with the Imperial General Headquarters officials to formulate a new policy, and this is what was decided:

Japan would continue the war and push her expansion toward Australia and in the South Pacific to Samoa and other Western colonies. She would also seek to become self-sufficient with the help of the Greater East Asia Co-prosperity Sphere. The Navy wanted to invade Australia, but the Army did not have the troops to do it. The Navy wanted to take Hawaii, but the Army again did not have the troops. Nevertheless the Navy was going to plan for invasion of Midway atoll, partly to set up a future invasion of Hawaii, and partly to draw the remaining American fleet out from Pearl Harbor to destroy it once and for all.

The Army wanted to expand to the Aleutians (to prevent their use as a base for bombing Japan) and the Navy agreed to tie that into their Midway operation. So for the spring the operations would be Aleutians, Midway, Port Moresby in New Guinea, then New Caledonia, Fiji, and Samoa. Also, the Army would move as fast as possible to "settle the China incident." In January 1942 Prime Minister Tojo had announced that a general election would be held at the end of April. He and the Army both wanted to consolidate their strength, although at this point Tojo's ambitions began to diverge from those of the Army's rulers. Neither the premier nor the generals wanted opposition within the Diet. Tojo summoned a select group of civilian supporters of the Army and asked them to present a list of "patriotic candidates." This group was largely drawn from the Imperial Rule Assistance Association, an organization Tojo found it possible to manipulate.

This group scoured the country for proper candidates, but they did not find enough of them to completely supplant the existing membership. Their problem was that the incumbent Diet members were firmly entrenched in their constituencies. In many areas a Diet seat was much like a feudal fief, handed down from father to son. When the list was finally completed it included 235 incumbent Diet members, 18 former members, and 213 new candidates.

The government could not prevent independents from running without official sanction. The Meiji constitution guaranteed that right and to put it aside would have distressed the entire nation and cost the government and Army much support in the countryside. So 613 independent candidates did run, and the total number of candidates, 1079, was the highest ever recorded in Japan. In Tokyo 100 candidates competed for three seats.

Tojo tried to control the elections but did not entirely succeed. The Army had special funds, which it had been using for years to suborn politicians and bribe newspaper editors on its way to national control. Now Tojo found Y5000 for each of his favorite candidates. This was then an enormous amount of money to pour into a political campaign. More important than the funds was the use of official power to try to sway the elections. The Home Ministry told the police to suppress any criticism of the government, and censorship was invoked. In one day six rallies were suspended in Tokyo alone. The radio urged people to vote for the "patriotic candidates," and the press, which was controlled by the government, not only by censorship and bribery but by intimidation, urged the election of Tojo's list. But 600 Japanese dared stand up and be counted against the Tojo government. One candidate was Takao Saito, who had been expelled from the Diet in 1940 for criticizing Army operations in China. When the police confiscated his campaign material he went to Tokyo and complained to the Home Ministry; his campaign material then was reprinted, but in a form watered down sufficiently to pass censorship.

But in Nagasaki and Kagoshima candidates were mistreated and refused permission to hire halls for speeches. One candidate in Nagasaki was arrested, for what no one quite knew, so he had to be released.

Another candidate was arrested for praising the Americans' humane treatment of prisoners of war, which was, of course, a slap at Japanese practices. The government was already aware of criticism at home and abroad of its treatment of such prisoners, particularly by the Army. The general's instinctive reaction was to suppress dissent.

One odd factor in the 1942 election was the appearance of a special list of 46 candidates of the right-wing Society of the East established by Seigo Nakano, who was an admirer of Hitler. Nakano had been a member of the Imperial Rule Assistance Association until he discerned that it was not going to become a totalitarian party in the Nazi model, as he had expected. So he broke away and became a right-wing opponent of the Tojo government. Yet he could not be accused of lack of patriotism, for patriotism was his motto. He accused Tojo of betraying the patriotism of the people and of carrying out bureaucratic oppression.

The Nakano group was supported by the Great Japan Imperial Rule Assistance Young Men's Corps, which had been founded with the support and financial backing of the Army only a few weeks after the war began. Its function was to enlist young men for activities like those of Hitler's storm troopers—the terrorization of those who questioned Army control of Japan. Its role in this election of 1942 was to intimidate opposition candidates, for the Army was still trying to establish a Nazi-type party to support its own rule. The leader in this effort was Lt. Gen. Akira Muto, head of the extremely powerful Military Affairs Bureau of the War Ministry and one of the three chiefs of the Army cabal who had chosen Tojo as candidate for war minister. As we shall see, these generals soon began to believe that they had created a monster. Each month the cabal became less certain of its control over Tojo.

Only seven members of the right-wing Society of the East were elected. In April, in connection with the election, Tojo made his first quiet bid for power by unseating Muto as head of the Bureau of

Military Affairs. The reason given, and swallowed by the generals, was that Muto had overreached in his efforts to Nazify Japan, and that the people would not support that program. Tojo used the objections of Finance Minister Okinori Kaya, State Minister Suzuki, and Chief Cabinet Secretary Hoshino to buttress his decision to remove Muto. He accomplished the demotion by a brilliant plot that Muto could not contravene.

General Takura Nishimura had proved to be a very bad soldier who would not take orders properly. He was the commander of the Imperial Guards Division, which had been part of General Tomoyuki Yamashita's 25th Army, which had conquered Singapore. Nishimura insisted that the Imperial Guards should be in the vanguard of the army. When this did not fit Yamashita's plans, the Guards virtually rebelled and went their own way. General Nishimura was one of the "tough" school, who encouraged his troops to rape, murder, pillage the civilians they encountered, and deal swiftly with wounded enemy and prisoners of war by killing them. Yamashita was opposed to his subordinate's policy and tried to discipline Nishimura, but after the battle of the Muar River, Nishimura ordered his troops to bayonet the enemy wounded for practice. The Guards killed more than 200 as they lay wounded on the battlefield. "I want my troops to behave with dignity," General Yamashita wrote in his diary, "but most of them do not seem to have the ability to do so."

Finally, General Yamashita took the matter of the Guards Division to Field Marshal Terauchi, and Nishimura was sent back to Japan in disgrace. The Imperial Guards Division was the only one of three divisions in Yamashita's army that did not receive an Imperial Rescript of commendation for its actions in the Malaya campaign. This was obviously painful to Emperor Hirohito because the Guards Division was the one he had counted on to put down the rebellious First Division in the Army's attempted revolution of February 26, 1936. At that time Hirohito had threatened to personally lead his Guards Division against the Army if the generals did not obey his commands.

Now, the Guards Division must be rehabilitated, and Tojo chose Muto for the task. It was a job that Muto could not refuse, for who could fail to honor the Emperor's wishes. Tojo had made the suggestion to Hirohito, who greeted it with approval.

So General Muto left his post of power and passed into the field, where Tojo made sure that he remained for the rest of the war. To the post of chief of the Army Military Affairs Bureau, Tojo now brought Maj. Gen. Kenryo Sato, an experienced military bureaucrat who had been serving on the government Planning Board. "General Sato enjoys the deep trust of Gen. Hideki Tojo," said the *Asahi Shimbun*. It was apparent that Tojo had made his first move to consolidate power. Since General Terauchi, too, had been sent into the field to become mollified with the rank of field marshal and to direct the armies in the Pacific and Southeast Asia, he had been effectively removed from control of Army policies. Now Tojo had only to deal with Field Marshal Sugiyama, the chief of the Army General Staff and commander of Imperial General Headquarters; he outranked Tojo in terms of service and position. Sugiyama was a formidable character, but Tojo knew that Emperor Hirohito both feared and distrusted Sugiyama, so in this struggle to take over the Army Tojo had the Emperor as an ally. The election was not creating as much interest as Tojo had hoped, for he wanted to use the results again in the consolidation of his power. With the Imperial Rule Assistance Association as a base he expected to have a Diet that would not criticize and would in no way impede the progress of the war as it was to be managed by the Army—his Army. But because of the strong government propaganda campaign for the list of favored establishment candidates the voting public seemed almost totally apathetic.

Then came an event, on April 18th, that changed the entire picture. Japan was bombed for the first time in its history.

That day sixteen American B-25 medium bombers led by Lt. Col. Jimmy Doolittle of the U.S. Army Air Corps took off from the carrier USS *Hornet* about 600 miles from Japan, bombed the cities of Tokyo, Yatiasaka, Yokohama, Nagoya, and Kobe, and then headed off to land, if possible, on airfields in China. In fact, the aircraft crashed, crash-landed or ditched in the sea off the China coast. The air raid had been conceived by American army and navy authorities to give a badly needed boost to American civilian morale. All over the Pacific the Japanese had appeared just then to be invincible. The bombing of Japan did just what the psychological specialists in the U.S. government expected. Americans cheered. When asked at a press conference where the American airplanes had come from to bomb Tokyo, Roosevelt had grinned and said "from Shangri-La," which was the name of a Tibetan Eden in a movie that was currently popular. All Americans were buoyed by the event. But in Japan the effects were enormous too.

That day, Prime Minister Tojo was visiting Utsunomiya, about sixty miles from Tokyo, to inspect an airmen's training school. He had gone by train from the capital because the weather was deemed unsuitable for flying; the American raid then was quite a surprise. He hurried back to Tokyo to report to the Emperor and apologize for the event.

To the Emperor, Tojo promised a complete investigation; it began immediately. Chiang Kai-shek had correctly anticipated the Japanese reaction to the Doolittle raid and had warned his ally against carrying it out. But the American planners had not listened; they had been insistent on what even some admirals and generals called a "stunt." They'd gone ahead because President Roosevelt wanted it. Chiang had forecast gloomily that the raid would result in the reprisal deaths of thousands of Chinese.

And so it did.

Tojo had ordered the investigation, and General Sugiyama turned to it with a will. By April 21 it was determined that the planes had taken off from an aircraft carrier. Maps recovered from some of the wrecked aircraft and interrogations of the captured American airmen convinced the intelligence officers that the B-25s were headed for Chuchow. Sugiyama then ordered General Hata, the commander of the China Expeditionary Army, to destroy the Nationalists' central China air bases. The specific targets were to be those in Chekiang province at Chuhsien, Lishui, Chinhua, Lungyu; in Kiangsi province at Kanhsien, Nanchang, Suichuan, and Yushan; and in Hunan province at Hangyang, Chuchow, and Chihkiang.

Hata's effort was called Operation Che-Kiang (for Chinese characters from the names of Chekiang and Kiangsi provinces). The attacks would be carried out by the 13th Division, stationed at Shanghai, and the 11th Division, at Hankow. They would move along the He-Kiang railroad from east and west respectively. So the operations began in May, and a general offensive was launched as well. But the principal missions of the Japanese troops were to destroy the airfields and punish the Chinese. In the course of the next few months 250,000 Chinese would lose their lives in consequence of the Doolittle raid. Chiang Kai-shek then added a bitter postscript to his earlier protests:

"After they had been caught unaware by the falling of American bombs on Tokyo, Japanese troops attacked the coastal areas of China where many of the American fliers had landed. These Japanese troops slaughtered every man, woman, and child in those areas—let me repeat—these Japanese troops slaughtered every man, woman, and child in those areas, reproducing on a wholesale scale the horrors which the world had seen at Lidice, but about which the people have been uninformed in these areas."

*   *   *

In Japan, the Doolittle raid electrified the nation. Americans later said they believed this was the occasion on which the Japanese stopped believing their government, because they had been told that Japan would never be raided from the air. Such statements had been made in terms of the China war. When the war expanded, no responsible Japanese authority believed that nation would be safe from air raids, and the Emperor least of all. He quite expected them.

When this raid came, killing an estimated 50 persons—some of them children—it put the Japanese people squarely behind their government. The dull parliamentary campaign suddenly took on more importance, and on election day, April 30, 12 million of the 14.5 million eligible voters cast ballots. They returned 381 of the preferred candidates, who polled 66 percent of the votes. The independents received nearly a third of the votes, and the far right managed to elect only seven of its 46 candidates.

When the Diet met in May a new body was formed, the Imperial Rule Assistance Political Association, and 98 percent of the legislators joined it. So the Doolittle raid lent a new sense of purpose to the Japanese people, and served Premier Tojo's purpose very well, too.

9

The Imperial Way

From the days of his childhood, Emperor Hirohito had never believed in the theory of the divinity of the Emperor, which was developed from age-old national myth by the politicians of the Meiji era to strengthen the monarchy. He had argued the point with his principal tutor and advisor, Prince Saionji, but never to any reasonable end. In a very real sense the Emperor of Japan was a symbolic figure, and when the Army seized control of the government in the mid-1930s the new rulers found the notion of a living deity as their figurehead useful. And so, against the express wishes of Hirohito, it became national dogma.

Tojo was not the architect of this theory. It took a man with a great deal more imagination than he possessed to see how Japan could be reshaped into a militarist state by the Army—by convincing the nation's youth that their greatest ambition should be to die for Emperor and country.

The man who revived and refurbished the old Bushido doctrine was Gen. Sadao Araki. Half a generation older than Tojo, over the years he had held many important government posts, including that of war minister, but was most notable as a member of the *Kodo Ha* faction in the Army, during the struggle for power, and for his ability to survive politically when his clique failed. General Araki became minister of education in the Konoye cabinet of 1937, and from this vantage point revamped Japanese education to magnify emperor-worship and patriotism as its twin guidelines.

Much to Hirohito's disgust he found himself to be an object of religious veneration, and although he did not accept that concept, he was convinced that for the sake of national unity he must bear the burden of being god-emperor, as the Army demanded.

For the first few months of Pacific conflict, as noted, Premier Tojo also kept the home affairs cabinet portfolio, which controlled the police and the many patriotic organizations that were capable of creating so much trouble. But by the spring of 1942 it was apparent that the Army was in full control and that the Home Ministry could not exercise the power that it did in other countries. So Tojo gave up that portfolio to Michio Yuzawa, a senior bureaucrat who would hold the office for fourteen months. One of the principal tools of the Home Ministry in its exercise of authority over the people was its control of the Neighborhood Associations—local units that governed the daily lives of those on the homefront in matters such as rationing and civil defense. But neither Yuzawa nor any of the four men who followed him in that position made any attempt to increase the powers of the Home Ministry or to abuse them to challenge Tojo. The Japanese war effort was generally supported by the public all the way through the conflict.

The matter of dealing with conquered peoples and war prisoners had to be addressed from the very beginning, although neither Tojo nor anyone else in the Army had the prescience to see that they were dealing with an explosive and extraordinarily important issue. The Japanese had a concept of war and responsibility entirely different from that of the peoples of the West. In their struggle for control of China, the Japanese behaved with total abandon, following the new Bushido concept of the Army—kill or be killed. Chinese prisoners of war, if any were taken, frequently were dealt with summarily, often killed on the spot, because the Japanese forces could not be bothered with housing, feeding, and guarding them.

As long as this policy affected only Orientals, it is sad to say, the Westerners did not seem to get aroused. One monstrous example is the December 1937 Rape of Nanking, in which perhaps 200,000 Chinese died. The world knew about the atrocity, for foreign observers were there, but it created not nearly so much stir as the sinking of the American gunboat *Panay* by Japanese naval aviators near Nanking at the same time. Another example was the Doolittle raid, which as we have seen, was the Japanese rationale for taking the lives of a quarter of a million Chinese, but the reprisals raised few eyebrows in America.

But other consequences of the Doolittle raid amplified the West's concern about Japan's method of conducting warfare. Virtually no one had cared for a decade, yet suddenly the ferocity of the Japanese military became a matter of interest to Occidentals whose own sons now were directly affected.

In the Doolittle raid, two of the air crews were captured by the

Japanese, and immediately attention focused on the fate of such captives. Nothing was known at that time of the Bataan Death March, which was just then in progress, and reports of Japanese mistreatment of soldiers and civilians in Singapore, Hong Kong, and the Dutch East Indies were not yet clear. The world was only slowly learning of the calculated savagery of the supremely arrogant Japanese Army and its unconcern over the world's reaction.

In fact, a previous Japanese government had publicly committed the nation to a civilized policy regarding civilian internees and military prisoners of war. Japan had attended the Hague conference in 1907 and signed the Fourth Hague Convention, which promulgated "Regulations Respecting the Laws and Customs of War on Land." Under this pact prisoners of war were to be housed in healthy surroundings, allowed exercise, and fed as well as the troops of the capturing nation. They were not to be chained or manacled, and they were not to be used as slave labor.

Later, in 1929, the rules were augmented in the Geneva Convention covering prisoners of war. This was signed by almost all nations that year, but Japan did not adhere, although a Japanese representative had participated in drawing up the compact. Neither, however, did the Japanese government actually reject the convention. The civilian government wanted to accept the Geneva covenant, but the military wanted to reject it. Because such an issue could cause the fall of a cabinet if the Army were to withdraw the war minister, which we know it was quite capable of doing, the civilians were afraid to press.

In the struggle for power between civilian and Army groups in Japan, the Geneva Convention was conveniently put aside as too explosive an issue to interject into a tense situation. The Army's objections were explained in 1934. The military opposed the signing of the convention because prisoners of war then could not be punished as severely as could Japanese soldiers for infractions of Japanese Army discipline, and therefore the Japanese military code would have to be revised. For example, a Japanese soldier who deserted was subject to the death penalty, but a prisoner of war who tried to escape could not be so punished under the Geneva Convention.

This argument was nonsense, of course. All other countries had their own systems of military discipline, but they were not deemed to be contravened by the special treatment willingly accorded war prisoners. The rejection by the Japanese military of the Geneva Convention was indicative of the enormous schism in that country's society. The Japanese society had adopted the dress and ways of the West in the nineteenth century—part time. The Army and Navy had accepted the ways of the Western armies and navies. But in the 1920s the Japanese military had reverted to planned savagery, discarding the manners and military mores learned from the West. The symbol was General Araki's discarding of the Western-style sword when he was minister of war in 1931. The Western-style sword had become almost entirely a dress uniform accoutrement after cavalry disappeared from the military scene, and the readoption of the samurai sword, which was definitely regarded as an infantry weapon, was symbolic of the Imperial Army's attempt to promote a new Bushido, whose relationship to the Bushido of the past was only superficial.

So Japan went into the China war with uninhibited ferocity; terrorism and cruelty became two of the major weapons used against the Chinese. When the Pacific war began, the Americans, British, Canadians, Australians, and New Zealanders announced that they intended to treat Japanese prisoners of war in accordance with the Geneva Convention, and asked Japan for a guarantee of reciprocity. Foreign Minister Togo gave that guarantee, with the knowledge of Prime Minister Tojo. But almost immediately other difficulties arose between those two men over the management of affairs with the newly conquered countries, and their relationship became cold and formal. Tojo no longer sought Togo's advice nor did he honor the foreign minister's legal and moral commitment to the Geneva Convention.

This change was first apparent very early in the Pacific war, as the Japanese rolled up one victory after another, and the Imperial Army leaders began to think of themselves as omnipotent, so swollen with success had they become.

When Hong Kong was captured on Christmas Day, 1941, Japanese troops entered St. Stephen's College, then used as a military hospital, and bayoneted approximately seventy prisoners, tortured and mutilated others, and raped the Chinese nurses. The same pattern was followed when the Japanese captured Singapore in February 1942. The troops surged into the Alexandra Hospital, bayoneted every person they saw, entered the operating room, where an operation was going on, and bayoneted the patient, the anesthetist, and the surgeon. From there they moved through the hospital and killed every person they found. When the Japanese captured Java in March 1942 they behaved in exactly the same way, bayoneting, raping, murdering and looting. This all was obviously official Japanese military policy; dozens of similar cases ultimately came to light. Mistreatment of prisoners was standard; decent treatment of prisoners was rare, and depended almost entirely on the goodwill of the local commander, and even he could not always control his soldiers.

In Java, one line officer asked the commander of the Imperial Army 36th Division if he could have an American prisoner of war to kill for practice. The division commander sent him two POWs, who were subsequently blindfolded, repeatedly bayoneted, and then decapitated with shovels by the Japanese soldiers, acting on the orders of their officers. But they did not need such orders, for it was inherent in their training from the beginning that the prisoner was not to be treated as a human being, but simply as "the enemy"; no mistreatment or torture was disallowed.

In Malaya and the Philippines, two humane commanders, generals Tomoyuke Yamashita and Masaharu Homma, were dismayed to learn that they could not control the inhuman activities of their military units. The Imperial Army system had made monsters of their men.

Further, in the Imperial Army's propaganda, they found it useful to humiliate the Western prisoners of war to impress Asians with the essential superiority of the Japanese. Prisoners of war then became pawns in Japan's political warfare, as is demonstrated by an event that occurred in Korea early in the war.

Against the will of its people, Korea had been annexed to Japan in 1910, and the Koreans had rebelled and revolted ever since. The Japanese Imperial Army formation called the Army of Korea was one of the strongest in the Japanese system, and one of its major functions was to maintain order in this colony. In early 1942 General Seishiro Itagaki was commander-in-chief of the Japanese Army in Korea, and General Jiro Minami was governor general of Korea.

On March 4th of that year, General Itagaki sent a telegram to the War Ministry asking for the dispatch of a number of prisoners of war for his political use:

> As it would be very effective in stamping out the respect and admiration of the Korean people for Britain and America, and also in establishing in them a strong faith in victory, and as the Governor General and the Army are both strongly desirous of it, we wish you would intern 1000 British and 1000 American prisoners of war in Korea.

The next day Tojo's War Ministry responded. A thousand white prisoners of war would be sent immediately to Korea. The message was premature; it was August before the first batch of prisoners arrived. They were British and Australians captured at Singapore.

These troops had been five weeks in the Japanese transport *Fukai Maru*. They were disembarked and sprayed with disinfectant, photographed by Japanese newsmen, and mustered on the wharf for inspection. During the inspection watches and rings and anything else of value was taken by the *Kempeitai*, the military police, and not returned.

Then the prisoners, including the sick, were formed into a column of fours, and marched through the city of Pusan with a mounted Japanese officer at the head of the column and Japanese guards all around. They were marched all day in the hot sun with two breaks at schools, where children were encouraged to come up and jeer and spit at them.

Then the POWs were taken to the railroad station, given *bento* (box lunches) which they ate on the platform, and another *bento* which they took on the train with them. They then left for Seoul. On arrival they were marched through this city, too, before a crowd of 120,000 Koreans and 57,000 Japanese. Then they entered the prisoner of war camp where they were to stay.

As reported to Tojo's Ministry of War in Tokyo, this program had the desired results. Itagaki's chief of staff quoted two young Koreans who had watched the parade:

"When we look at their frail and unsteady appearance, it is no wonder that they lost to the Japanese forces," said one.

"When I saw young Korean soldiers, members of the Imperial Army, guarding the prisoners, I shed tears of joy," said a second young man.

So, said Itagaki's chief of staff, "On the whole it seems that the idea was very successful in driving all admiration for the British out of the Koreans' minds and in driving into them an understanding of the situation."

This program was deemed so successful that it was repeated many times in many places.

By the middle of March 1942, official Japan knew about the many protests that had come in against this sort of treatment, and British Foreign Minister Anthony Eden had raised the issue in the House of Commons. Word of that had gotten back to the Imperial Palace in Tokyo and was discussed by Lord Keeper of the Privy Seal. Also, because there were so many complaints and inquiries from abroad about the fate of prisoners and internees, Prime Minister Tojo created a special office of information in the war department to deal with the questions. But there is little if any evidence that the complaints made any difference, for time after time the Japanese authorities rejected them as untruthful or unfounded. After the war the allegations were found to be all too truthful and well founded.

When the war ended, Tojo indicated that it was a complete surprise to him to discover that Japanese military commanders had tolerated and encouraged the mistreatment of prisoners. The Japanese Army system, he said, gave great latitude to local commanders to do as they wished. That was true because that system, as he was well aware, totally disregarded the Geneva Convention and the rights of POWs and internees. It was uncomfortable to be called to account, and Tojo showed this, but he also refused to acknowledge any sense of guilt, which was quite in keeping for the savage son of a savage system. After all, Tojo's rise to prominence had been as commander of the *Kempeitai* in Manchuria, an organization notorious for its methods.

The Doolittle raid, as noted, had created a furore in Japan. Two of the air crews were captured in China; one crew was taken to Shanghai and the other to Nanking. Later the fliers were transferred to Tokyo and thrown into cells at *Kempeitai* headquarters. All these Americans were tortured into making false confessions of wrongdoing against the Japanese.

The propaganda value of the humiliation of the Americans was appreciated by the Japanese military authorities; it abetted their campaign to belittle the white men and break the will of the Chinese.

Prime Minister Tojo's day-to-day activities showed very clearly his role in the war effort. He was completely aware of what was happening with the Doolittle fliers, because General Sugiyama insisted that they be treated as war criminals. Tojo had suggested that the matter be dealt with promptly, but Sugiyama insisted that the current military code of justice did not have adequate provision for such "crimes" and insisted also that a special example be made of the Doolittle fliers to discourage future raids on Japan.

Prime Minister Tojo, functioning as war minister, acceded to Sugiyama's demands, and put the wheels in motion for the changes in the code of justice. These would mandate imprisonment for at least ten years or even death for air attacks.

While the fate of the Doolittle fliers was being written in these *ex post facto* regulations, Tojo went about his routine. Much of what he did was ceremonial, such as a trip to Kyushu in April. His visit to

Kagoshima on April 1 was a case in point. In the morning he visited the prefectural offices, and greeted the officials who had assembled to meet him. Then he held a newspaper interview, and made a speech to the prefectural workers. Next he reviewed the troops and made another speech about the war effort. After that there was a luncheon party of some fifty people, and then more meetings. At five o'clock he toured the naval base and one of the ships, and at six o'clock he visited the naval air base. That was how it went day after day on the Kyushu trip—meetings and ceremonial meals, the purpose of which was to enhance the war effort.

His major responsibility was to keep the government going. Unlike in Germany and Italy, the Japanese Diet met regularly all during the war, and in several special sessions to settle matters of the budget. That is not to say that Japan was not a police state. It most definitely was. The first major bill Tojo presented after the outbreak of war was the Press, Publication, Assembly, and Association Special Control Law; it banned any of these activities that were not specifically authorized by the government. In other words, the control of public activity was total. This omnibus bill was railroaded through the almost supine Diet after only one day of debate on December 17, 1941. Another Tojo bill, which brought in administrative reform and decreased the power of the bureaucracy to stall action by the government, was later passed after three days of debate.

As was the Japanese custom under the Meiji Constitution, the wartime Diet almost automatically enacted all legislation offered by the government.

All this had been foreseen by Prince Konoye when he was prime minister. The National Mobilization bill of 1938 had put Japan on a war footing. In 1940 the political parties had been dissolved and the Diet assumed what the government liked to call a "national" appearance. In fact, even before Tojo's assumption of the premiership police state tentacles were pervasive. Theoretically Diet members had immunity from prosecution for anything they said in the House, but actually if they overstepped the marks set by the Army they were expelled from the parliament. In March 1938 Suehiro Nishio, a member of the Social Mass Party, which was akin to the Nazi Party in Germany, called on Prince Konoye to emulate Hitler, and he was expelled by the Diet Discipline Committee. In February 1940 Dietman Takao Saito was expelled for criticizing the Army's conduct of the war in China. In November 1941 Member Taneo Miyazawa was expelled for criticizing the military budget. And yet embers of independence still glowed. Both Nishio and Saito were reelected to the Diet by their constituents.

In September 1941, the government had achieved a new level of control of the legislative processes—again under the Konoye regime—when the Diet Members Imperial Assistance League was formed under the auspices of the Imperial Rule Assistance Association, which Konoye had set up to guide every level of Japanese political life, from the neighborhood association to the national legislature. Three hundred and twenty-six members of the Diet joined, or 70 percent of the total. What of the other 30 percent? Outstanding in this group was the Association of the Like-minded, a liberal group led by Ichiro Hatoyama, with 36 representatives in the Diet. These dissidents represented considerable economic power and prestige, from the *Japan Times*, the most important (and independent) English-language newspaper, to the son of the late Prime Minister Inukai—that premier had been assassinated for his stand against the Army in 1932. These people continued to function during the war, although their activity was limited and they were under constant observation by the "thought police." So, as noted, Japan was never a dictatorship in the Western pattern, although the Army had seized and maintained control of the war effort and more and more wrested control of foreign affairs.

One of Tojo's major tasks in his role as prime minister, but actually representing the Army, was to take control of Japan's foreign affairs from the basically liberal foreign office, which had fought the Army over China policy and lost. This was the subject of his dispute with Foreign Minister Togo. After 1938 the Foreign Ministry had been relegated to the position of propaganda agency for Army policies, a state of affairs that caused a constant smoldering among the foreign office bureaucrats, but about which they could do nothing. From time to time, however, the foreign office did manage to interfere and sidetrack some Army policies. Of course, the closure of the Japanese embassies in the United States and Britain and all the commonwealth dominions decreased the prestige of the foreign office. In Germany and in Italy military missions represented the most important aspects of Japan's relationships with those countries. Only in the Soviet Union, where there was violent distrust of the Japanese Imperial Army, did the Foreign Ministry have influence. Having learned a bitter lesson from the abortive attack on Russia at Nomonhan in 1939, and recognizing the impossibility of fighting in the north as well as in China and the south, the Army was temporarily content to let the foreign office manage this segment of affairs.

But not the rest. The conquest of the Philippines, the Dutch East
Indies, and Malaya, and the occupation of Indochina, raised the issue
of which government agency would deal with these areas. The Foreign
Ministry was theoretically in charge of Japanese relations with Manchukuo (where the Kwantung Army actually ran the show), with
Nanking China (where the China Expeditionary Army held the real
power), and with Thailand. The establishment of local governments in
these conquered areas caused the Foreign Ministry to demand control,
which was the last thing the Army wanted. So as representative of the
Army, Prime Minister/War Minister Tojo's task was to secure Army
control, preferably without martial law, because that would tie up too
many Japanese troops, and the troop manpower barrel was already
running low.

In the spring of 1942, after the rapid conquest of Southeast Asia and
the drive deep into the South Pacific, difficulties arose between Tojo
and Togo. Following the demand by the Army leaders, Tojo had moved
to establish the Greater East Asia Ministry, to handle relations with
the new countries that now comprised the Greater East Asia Co-
prosperity Sphere, and which would be the nucleus of the New Asia.

At the end of April delegates from Thailand arrived in Tokyo to
negotiate a treaty of alliance with Japan. The purpose was to bring
Thailand into the Co-prosperity Sphere, but also to secure such military assistance as would be valuable to Japan. One of the primary
matters was the construction of a Bangkok to Rangoon railroad, one
which would give the Japanese an overland route to supply their forces
in Burma and ultimately, as the plan went, to stage an invasion of
British India.

That spring of 1942 Tojo made a trip to Southeast Asia to see for
himself what had been accomplished and to examine some of the
problems. He went from Japan to Shanghai, thence to Taiwan, and
Saigon. The latter city was the headquarters of General Count Terauchi, and it must have been on this visit that one of the most controver-
sial of matters came up. Tojo had been sympathetic to the plight of the
prisoners of war captured in the lightning campaigns in Southeast Asia.
He had observed to his secretaries that the Australians, the Dutch and
the British had fought very hard. His opinion of their leadership may
not have been very high, but he respected bravery in the field. He had
said to his secretaries at the dinner table that he believed the enemy
prisoners should be dealt with gently.

But others in the Japanese Army establishment did not share Tojo's
attitude, and Count Terauchi was among them. Terauchi was to be held

responsible for the building of the Bangkok-Rangoon railroad and he was wondering how he was going to do it. Japan did not have the resources to bring thousands of vehicles and pieces of construction equipment into Southeast Asia. The job would have to be done by hand labor. Tojo was asked how he felt about the employment of prisoners of war on such essential tasks and he gave a reply that he later indicated he thought was noncommittal. During the war, the premier said, everyone would have to work.

And from this rather equivocal stand the Army emerged with a policy of slave labor for war prisoners—a policy that was matched in cruelty only by the German treatment of the Soviet and Eastern European prisoners and civilians who came into their hands.

The fact was that in the matter of local military government the Japanese tradition, dating back to the first Sino-Japanese and the Russo-Japanese war, had been to give area army commanders full responsibility and authority to deal with all problems. Only if matters reached so parlous a state as to be scandalous or if somehow a matter came to the attention of the Emperor would Tokyo interfere.

In the Saigon area, Tojo met with Army and Navy officers, and inspected the troops. He discussed military affairs in his capacity as war minister, but he did not interfere with the local command. His function was not that but to see how matters stood in terms of supplies, equipment, and manpower, and to promote the Greater East Asia Co-prosperity ideal.

From Saigon Tojo went on to Bangkok, where most of his time was taken up with the furtherance of the alliance with the Thai, and attempts to convince their authorities that Japan really did intend the Greater East Asia Co-prosperity Sphere to bring prosperity to all the member states—that it was not simply a means for the Japanese government to milk the Asian nations. A number of projects of benefit to the Thai were discussed, among them the modernization of their capital.

From Bangkok Tojo then went to Singapore, which had been re-named Shonan ("Glorious South") by the Japanese. The Imperial Navy at this point had high hopes to make of Shonan the Japanese naval bastion that Singapore had been for the British.

On May 24 Tojo was in Palembang and Batavia; the next day he traveled to Surabaya, and Balikpapan. He visited a division that had a prisoner of war camp under its command, and issued a statement that in its essence was to be repeated many times:

"The present situation of affairs in this country does not permit anyone to lie idle, doing nothing but eating freely. With that in view, in dealing with prisoners of war, I hope you will see that they are usefully employed."

On the 27th he visited the commands at Davao and then went on to Manila, where he spent two days. There was some talk about the unsatisfactory nature of the campaign to take the Philippines, for which the Imperial Headquarters blamed General Homma. Tojo had reports of Homma's softness to the enemy (and he also had reports on the Bataan Death March, which he ignored), but it was not his responsibility or his place to take sides in a dispute within the Army, and at this point Tojo was too unsure of his power to do so. In fact, a young Colonel Masanobu Tsuji, who had already cost General Yamashita his command in the Malaya area,* was now after General Homma. Tsuji was the architect of the Bataan Death March. He had read the Army handbook prepared by General Tojo when he was war minister in the Konoye cabinet, to encourage the troops to greater effort. Tsuji was inclined to quote the parts calling for perseverance and staunchness to death; he also held Japan's enemies in contempt because they had surrendered rather than die. Tojo professed no such standard for the enemy, although his concern for the humane processes was as minimal as that of any other Japanese Army officer.

Back in Japan before the battle of Midway, Prime Minister Tojo issued instructions to newly-appointed commandants of prison camps:

> In Japan we have our own ideology concerning prisoners of war which should naturally make their treatment more or less different from that in Europe and America. In dealing with them you should, of course, observe the various regulations concerned and aim at an adequate application of them. At the same time you must not allow them to lie idle doing nothing but enjoy free meals, for even a single day. Their labor and technical skill should be fully utilized for the replenishment of production, and a contribution thereby made toward the prosecution of the Greater East Asia War for which no effort might be spared.

These instructions, when read in connection with the rules concerning prisoners, which focused more on their punishment for infractions of

---

*Colonel Tsuji, one of the most aggressive of the young officers, had informed Tojo as war minister, that Yamashita was "soft on the enemy." This had played into Tojo's hands and enabled him to transfer Yamashita to exile in a remote post in Manchukuo on the pretext of guarding against Russian attack.

rules than their well-being, were a green light to the camp commanders and army area commanders to treat prisoners exactly as they wished.

Tojo was not consulted about actual operations in the war and had no responsibility other than to report to the Emperor. This he did regularly, using information supplied to him by the Army and the Navy ministries. Otherwise this spring and summer of 1942 Tojo's principal effort was devoted to establishment of the Greater East Asia Co-prosperity Sphere. The foreign minister wanted to control relations with the Philippines and the other countries involved, as we have seen, but the Army strenuously objected to this notion. The Army wanted a separate ministry for Greater East Asia, and the Army won out. After having once suggested that Tojo resign as prime minister because of the difficulty, Foreign Minister Togo was the one who resigned. He had learned that the Emperor was concerned about this contretemps and wanted it resolved without a resignation of the entire cabinet. So the Ministry of Greater East Asia was established, and became the most important civilian ministry of all.

The Doolittle fliers had been moved back to China—to Shanghai and Nanking. General Shunroku Hata, commander of the China Expeditionary Army at Nanking, had been told to delay the trial of these men until the new Army regulations were promulgated. In fact, Tojo's War Ministry told General Hata to "establish the law" by trying these defendants under it. On August 13, the "Enemy Airmen's Act" was officially proclaimed by the Army and the Doolittle fliers were brought to trial under these rules. The trial was held on August 28. The accused were not told the charges (in English) and they were given no facilities for making a defense. All the accused were found guilty of crimes against humanity and sentenced to death by the Japanese military court. The findings were sent to Tokyo, where Tojo learned of them. He tried to soften the punishment, but General Sugiyama was adamant. The Doolittle fliers must be made into frightening examples to show other Allied fliers what would happen to them should they attack Japan.

Tojo then took up the matter with the Emperor, who recommended leniency. Once again the premier went to Sugiyama, who was obdurate at first, but who, when he heard of the Emperor's interest, compromised to the extent that the death sentences for five of the prisoners were reduced to life imprisonment. Still, three of them, Lt. Dean

Hallmark, Lt. William Farrow, and Sgt. Harold Spatz, were executed by firing squad on October 15, 1942.

They were only the first of many Allied airmen killed under this new law approved by War Minister Tojo.

10

The Dream: United Asia

The perception of the fundamental idea of a united Asia under Japanese leadership began in the 1920s in Manchuria. One of its leading exponents was Masayoshi Miyazaki, a graduate of Moscow University. In the 1920s he was an official with the South Manchuria Railway Company, that harbinger of Japanese expansionism. One of Miyazaki's converts was Lt. Col. Kanji Ishihara of the Kwantung Army, and the military man became the activist; he was the guiding spirit behind the Mukden Incident of 1931, which resulted in the wrenching of Manchuria away from China and the creation of Manchukuo.

The formation of Manchukuo led to the Japanese withdrawal from the League of Nations in the storm of criticism that assailed Japan, and her isolation from the Western powers. This isolation was amplified with the failure of the London Naval Conference of 1934, and the subsequent rush of Japan to strengthen her military forces on land and sea.

At this same time a number of study committees of Army and Navy looked to the development of a basic policy to cover Japan's ambition to lead the Asian nations out of colonialism. Not coincidentally, it was also to lead them into a new era in which Japan would be the leading power in a friendly, united Asia—an Asia which would have divested itself of ties to the Western powers, most particularly Britain and the United States.

In his book *Toa Renmei ron* (*The Theory of East Asian Federation*), Miyazaki virtually laid out what would become the Imperial Army's policy resulting in the China war and the Pacific war:

East Asian Federation is to my way of thinking a good and moral action, but I don't advocate it simply as social good and international righteousness. I do advance it because in the present stage of the history of the Orient, centering around Japan, and of the world, it is inevitable that it will be realized soon. I affirm that the East Asian Federation will be the essence of the Showa Restoration. . . . In brief it will be the achievement of the great mission of *Hakko ichiu* [all the eight corners of the world under one roof] and the denouement of the Showa Restoration. It seeks the liberation of East Asia through destruction of the Western imperialistic structure in the Orient. The first stage of the plan is to create a New East Asia Structure, combining Japan, Manchukuo and China, and also to create a new order in our own country which will be closely related.

Miyazaki held that this program was the revolutionary solution to Asia's problems, all of which centered around Western colonialism. "The first task is to completely liquidate all the vestiges of the idea of imperialistic aggression and return to Mahayana [Buddhism]."

It was natural for Japan to lead this movement, for Japan was the only country in Asia with a modern economy and a modern military machine. It was Miyazaki's aim that Japan achieve this leadership without any selfish motives, to displace the role of America and Europe with that of Japan. China's negative attitude toward Japan, the federationists held, was the result of European and American pressures. Japan had been subject to similar pressures because the island nation had not previously had the power to expel the foreigners from Asia.

As it turned out, the federationists believed, the structure of the modern Japanese government had been a mistake. Germany, Italy, and the USSR had made great strides in building their military power, because they had dictatorial governments. The liberalism of the Japanese political system had been its weakness, delaying Japan's military buildup for years, and thus postponing the day when Japan could push the British and Americans out of Asia. By 1936, the year that Miyazaki's book was published, the Army was in the process of wresting power away from the civilian government. The abortive 2-26-36 Incident presaged that wresting of power by the intimidation of the civil authorities. An American newspaper reporter termed the phenomenon "government by assassination," and he was not far wrong; assassination and the fear of assassination loomed over almost every politician who dared speak out against the burgeoning of Army power.

One other development within the Army hastened the rise of the *Gumbatsu*: the military combination of the *Tosei Ha* (Control) and *Kodo Ha* (Imperial Way) factions of the Army. This came about after the 2-26-36 Incident because in their miscalculation the *Kodo Ha* endangered the whole Army, and the *Tosei Ha* leaders also saw that almost all of the young officers were on the side of the *Kodo Ha*. So the factions merged, with *Kodo Ha* influence predominating; the Imperial Way with its Emperor-worship became the Army way.

In April 1936 a Navy committee laid the groundwork for a national military policy "to expand the national government internally, and externally to ensure Japan's position on the continent." Japan should also move south [for oil], expand her power, and assure peace in East Asia. To accomplish this, Japan must have a centralized national policy, treading softly at first, so as not to arouse the sleeping great powers [Britain and the U.S.].

Manchukuo, the Navy planners readily admitted, had "the structure of an independent nation and the reality of an indivisible relationship with Japan." Manchukuo was to be the starting point for the Greater East Asia plan. The existence of Manchukuo would help to persuade China to a new policy of cooperation under Japanese leadership.

Japan's relationship with China would depend on enlightened self-interest. She should give economic and technical aid to China and make that vast land self-reliant. At the same time, China must be made friendly to Japan and must rely on Japan for protection against the influence of the U.S. and Britain. Moreover, the five provinces of North China and Inner Mongolia must be a bulwark against the Soviet Union for Japan. The nature of the policies advanced by the planners were as follows:

1. Towards Southeast Asia: Strengthen Japan's national defense through the acquisition of resources. Help solve the Japanese population pressure problem (projected to become serious in the ensuing decade) by providing room for major overseas resettlement of Japanese.

2. Towards the Soviet Union: That state must be restrained against advancing in the Far East and communization must be resisted.

3. Towards Britain: Japan should move to replace British influence where possible, form close ties with British colonies to control Britain's anti-Japanese policy, and take advantage of developments to erode British power without openly twisting the lion's tail.

4. Towards the U.S.: Resist America's traditional Open Door policy in the Far East, make military preparations, and persuade the Americans to recognize Japan's special position in Asia. At the same time to establish friendly relationships on the basis of "mutually dependent economic relationships."

By June 1936 the Imperial Army had assumed a more belligerent stance: "Our national policy is to establish our status as the protector and leader of East Asia. To do this we must have the power to expunge the pressure of the white races in East Asia."

Unlike the Navy, the Imperial Army still regarded the Soviets as the primary potential enemy of Japan, and advocated preparations for war with the USSR. But the keystone of Japanese Army policy was the restructuring of and then friendship with China. Ultimately, the Japanese expected to fight "a great decisive war with the United States."

By midsummer 1936 the Army had come to power, and at a five ministers' conference, which represented the powers that controlled Japan, several points were brought out. These points reflected the preceding months' work by the military planners.

1. The Imperial Way had become the policy of Japan. The Soviets were still seen as the primary enemy on land, but ultimate conflict was expected with the U.S. and Britain.

2. Japan should be the stabilizing power in East Asia.

3. Japan's diplomatic policy should be aimed to achieve Japan's military aims.

4. Japanese public opinion should be shaped to that end.

5. Industry and business should implement national policy.

On December 22, 1938, Prince Konoye, then prime minister, proclaimed the New Order of East Asia, which embraced Japan, Manchukuo and China. This was at the point that the Japanese had finally given up on trying to reach an accommodation with Chiang Kai-shek and had set the wheels in motion to support the Nanking government of Wang Ching-wei, but had not yet decided definitely on the move south. What Japan wanted from China was freedom of trade and movement, and Konoye denied any territorial ambitions:

"If the object of Japan in conducting the present vast military campaign be fully understood, it will be plain that what she seeks is neither territory nor indemnity for the costs of military operations. Japan demands only the minimum guarantee needed for the execution by China of her function as a participant in the establishment of the New Order."

By April 1939 the Navy-sponsored National Policy Research Committee's position paper reflected further developments in nationalistic thinking. The move south was now to support the China war and should yield resources Japan needed. This was to be done by establishing industries and creating trade opportunities, by promoting friendship with the peoples of these southern areas, and by promoting projects for Overseas Chinese in these areas.

Now, too, the Japanese began to name the places that interested them: the Philippines, Siam, Netherlands Indies, Malaya, and more particularly Sumatra, the Celebes, New Guinea, Mindanao, and Borneo. Their planning took a more aggressive stance, aimed at "driving out British and French political and economic power, and making the Dutch rely on Japan, promoting Philippine independence."

They would do this by upgrading their consular offices to diplomatic status, by efforts to promote friendship with local peoples by cultural exchanges and activities, by banking activity, promoting Japanese travel and by expanding cultural friendship organizations.

With the outbreak of the China Incident, the Imperial Army had come into its own, and the military control of the government had been achieved. Japan then would proceed to assure an Asia for the Asiatics, and bring China around to the same attitude, after which the strength and power of the East Asia Federation would be secure. This was the theory. It dominated the Kwantung Army, and with the dispatch of General Tojo to Manchuria in 1935, he too had become a convert to the theory. He was also a firm member of the *Tosei Ha* faction, and when the factions merged his star continued to rise because he was regarded as the least ambitious and most trustworthy of the generals.

But the practical implementation of the policy, under the concept of the Greater East Asia Co-prosperity Sphere, was first enunciated by Prime Minister Konoye in July 1940. His vague allusions were given more substance on August 2 in a radio broadcast by Foreign Minister Yosuke Matsuoka, who had been closely allied with Tojo in Manchuria. By 1940 the concept of Greater East Asia had broadened to include not only China and Manchukuo, but the Dutch East Indies and French Indochina.

As war minister, General Tojo endorsed this concept, but when he became prime minister he took it further. As noted, on January 21, 1942, Tojo addressed the Diet on the subject, and included in the sphere Malaya, Burma, and the Philippines. Soon the sphere was widened to include India.

By that time, Japan had conquered Hong Kong and Malaya and was well along in the occupation of the Philippines, with the American resistance limited to the Bataan peninsula and Corregidor.

The whole military point of the Pacific war, Tojo said, was to secure strategic bases in Greater East Asia and to bring under Japanese control the resources she needed most (rubber, tin, and above all oil). In cooperation with Germany and Italy, Japan was determined to bring America and Britain to their knees, and expel them and their influence from Asia. Although General Sugiyama and the others at Imperial General Headquarters were flushed with victory and cocksure of success, Tojo himself was under no such illusions about the future of the war. He saw it as a herculean struggle, against great odds. He saw a need for more than the short-term military advantages. They must enlist the people.

"We must, therefore, be prepared for difficulties of various sorts which may arise in the future, and that the present war will become a prolonged one. Accordingly this war remains indeed to be fought hereafter. In order to fulfill the purpose of the war, the whole nation must persevere, in whatever difficulties and tribulations with a firm conviction of ultimate victory and thus serve the country."

Already, even as the Imperial forces fought on land and sea, the practical formation of the co-prosperity sphere was under way. It was to be raised to the practical level through the cooperation of the peoples of the Asian lands.

Tojo, in this speech to the House of Peers, outlined the steps by which Japan would achieve this new order.

First, Japan would take control and retain control of the areas that were absolutely essential for the defense of Greater East Asia. But other areas, which she might occupy for a time, would be dealt with in accordance with the tradition, culture, and circumstances of each people. In time, he said, Japan looked forward to the independence of all these peoples within the framework of the alliance. It was, in other words, ultimately to become a United States of Asia. Japan would undertake first to eradicate all the British influence from Hong Kong and Malaya. For the time being, but only temporarily, that meant Japanese control.

As to the Philippines, Japan would give them the independence they had been promised by the United States, in exchange for their adherence to the Greater East Asia Co-prosperity Sphere. The same treatment would be accorded to Burma.

In the Netherlands East Indies (where the Japanese had just landed) and Australia (where they had not landed yet) the people would have to make up their own minds. If they continued to resist Japan, then the

Japanese military machine would crush them. But if they joined Japan in its intentions to create this new Asian world, then Japan would do everything possible to help them.

China remained the great sorrow of Japan, Tojo said, because the regime insisted on clinging to the old colonial tradition. Chiang Kai-shek would have to be destroyed, and China brought onto the right track under the Nanking government.

By this time the Greater East Asia Co-prosperity Sphere was already in existence, theoretically serving the interests and with the coopera-tion of Manchukuo, Nanking China, Thailand, and French Indochina. For the moment Japan would have to maintain military government in much of the area of Asia, but preparations for the future were already under way, and the scope of civilian participation would steadily be expanded.

That Tojo speech brought jeers from the Western Allies and from the fastness of Chiang's inland capital Chungking, but it should have brought shivers. If the Japanese could achieve what they promised, they would create a revolution throughout East Asia. But the Japanese had one extremely difficult self-imposed hurdle to overcome. That was the intractability and arrogance of the Imperial Army, and it threatened the entire cooperative scheme.

Virtually every responsible public figure in Japan supported a New Order for Greater East Asia—one which would see Japan leading the Asian countries out of colonialism. Foreign Minister Shigenori Togo was one of these leaders who espoused wholeheartedly this concept, and in the beginning of their association he and General Tojo had no conflict. But they would soon fall out over the Army's methods.

Togo was on record as favoring the leadership of Japan "as an advanced nation of East Asia." On January 21, 1942, he had so said to the Diet in a major foreign policy speech detailing Japan's war aims and bringing to the fore Japan's intention to cooperate with *non*-Asian nations also in the development of East Asia.

But even as Togo made that speech, it was apparent to him that his views and those of General Tojo and the military were diverging rapidly. Togo accused the generals of being "increasingly drunk on the military successes," although Tojo, he said, was still very cautious. But Army Chief of Staff Sugiyama and the other generals of the high command were eager to decide the future status of the southern areas by installing military government more or less permanently. Foreign Minister Togo objected to this plan, as destructive of the intent of the New Order, converting an ideal to a tool of the Army.

Tojo supported him. A liaison conference was held between the military and the cabinet, and Tojo supported Togo's position, which carried the day.

Togo saw, however, that the Army was going to take the direction of foreign policy out of the hands of the foreign office. In May 1942, Togo began to hear talk in Army circles of the establishment of a new ministry to manage relations with the new territories acquired during the war. Already the demands of empire had diminished the Japanese foreign office. Korea was a colony governed by a general. Taiwan was virtually the same and so was Sakhalin. Manchukuo maintained the façade of independence, but the truth was that the commander of the Kwantung Army was also the ambassador and actual governor of Manchukuo. The China Expeditionary Army controlled the relationships with the Wang Ching-wei government of China. Since this would be an outright invasion of the prerogatives of the Foreign Ministry, Togo objected. The talk persisted and soon Togo realized that the Army intended to manage this new ministry. It would take over all affairs relating to Manchukuo, China, Thailand, Indochina, the Netherlands East Indies, the Philippines, Malaya, the Kwantung-leased territory, and the mandated islands of the South Seas. What would this leave for the Foreign Ministry? The parts of the world most important to Japan would have no relationship to Togo's office. The Manchuria Affairs Bureau, the Asia Development Boards and the Ministry for Overseas Affairs would all be abolished and their duties put under this new Greater East Asia Ministry, which would then become the key agency in Japanese foreign policy.

When the foreign minister was sure that this transformation was more than idle talk he went to the premier with his objections. Tojo listened gravely and promised to consider them. But when the prime minister aired the objections to General Sugiyama and the other leaders of the military clique (*Gumbatsu*), they rejected the Togo position out of hand. It was impasse. The Army had always had difficulty with the foreign office; the diplomats had stood in the way of the generals' manipulations time and time again; they had almost put a peaceful end to the China incident without a victory. The Army would have liked nothing better than to eliminate the Foreign Ministry altogether—it was rotten with liberals, said the generals—and this new move was the closest they could come to doing so.

Then came changes in the war, and these began to make the leaders of the *Gumbatsu* nervous. First, in May, was the unnerving affair involving Port Moresby in New Guinea. Planning a landing and the capture of that port, the Navy ran into serious opposition from the Americans at the battle of the Coral Sea. Although the Japanese claimed a victory, the high command was not so sure. And a few weeks later their uneasiness was confirmed. Because the carrier *Zuikaku* lost too many aircraft and the carrier *Shokaku* was damaged in the battle, they could not participate as they'd been expected to do in the early June battle of Midway. These ships could have made all the difference; what was anticipated as an easy victory turned into a shocking defeat for Japan. The naval ministry was so unnerved by the defeat that even Prime Minister Tojo was not informed for several days.

Following this disappointment, on August 7 the Americans landed troops on Guadalcanal in their first military offensive of the war. And though inclined to make light of this at first as just an American raid, Imperial General Headquarters soon had to take a more serious view. Although they had no lack of confidence of victory, the going seemed to grow more and more difficult. General Sugiyama, then, was in no mood to compromise on Army control of captured territories, and so the creation of this new ministry continued apace.

When Tojo had this word from the Army, he sent his chief cabinet secretary, Naoki Hoshino, to see Foreign Minister Togo. Hoshino carried with him the draft of the bill establishing the Greater East Asia Ministry, and told Togo that the prime minister wanted to get it through the cabinet at the meeting on September 1, just three days away. The foreign minister wanted to delay at least a week, but Hoshino said that Tojo was insistent. Togo saw Tojo at a dinner party on August 31, and again the premier refused to accept any delay.

So at the cabinet meeting on September 1, the plan was brought up. Togo aired his objections:

1. The division of the world into two parts, East Asia and everywhere else, would make it impossible for Japan to carry on a unified foreign policy.

2. The notion of "pure diplomacy" (the proposed new foreign office function) did not make any sense at all.

3. The East Asian countries, seeing that they were treated differently from others (and it could not be long before they would learn that the new ministry was really controlled by the Army), would not trust the Japanese government.

4. This ministry would really be an extension of the old Asia

Development Boards, which had aroused the antipathy of China and failed utterly.

5. This reorganization was a waste of time.

General Tojo, who answered the Togo arguments, said the Asian countries should be treated differently because they "were Japan's kin." Other cabinet members also intervened in favor of the new ministry.

After the meeting had failed to reach agreement, Tojo suggested that Togo resign. Togo suggested that Tojo resign. Again there was impasse. Togo feared that the whole of Japanese foreign policy would now become an extension of the Greater East Asia Co-prosperity Sphere of which Tojo seemed so enamored. He did voice his fear that this would also be nothing more than an extension of Army policies.

But most important, Togo wanted to force the resignation of the entire cabinet because he had lost faith in Tojo's ability to direct the war to a successful conclusion. He did not quite understand Tojo's problem with the generals and how Tojo was even then maneuvering to assume the power once held by the cabal of three.

To the foreign minister, Tojo represented weakness, a man who "labored mightily at advertising the initial successes of the war but was guilty of flagrant nonfeasance in carrying out urgently needed moves for increasing fighting power. Under such a premier ultimate victory in the war was not to be hoped for."

That night, Finance Minister Kaya called on Togo and tried to persuade him to reconsider. Then General Sato, the chief of the Army Bureau of Military Affairs, and Admiral Oka, his opposite number in the Navy, came to try. Togo was firm. Finally Navy Minister Shimada came and said that the Emperor wished Togo to resign because he did not want a change of the whole cabinet at that time. So Togo relinquished his post, and Prime Minister Tojo went ahead with the new Ministry of Greater East Asia, for which he and the Army had such high hopes in securing Asian peoples' support for the war, and (in Tojo's view but hardly the Army's) creating the new world of freedom for Asians that Japan wanted when peace was restored.

The next day, September 2nd, the now former foreign minister outlined the course of recent events, including all his objections, to his former staff. He did so in front of Prime Minister Tojo, who had temporarily taken over the foreign office portfolio.

And so the Greater East Asia Ministry was born, with Kazuo Aoki chosen as minister, serving under the watchful eye of the Army and the cynical gaze of the emasculated foreign office, whose diplomats never did come to trust the administration of the Greater East Asia Co-prosperity Sphere. From the beginning it was as Togo had prophesied: the peoples of Asia found the Japanese Army arrogant and cruel to conquered and "allied" local civilians wherever the military operated and exercised control.

By the autumn of 1942 this area was huge, about one and three-quarters million square miles in size, and with a population of 1,500,000,000 people, not including Manchukuo or China, which were also destined to be part of the picture. It included French Indochina, Malaya, the Philippines, Thailand, Burma, India the Netherlands East Indies, British Borneo, and Portuguese Timor. What remained to be seen was what use Japan would make of these new territories, and what she would do to attract the allegiance she so desperately wanted from their people.

11

Tojo Deals Out One Enemy

On August 8, 1942 (Tokyo time) the American First Marine Division had landed on Guadalcanal and seized control of the new Japanese naval airfield there. It also wiped out the Japanese seaplane base on little Tulagi Island 19 miles north across Lunga Strait. That day Prime Minister General Tojo was in his office as usual. His first duty was to go to the Imperial Palace to accept a new Imperial Rescript. As was the custom, he then went to the Meiji shrine and the Yasukuni shrine to pray in company with Navy Minister Shimada.

The rest of the day was spent in his capacity as war minister, exchanging information with General Sugiyama and others at Imperial General Headquarters. It was known that the Americans had landed; the radio station at Tulagi had broadcast a warning just before it was shot off the air, but it was not known how large a force had landed, or what the American intention might be. The landings were not a big surprise to the Army because the Americans had attacked the seaplane base in May, during the preliminaries to the battle of the Coral Sea. The Navy, which had manned both the airfield at Guadalcanal and the Tulagi base, seemed to believe the landing was a raid.

That day the Japanese were sending a convoy from Truk to New Guinea to strengthen the Japanese forces that had landed at Lae and Salamaua earlier. Navy and Army had not given up their intention to capture British New Guinea, although the plan had been set back by the confusion resulting from the battle of the Coral Sea in May and the outright defeat of the Japanese Navy at the battle of Midway in June. Now the Navy called the convoy and diverted it to Rabaul, the big Japanese base on New Britain Island, there to await developments. When Admiral Yamamoto had learned that a large American naval force, including three carriers, was in the vicinity of Guadalcanal, he ordered Adm. Gunichi Mikawa, commander of the 8th Fleet at Rabaul, to attack the Americans immediately and destroy their carriers and transports. Mikawa dispatched a force of cruisers and destroyers to do so.

Neither Imperial Headquarters nor General Tojo were very much concerned about the American landings, Tojo so little that in the account of his day-to-day activities kept by his two secretaries, Guadalcanal is not even mentioned on August 8. The Army was swollen with months of victory, and the premier had no good reason to revise his long-standing ill-founded lack of regard for the fighting qualities of Americans.

Imperial General Headquarters, too, was of the opinion that Western soldiers were soft. Gen. Masuharu Homma could have enlightened them—his 14th Army had run into more than a little difficulty in the conquest of the Philippines. But what one sees often depends on what one wants to see. General Sugiyama and others at Imperial General Headquarters had sent Col. Masanobu Tsuji to Manila, and he had reported that the slowness of the Japanese victory (two months behind schedule) was the fault of Homma's bad organization, not the Americans' fighting ability. So Imperial General Headquarters remained blissfully unaware that the Americans were preparing to give them a real battle for Guadalcanal. On the scene, at Rabaul, Gen. Haruyoshi Hayakutake's 17th Army leaders knew so little about the American military organization that when they discovered that American Marines had landed on Guadalcanal, they had to ask a Navy liaison officer "What is a Marine?"

In the consultation within the Army about what to do to dislodge the Americans from Guadalcanal it was decided that this really did not demand more than a relatively small competent unit. Such a unit was ready and waiting. Col. Kiyonao Ichiki, commander of the 28th Infantry Regiment, had put together a well-trained force that had been scheduled to undertake the capture and occupation of Midway Atoll in connection with the Japanese naval action there to rout out the American fleet. When the Midway battle had turned into a Japanese rout instead, Colonel Ichiki's men had been taken to Truk, where they were landed—a compact striking force that could be used anywhere, perhaps in New Guinea. But now that this troublesome matter had come up at Guadalcanal, General Sugiyama proposed to use the Ichiki Detachment to clean up Guadalcanal, which they were expected to do a day or two after their arrival there. Ichiki was alerted, and arrangements were made to land him and his advance echelon—about a thousand men. The rest of the regiment, which was in Guam, might be brought in later if they were needed, a contingency Sugiyama believed most unlikely to be exercised.

General Tojo heard the Army's plans and he saw no reason to make any suggestions, or to change his own plans. He was scheduled to go to Nikko on August 9. He travelled by train from Ueno Station, and put up at the Kaneya Hotel. While he was en route he had a message from Imperial General Headquarters announcing the great Japanese victory in the naval battle they would come to call First Guadalcanal and the Americans called Savo Island. It was true, the Japanese had smashed the American cruiser force at Savo Island, sinking or badly damaging five Allied cruisers and a destroyer with no loss to themselves.

In Nikko Prime Minister Tojo made a speech to an assembly of retired Army and Navy officers. The next day he returned to Tokyo, got the details of the victory from Imperial General Headquarters, and that night attended a victory dinner. There was absolutely no concern about the Guadalcanal situation.

On August 18, the Ichiki Detachment was landed at Taivu Point, about 20 miles east of the American position on Guadalcanal; they reconnoitered and concluded that there were only about 2000 Americans on the island. So on the night of August 20/21 they attacked westward along the Ilu River, and were virtually annihilated by the withering Marine fire. Colonel Ichiki committed suicide, and his bedraggled remnants moved into the jungle to regroup. The Japanese naval forces continued to win battles and skirmishes in the area apparently at will; Japan's air force controlled the skies there in these first few weeks, but the Japanese Army was not in evidence.

One reason for this was the command situation. Until now Guadalcanal had been considered a Navy outpost, and the Army had no responsibility. General Hayakutake, the commander of the 17th Army, was busy planning the capture of British New Guinea and was having difficulty with an Allied offense that was developing there. He was not giving much attention to Guadalcanal. After the debacle, the Ichiki Detachment was supplanted by the Kawaguchi Brigade, a larger force. But the brigade's ships were found by American planes and bombed and strafed until two-thirds of the vessels were lost, along with most of the supplies for the 4000 Japanese who managed to get ashore.

When Maj. Gen. Seiken Kawaguchi's force got to Guadalcanal General Hayakutake offered to send a whole division but the brigade commander said he could not possibly use so many troops for the job at hand.

The weeks dragged on. The Marines held on by their toes, beating off one attack after another as the Japanese filtered in troops a battalion at a time. The Japanese seemed never to learn what they faced.

Guadalcanal still was not deemed important enough for General Tojo's secretaries to make any special mention of it in his journal. During August and September he was much more concerned with the Greater East Asia Ministry, which had many problems of organization. More than any other cabinet member, Minister Aoki worked with Tojo to pursue this dream of Asian cooperation. But the dream was already going sour, because the Army commanders in the occupied areas insisted on having matters their own way. Thailand was not happy with the constant transit of prisoners of war and coolie labor to build the rail line; obviously it was slave labor. In the Philippines and in the Dutch East Indies the military occupation regime's treatment of civilians was often cavalier, and sometimes extremely cruel. It had been hoped that the Japanese Army would be seen by Asians as a great liberator. But already, a few months into the war, the Japanese Army had a deserved reputation for monstrous behavior. Tojo had played an important part in this creation. It was he who had authorized Count Terauchi to use prisoners of war in this fashion, and the premier/war minister carefully refrained from inquiring what happened to the prisoners after they were so employed. The rumors were already getting out about neglect and actual mistreatment to the point of murder, but having insulated himself with the appointment of the Special Information Committee as a part of the War Ministry, Tojo subsequently ignored the entire problem.

On Guadalcanal the war now was going badly. While Admiral Yamamoto's cruisers and destroyers and even battleships bombarded Henderson Field and the Americans around it night after night, the Army promised an offensive that would take the airfield. Yet the Army failed time and again. The American leadership in the South Pacific had faltered and Adm. William F. Halsey came in to take over, raising American morale considerably. The Marines still were hanging on, never sure of supply and harried by Admiral Yamamoto's fleet on sea and his planes in the air.

Almost every week Prime Minister Tojo went to the Imperial Palace to brief the Emperor and always he was asked what was happening to the Army on Guadalcanal. He gave the Emperor reassurances which were satisfactory for a time. He really did not know. Imperial General Headquarters was withholding information from him.

All through September Tojo waited for news of the great Guadalcanal victory the Army promised, but it never came. The real problem was a failure of the high command to understand the enemy. The Americans had about 25,000 troops on the island by the end of September and their air forces were growing stronger.

The Japanese fed a division into Guadalcanal, and then another, until they, too, had about 25,000 troops on the island. But as the battle continued, the American supply situation began to improve and the Japanese supply situation worsened steadily.

Questioned by the Emperor, by October 1 the Imperial Army had begun to consider the Guadalcanal campaign a matter of national pride. It must be won. More troops were brought in until the Japanese had 28,000 men on the island, but they could not win a battle, in spite of many attempts. By November they were hungry and soon they would be starving. The Navy, in its efforts to resupply the troops, resorted to packing food in steel drums and trying to drift them ashore. Finally that month Gen. Hitoshi Imamura was brought down from Java in the Dutch East Indies to take over the Guadalcanal battle. He was given charge of the 8th Area Army and he would have two armies with which to fight the battle. But now nothing seemed to help. The Japanese had lost an enormous amount of shipping in the preceding twelve months to submarines and air attack in the South and Southwest Pacific.

As the year 1942 approached its end it was apparent in Tokyo that the war had taken a turn very much for the worse since late summer. When Emperor Hirohito opened the session of the Diet in December he was extremely serious: "Now the war situation is grave," he said. "All of us ought to be of one mind: strengthen the national power and destroy the inordinate ambition of the enemy."

But at long last real information about what was happening on two principal war fronts was filtering into Tokyo. General MacArthur and the Australians had finished their attacks in New Guinea by wiping out the Japanese forces in Buna and Gona, which really meant that the whole Japanese effort against New Guinea had failed. On Guadalcanal the troops were starving. Colonel Tsuji, the gray eminence who had brought down generals Yamashita and Homma, came down to Guadalcanal, conferred with Admiral Yamamoto at Truk, and went back to Tokyo, confounded for the first time. He was not faulting General Hayakutake, who was directing operations on Guadalcanal. He was not faulting Imamura, who directed operations in the total South

Pacific. Tsuji told of a strong and united enemy, much stronger than anyone in Tokyo had believed, and of how the Navy could not supply the troops. The Army, hastened by the Emperor's open disapproval of their activities, now demanded a major push on Guadalcanal. They came to General Tojo, as war minister, and demanded that he find them 600,000 tons of ships from the civilian economy for the Army's use. General Tojo responded as prime minister and said he could not denude the civilian economy to meet such a request for a lost cause. Now Gen. Shinichi Tanaka, the Army chief of operations, came to meet Tojo to personally demand the ships. Tojo refused. Tanaka went away and came back with the support of Col. Takushiro Hattori, the Army operations expert, who testified that the cargo vessels were absolutely essential to save Guadalcanal.

"Then Guadalcanal must be evacuated," declared Prime Minister Tojo.

"No," replied Tanaka, "Guadalcanal will not be evacuated. The battle will be won."

"I cannot give you the ships," said Prime Minister Tojo.

"You are a bloody fool!" retorted the dogged Tanaka, leaving an angry Tojo as the equally angry operations officers stomped back to Imperial General Headquarters.

Prime Minister Tojo sensed that he faced a very real crisis; he had faced another just a few days before. Gen. Kanji Ishiwara had long been one of Tojo's detractors. He was four years younger than the premier, and he was a brilliant strategist who some said should have Tojo's job as war minister. He preached that Japan should stop fighting China and ally herself with Chiang Kai-shek. He had once described Tojo as "an enemy of the people who should be arrested and executed," and for that remark Tojo had a year earlier invoked his power as war minister and put Ishiwara on the retired list.

But there were many in the military establishment who resented Tojo's treatment of Ishiwara, and a few days earlier Tojo had brought him to the office of the prime minister and tried to persuade him to change his views and join Tojo's team. Ishiwara had responded by telling Tojo that he was just as incompetent as Ishiwara had always believed, and the best thing Tojo could do for the country was to resign.

These rebellions disturbed Tojo because he was beginning his struggle for control of Imperial General Headquarters against General Sugiyama. He could do nothing to General Ishiwara except have him arrested on trumped-up charges, and the Army would quickly see through that plot. But he could punish Tanaka and he did. A few days later, General Tanaka was whisked off from his all-important Army operations post and sent down to General Count Terauchi in the Southern Army Command. Tojo had already dealt with Count Terauchi, he thought, by appointing him to that military command, which was thousands of miles from Tokyo. It would be a good idea to have another enemy consigned to that outpost, too.

And having dealt with General Tanaka, War Minister Tojo then appointed Maj. Gen. Kitsuju Ayabe to the post of deputy chief of staff of Count Terauchi's Southern Army, just to keep an eye on both of them. This was his second big challenge to General Terauchi, until lately one of the two undisputed leaders of the *Tosei Ha* bloc and the *Gumbatsu*. Tojo was not quite ready yet to challenge General Sugiyama, a charismatic leader whose following was very strong in Tokyo army circles, where Tojo's name had never caused a ripple of enthusiasm.

He was now strong enough to enforce his will on the Army in the southern area, where Imperial General Headquarters had made a botch of the job, neither capturing Port Moresby and winning control of New Guinea, nor regaining control of Guadalcanal. Here it was the first anniversary of the war, and the tide of victory had already receded. Some were claiming that the war was already lost.

On December 31, 1942, General Tojo presided over an important conference of the Imperial General Headquarters. He caused it to be held not at IGHQ, where General Sugiyama would be on his own turf, but at the Imperial Palace, with the Emperor in attendance. Attending were the chiefs of the Army and Navy general staffs; the deputy chiefs of staff; the chiefs of the Operations Bureau, and the heads of the operations sections, which had recently been stacked by General Tojo; and the ministers of war and Navy. Since the minister of the Navy was known always to follow Tojo's lead—so much so that he had a bad reputation with his fellow admirals—it can be seen that Tojo had the edge for the conference. Besides, the Emperor's dislike of General Sugiyama had not been lessened by the series of embarrassments caused by misinformation about the Guadalcanal campaign all the way through.

General Sugiyama knew better than to raise the issue of Guadalcanal again, for the shortage of shipping was a sore point with the Navy as well as with the Army, and the Navy blamed the Army for loss of many ships in the Guadalcanal and New Guinea campaigns.

The conference met for an hour and forty minutes and Tojo did most of the talking. At the end, the conferees agreed that the Guadalcanal operation would be suspended and the island evacuated at the end of January. A new line of defense would be established north of New Georgia and Isabella islands.

More important in the long run, for the attack on Australia, was the capture of New Guinea; Japan would turn her attention to that problem. Lae, Salamaua, Madang, and Wewak would be reinforced. Important trails and centers in eastern New Guinea would be captured in preparation for a new drive against Port Moresby. The Buna area, where there still were Japanese troops, would be evacuated and the troop positions consolidated. In the Solomons the Army was to go on the defensive, but in New Guinea the offensive was to be resumed.

Basically Tojo dictated all this, and the others listened and responded. He spoke to the point of the military situation and noted that the Army high command was not responsive to the needs of the country at large in the war. The shipping problem was a case in point: civilian needs were not being met, and yet the Army was demanding ever higher numbers of ships for its purposes. This would have to be changed.

For five years, since the outbreak of the China war, the Army had had its way, always depending on its trump card, "the requirements of the high command," to get its own way. But now with the war taking a different turn, the requirements of the generals were just one of the factors to be considered by the government. And it was the government, not the Army high command, that had to run the country, General Tojo said.

Here was the opening salvo in Tojo's bid to unseat General Sugiyama as the chief of the *Gumbatsu*. It came at a time when the Army spirit and Army prestige were at a low ebb. The dismal failure at Guadalcanal was the cause for which the generals could blame no one but themselves.

So, as the year 1942 drew to a close, one could not say that Prime Minister and War Minister Tojo had won control of the Army. Yet, it was quite obvious that General Sugiyama would never attain the sort of shogun's powers that seemed almost within his grasp a few months earlier. His reckless management of the Imperial General Headquarters had cost Japan dearly and thrown the whole Southern Pacific military operation into confusion.

Tojo now intended to turn his attention to strengthening the Japanese economic position by making the Greater East Asia Co-prosperity Sphere work for Japan.

12

The Changing Dream

The Japanese Pan-Asia concept with Japan as the leader of the Asians, as noted, went back to the days of Commodore Perry and the forcible opening of the island nation to Western trade and influence. Virtually all Japanese, including the Emperor, subscribed to the goal. So, after Prince Konoye gave utterance to the plan for a Greater East Asia Co-prosperity Sphere, the program gained steadily in the public eye. By early 1941 the Japanese were feeling enormous diplomatic and economic pressure from the Western powers, and at the same time were bogged down in a China war that was proving to be a staggering burden, but one that the military would not relinquish. So the "enlightenment" aspect of the Showa Reformation became more and more popular, a move involving the rejection of the foreign colonialism and the assumption by Japan of the leadership of a new Asian bloc of nations that *might* extend to include Australia and New Zealand as equals, but not masters.

Asia for the Asiatics was the announced foreign policy of Japan. The Imperial Army, however, was not so certain that the policies advocated by Tojo's government and accepted by the people and the Emperor would actually fit into their scheme of conquest. This was a matter taken up on November 20, 1941 at a liaison conference between Tojo and his civilian ministers on one side and the Army on the other. Everyone agreed that military government would have to be instituted at first in the conquered territories to restore order, expedite the acquisition of resources, and ensure the economic self-sufficiency of the Army. But Tojo's people insisted that the administrative organs of the military government should later on be switched over to civilian administrative machinery, and the Army reluctantly accepted that demand, particularly when Tojo invoked the name of the Emperor in the words "Imperial policies."

But the Army was not willing to be "soft" on the people of the new areas. "Economic hardships imposed upon civil livelihood as a result of acquisition of resources vital to the national defense and for the self-sufficiency of the occupation troops must be endured, and pacification measures against the natives shall stop at a point consistent with these objectives." That was how the Army saw the future.

As to independence, that cornerstone of the political thinking about the Greater East Asia Co-prosperity Sphere, the Army had serious reservations:

"Native inhabitants shall be so guided as to induce a sense of trust in the Imperial forces and premature encouragement of native independence movements shall be avoided."

This the Army insisted on despite the fact that that same Army had already dispatched agents to the territories that would be invaded, to encourage the people with promises of independence and cooperation with Japan.

And the Army, not content with this subversion of its own past policies, soon adopted an even harder outlook vis-à-vis the new territories. On December 12, four days after the opening of the war, another liaison conference was demanded by the Army. At this meeting the generals insisted on carving the targeted territories into administrative regions: Area A would include the Dutch East Indies, British Malaya, Borneo, and the Philippines; Area B would include French Indochina, Burma, and Thailand. The Army was willing to refrain from setting up military governments in Area B, for the moment at least, but gone were all the old promises of freedom and responsibility for the peoples of Area A.

In fact, the Imperial Army was changing a policy that it had been implementing secretly in its own way in the field. After the Japanese occupied China's Hainan Island, which they intended to use as a base for the invasion of Malaya, Imperial General Headquarters' Intelligence Section set up several training camps for the development of fifth columns and liberation armies for the targeted countries of Burma, Malaya, and the Dutch East Indies. Each of these camps developed its own ideology. Each Japanese unit was convinced to truly believe in its mission of liberating these European colonies, making them independent. Every one of the men who would go into the field had to swear an oath of allegiance to "his" national army.

One such was Maj. Iwaichi Fujiwara, who was assigned to develop the relationships with the Chinese and the Indians in Malaya. He soon found the Chinese intractable. He had been sent to Bangkok very early—in 1940—to begin this undercover work before the invasion of Malaya. Then he went to Hainan, from which he would accompany General Yamashita's force on the invasion of Malaya. Before the war began, Major Fujiwara conceived of establishing an Indian National Army that would lead the British colonial dominion of India to independence within the Greater East Asia Co-prosperity Sphere. Here was his creed:

> With both enemy and inhabitants alike who have been pressed into cooperation with the Japanese Army amidst gunpowder and smoke we must forge the basis of a new friendship and peace. We must spread this among the enemy and find allies among the enemy. So long as the Japanese Army fights we will not tire, we must go on adding enemies to our allies among the inhabitants. Japan's war will truly liberate inhabitants and POWs. Unfortunately they have to be made to realize that it is a righteous war in which the aspirations of the people will be achieved, and we will have their sympathy. Defeat in this ideological war, even though we achieve military victory, would mean that we could not attain complete victory. Regardless of the significance of the war, people who participate in this kind of work behind those in the independence movements of various nationalities must have enthusiasm and faith in the movements. And we must be humble and modest. . . .

Major Fujiwara made plans to move behind enemy lines to enlist Indian soldiers of the British Indian Army into the Indian Independence League. He intended to foment favorable political activity among a broad range of Indian nationals, but would start with those residing in Thailand and Malaya. At the outbreak of war the tempo of this activity should be increased among both the military and civilian constituencies.

Major Fujiwara's efforts were not confined to the Indians. He also was in charge of the formation of a Malay fifth column to work against the British. This was known as the *Kesatuan Muda Melays*, or the Malay Youth Movement. The members wore an armband with an F on it and were known as F men. The unit itself was called F-Kikan. Major Fujiwara's influence was great and wide: one of his principal converts was the Sultan of Pahang, who joined forces with the Japanese side against the British.

Once war began, the first work would be among colonial army POWs, instilling in them an appreciation of the Indian independence movement while making them aware of Japan's ideals for the Pan-Asia movement: prosperity and harmony "which transcends all conflicts and rivalries."

Fujiwara warned his Japanese colleagues against saying or doing things that might engender in the indigenous peoples a consciousness of any Japanese superiority or control. Neither must the Japanese display the pride of victors or conquerors. That way led to disaster: "The people of Greater East Asia must build a peaceful sphere wherein after being released from control and oppression all nationalities' political aspirations and cultural traditions will be enhanced in a free and equal relationship, and wherein the prosperity and progress of all Asia will be promoted. The Japanese, who undertook the leadership, must take the responsibility."

Major Fujiwara recognized the brutal nature of the Imperial Army and warned that those Japanese concerned with the Greater East Asia movement must mediate between the peoples of Asia and that Army, and ensure that the Army not behave toward these new potential friends as it had behaved and still behaved toward China.

When the war began, Major Fujiwara went into Malaya with the Yamashita force and began his work. His first proselyte was British Indian Army Capt. Mohan Singh, who had been captured in one of the early battles in Malaya. Together they began enlisting POWs.

Fujiwara then turned most of his attention in Malaya's chief city Singapore to the establishment of the Indian movement, and one early result was the Azad Hind government that was set up. Soon Indian Independence League centers were to be found in virtually every city and town in Malaya.

Because the Chinese refused the initial Japanese overtures, Fujiwara had nothing to do with the large Chinese community in Malaya. The Army handled the Chinese itself. The generals decided that the Chinese were inimical and assumed the same manner it had adopted in dealing with the Chinese in China. The adherents to Chiang Kai-shek's Kuomintang were hunted out and killed. So were the Chinese Communists. So was anyone who had fought against the Japanese in the war.

Consequently, from the very beginning Malaya was a perpetual thorn in the side of the Japanese Army, as the ethnic Chinese went underground to become guerrillas. And as the continuation of a vicious circle, this was another reason for the cruelty the Japanese Army visited on the Chinese community of Malaya, sending thousands of them to work on the notorious Rangoon-Bangkok railroad. This effort cost the lives of nearly 100 coolies for each mile of construction. So many were killed that mass graves are still occasionally unearthed, with bodies of the Japanese-executed laborers showing evidence of hands tied behind backs.

At the beginning of their occupation, the Japanese decided to utilize the framework of the previous administration, with Malayan faces replacing British. This worked very well, and the Malays began to feel a sense of independence and well-being that told them the Greater East Asia Co-prosperity Sphere could become a welcome reality.

By that time Major Fujiwara's work had centered on the Indians. Fujiwara explained what he said were the aims of the Japanese Army regarding aid to the struggle for the independence of India and the procedures for Imperial Army cooperation. He also told the Army that the defeat of Britain would be hastened by the defection of India. It was necessary that India be brought into the Greater East Asia Sphere, along with Burma.

Another who was active in promoting the Japanese view was Col. Keiji Suzuki, who was so imbued with the dream of Burmese independence that he took the Burmese name of Bo Mogyo. Imperial General Headquarters established Suzuki's intelligence unit, calling it the *Minami Kikan* (Southern Unit). This unit was not subordinate to the Japanese Army command in Burma, and thus was greatly resented by that headquarters staff there. Suzuki claimed his authority came from Prince Kanin. The prince was a general who had served as Army chief of staff until 1940, and when the war began was serving as military councilor to the Emperor. The colonel insisted that his authority thus came directly from the Throne, outside the Army chain of command.

He organized the Burma Independence Army, and made Aung San, a Burmese, his second-in-command. He taught independence of spirit and action in the early months of 1942 after the Japanese conquered Burma and drove the British out. By May 1942 Colonel Suzuki was in serious conflict with the Japanese Army in Burma. Colonel Hiraoka, the Japanese Army liaison officer to Ba Maw, the leader of the government installed under the Japanese, told Ba Maw that Suzuki was becoming a very bad influence, and teaching the Burmese some very wrong-headed ideas. One of these was *genuine* independence.

One day Suzuki spoke to U Nu, another Burmese patriot. "Don't be worried about independence," he said. "Independence is not the kind of thing you can get through begging for it from other people. You should aim for it yourselves. The Japanese refuse to give it? Very well then, tell them that you will proclaim independence and set up your

own government. What's the difficulty about that? If they start shoot-
ing, just shoot back.''

Colonel Suzuki tried to operate quite independently of the Japanese
Army in Burma. His units followed the Japanese advance, and took
over police action in the conquered territory, or tried to. But there
they began to run afoul of the Army's policy that allowed no room for
cooperation with subject peoples. And when the Japanese attacked
their ally, the less than fully obedient Burmese army in Moulmein, a
very hard blow was struck against the spirit of Burmese independence
under Japanese patronage, although Colonel Suzuki tried to persist in
his efforts. By midsummer 1942, all his activity in behalf of Burmese
independence was being challenged by the Imperial Army headquarters in Rangoon.

Gen. Hitoshi Imamura set up his military government in Batavia, in
March 1942. He was already a disciple of the Greater East Asia Co-
prosperity Sphere concept. He had, after all, served as chief of staff in
the Kwantung Army, where the idea was gospel, and where Manchukuo was regarded as the central core, along with Japan. Acting with
the authority vested in him as an area army commander, General
Imamura made all the right decisions. He did not like the concept of
military government espoused by Imperial General Headquarters, so
he did not follow it. Instead he adhered to the top policy being
developed in Tokyo by Prime Minister Tojo and the new Greater East
Asia Ministry that was forming. He brought the Indonesian leader
Achmed Sukarno out of a Dutch prison, where that nationalist was
being held on political charges, and had a long talk with him at his
headquarters. Would Sukarno cooperate with the Japanese? If so he
would be consulted by Imamura on any actions the military government proposed to take. Sukarno thought over the matter, and said he
would cooperate—with one proviso. When the war ended, he said, he
would reserve the right to take whatever political action he then
deemed appropriate.

Imamura could see that Sukarno meant that real independence for
the Indonesians was his goal. But this did not trouble Imamura,
because, theoretically, it was also the goal of Japan. Still, Imamura
was too smart not to realize that the Imperial Army intended to use
the Co-prosperity Sphere for its own purposes. But he also saw how
much easier his lot would be with the cooperation of the Indonesians,
and so a deal was struck. Within a matter of weeks Indonesian
nationalists were appointed to powerful military government posts
equivalent to jobs previously held only by the Dutch. Imamura estab-

lished an advisory council with five Japanese and ten Indonesian members. He told the Indonesian people that the days of colonialism had ended, and they began to believe.

But then Imamura began to receive criticism from Tokyo. Imperial General Headquarters did not like the idea of Indonesian independence. General Sugiyama dispatched an investigation commission to Batavia. When they arrived they soon found that the Japanese occupation was proceeding more smoothly there than anywhere else, and that the extraction of the resources that Japan wanted was moving ahead at a good pace. So the commission went back to Tokyo and, to the surprise of General Sugiyama and his associates, recommended that IGHQ do nothing but close its eyes to what Imamura was doing in the recently Dutch archipelago.

Thus although the Dutch and many of mixed race who had cast their lot with the Dutch were treated abysmally, in accustomed Imperial Army fashion, the Imamura occupation was the most successful of all the Japanese conquests.

Theoretically, Thailand was independent within the framework of the Greater East Asia Co-prosperity Sphere. And since the Thai offered no trouble to the Japanese military occupation, there was no military government, but a dealing between the Imperial Army and the Thai government. The Thai people were not impressed into the work gangs drawn from Malaya and elsewhere in Asia to slave along with the western POWs on the Rangoon-Bangkok railroad. The Japanese relationship with Thailand then was as close to a real alliance as the Japanese had in Asia, and several Thai naval vessels served under the Japanese naval command in the South Pacific.

In Tokyo that spring of 1942, the *Zaibatsu*, the industrial cartels, embraced the Greater East Asia Co-prosperity Sphere concept. First the industrialists established the Economic Federation of Japan. That organization, prompted by Prime Minister Tojo, set out to devise how the economic cooperation with the new empire would work. At Tokyo Kaikan, the great assembly hall in the middle of the city, a conference attended by Army, Navy, and foreign office officials met with many businessmen to project a program. Goals were set for the import of various raw materials from the new territories, and the industrialists took the responsibility for organizing the extraction of those resources.

Aichiro Fujiyama, president of the Japan Chamber of Commerce, initiated the formation of a Dai Toa Club in Tokyo; its purpose was to give important visitors to Japan from these other countries a place to stay while lending them a feeling of participation in Japanese life.

By the spring of 1942, then, the Greater East Asia plan was moving along, it seemed. The last segment to fall into place was the Philippines, which created some special problems for Japan. That was because the Americans had promised the Filipinos independence at about this time, and Prime Minister Tojo had made a similar promise when his troops invaded back in December.

On January 3, 1942 a Japanese miltiary government had taken over Manila. There were continuing promises of independence, but not much more. The Japanese were leery of the American influence of the preceding few decades and the effect that the democratization of Filipino politics had exercised on the people of the commonwealth. But until they could get the Americans out they moved slowly to establish any sort of permanent institutions. Bataan surrendered in mid-April and Corregidor fell in May. There still were hundreds of Americans and Filipinos who had gone to the mountains and the southern islands to live as guerrillas, and the Japanese more or less ignored these, except to send occasional expeditions to suppress them. Still it was late in 1942 before the Japanese could think of moving toward more permanent relationships in the Philippines.

In the West, where there was very little appreciation of the feelings of the people of East Asia, the Japanese call for a Greater East Asia Co-prosperity Sphere and Pan-Asianism was met with jeers. All this was simply a cloak for Japan's imperialist ambition against the world, said the Western critics.

And what of the government of these new colonies? How much Japanese participation would it take? The Tojo government in that summer of 1942 estimated that 30,000 Japanese would be needed abroad to staff the essential positions. By that time the Japanese conquests were as complete as they would be. The occupation of the Sphere had begun. Only Indochina and Thailand in the south were treated differently, without occupation forces, but with Japanese troop commands in these countries able to do very much as they wished, but not ordering the civil population about.

Each other country had its separate military administration under the supreme military commander of the area; that meant the Philippines, Malaya, Burma, Netherlands East Indies, and Hong Kong. Under the military commander, the government was organized by departments: general affairs, industry, finance, and transport. Under the central office of each department were prefectural and branch offices. The military maintained control of every branch, but employed civil administrators in Malaya, Hong Kong, and Indonesia. As noted, in Indonesia the local people had a great deal of influence and some power over their own affairs. In Burma and the Philippines, the military men were masked as advisors, but actual power rested in their hands.

Wherever possible, and it almost always was, the Japanese tried to use the existing government machinery, down to the stationery, but that did not fool anyone. It was a Japanese military government in every case. Except in the Philippines there were no existing legal political parties.

The Japanese set up political organizations conforming to their own Imperial Rule Assistance Association. In Burma it was the Dobama Sinye League. In Java it was the All-Java Cultural Movement, starting with 20,000 members in October 1942, but aiming for ten times as many. In the Philippines, the Japanese closed down the existing political parties because of their American influence and established the Kalibapi, the "Popular Movement for the Reconstruction of the New Philippines."

The guidelines of the Japanese government indicated that the existing religions, cultural institutions, and schools should be respected, and Tojo had authorized that specifically. In fact, religion was subverted to become a Japanese propaganda arm, and language and culture were turned definitely toward Japan. Japanese language schools suddenly appeared throughout the new empire, and in their various regions English and Dutch were outlawed and replaced by Japanese. The outlawing of English did not work very well. The Japanese often found that English was the only language in which they could communicate with the captured peoples. So English was actually much used although the Army kept up the pretense of abolishing its use.

By fall, Greater East Asia Minister Aoki had been given a policy: the scope of Greater East Asia's inner zone would be Japan, Korea, Manchuria, and North China; these regions would be developed intensely and populated in growing numbers by Yamato people—Japanese. The task of Southeast Asia was to supply raw materials and food for the armies. Each area, it had already been decided, would have to be self-sufficient during the war while also exporting to Japan. There was no time or energy to carry out the "*co*-prosperity" and this was also becoming clear to the peoples involved. Naturally, their enthusiasm for the Sphere began to wane, except under exceptional circumstances, such as that of India. In that case, Subhas Chandra Bose, the associate of Gandhi and Nehru, was suborned by the Japanese appeal to his ego, and showed great enthusiasm for the Japanese cause. But actually Bose had nowhere else to go.

By the autumn of 1942, then, not even a year after the opening of the war, the Greater East Asia Co-prosperity Sphere had changed from being an instrument of Pan-Asianism, to become an arm of Japanese empire, and it was apparent that the Japanese Army was going to exploit the conquered countries ruthlessly and without regard to promises. The various independence movements fostered by the Imperial General Headquarters for the preceding two years had already become an embarrassment to the Japanese, and the conflict between nationalists and the Imperial Army was beginning to become serious, particularly in Burma, which was the first country to become totally disillusioned with Japanese Army policy.

Tojo was well aware of the difficulties, but he was in no position at that moment to begin a quarrel with General Sugiyama and his peers within the Army. Sugiyama still held the cards, even though, as we have seen, at the end of 1942 the Army's conduct of the Guadalcanal campaign had brought Imperial displeasure and Tojo's determination to bring power into his own hands as quickly as possible.

13

The Collapse of High Hopes

Perhaps because of his training in the brutal system of the Imperial Japanese Army, General Hideki Tojo had very little concern for the treatment meted out by that army to the foreign peoples with which it came into contact in the Japanese war effort. Although he presided over the government from 1941 until the middle of 1944 he never made any inquiries as to what was really happening in the Greater East Asia Co-prosperity Sphere or to the prisoners of war captured by the Imperial forces. Although many complaints about prisoner mistreatment were received by the special office established in the war ministry, Tojo never asked any questions. It is inconceivable that what was happening was not known to him. Obviously he ignored the POW matter deliberately.

In the opening phases of the war, the Army behaved very much as it had behaved in China. The policies had been established long before the drive south in December 1941. On October 4, 1940—well before Tojo took over the reins as prime minister—the foreign office issued a secret memorandum on the subject "Japan's Policies Toward the Southern Regions."

The Japanese drive south was primarily to secure the petroleum resources she needed, which were located in Borneo, Java, and Sumatra. To try to make sure that the oil fields would be captured intact, Foreign Minister Matsuoka had issued a memo as severe as if it had come straight from Imperial General Headquarters, which must have been consulted.

"Were any of the important natural resources destroyed, all the persons connected with the raw material, and the [enemy] government officials concerned, would be severely punished as being the responsible persons."

On January 20, 1942, the Japanese who had landed on Borneo were preparing to take over the oil facilities at Balikpapan; they wanted to avoid a fight because they did not want the facilities damaged. Therefore two Dutch officers who had been captured in the earlier battles were brought into the presence of Maj. Gen. Kiyotake Kawaguchi, commander of the Borneo Expeditionary Force, and five other Japanese officers. They were told to deliver to the Dutch commander of Balikpapan the Japanese ultimatum to surrender the Dutch garrison there and deliver the oil facilities intact.

When the two officers conveyed the Japanese demands to the Balikpapan commander he replied that he was obliged to obey Dutch government orders to carry out certain specific demolitions. The Japanese then attacked Balikpapan, and with their greatly superior force, soon captured it. But the demolitions had been carried out and some of the facilities would not be available to Japan for months.

Kawaguchi's force then proceeded methodically to massacre the entire white population of Balikpapan. First, some of the Dutch soldiers had their arms and legs lopped off with samurai swords or were used for bayonet practice. Then the remaining whites were driven into the sea and those who did not drown were shot to death. When news of this massacre seeped to the outside world, the most terrifying aspect, and the reason the Japanese Army became thoroughly detested wherever it went, was that these actions were not taken in the frenzy of rage, but were considered Army policy in dealing with the vanquished.

To be sure, this policy antedated Tojo's leaderhsip; it had been decided by the Army shortly after the outbreak of the China war, when Chiang Kai-shek refused to yield to Japanese demands. But even then it was not totally new policy; the Kwantung Army had been among the most rigorous advocates and practitioners of terror, at an earlier time when Japan still was defining its policies toward China.

In 1928 the Kwantung Army had sent troops to Jinan, the capital of Shandong Province, China, "to protect Japanese life and property." Protect from what? From the Northern Expedition launched by General Chiang Kai-shek from Canton, to unify China and bring the warlords of the north under Nationalist government control. In the spring of 1928 Chiang had arrived at Jinan. And here the Japanese Army forever lost its chance to win Chiang over, although he had previously expressed his desire to cooperate with Japan, and just one year earlier had paved the way by breaking with the Chinese Communists.

Early in May after a confrontation of Japanese and Chinese troops, Chiang Kai-shek called for a meeting and it had been arranged at the office of his commissioner for foreign affairs, Tsai Kung-shih, and Chiang's foreign minister, Huang Fu.

But the meeting never occurred, because the Japanese were looking for an "incident" over which to attack the Chinese and defeat them. First they enticed Huang Fu to Japanese military headquarters and tried to force him to sign a statement that he knew the Japanese had fired on the Chinese because the Chinese were looting the people of Jinan. It was not true, and Huang Fu moreover refused to sign a separate statement on that he had even read the charges. Red-faced but afraid of Chiang's reaction, the Japanese let Huang Fu go. Back at Chiang's headquarters Huang Fu reported on the Japanese activity and Chiang knew that the Japanese were looking for trouble, so that night he moved his troops out of the city of Jinan. The next day the Japanese atacked Jinan and killed 13,000 civilians for no reason but terror. They also captured Tsai Kung-shih and took him to Japanese military headquarters. To frighten him they brought in a dozen Chinese and shot them in front of him. They ordered him to sign documents. He would not. They ordered him to kneel. He would not. They broke his legs with rifle butts, and he collapsed and shouted curses at them. They tore out his tongue and then, seeing what they had done, they killed him. All this was observed by a Chinese servant hiding in a closet, and when the young Japanese officers had left for the night, he sneaked out and went straight to Chiang's headquarters to report. Thereafter Chiang Kai-shek turned a deaf ear to any Japanese promises or professions of friendship. The Army had fouled its own nest.

All this occurred before Tojo was associated with the Kwantung Army. At the time he was in the transition period between staff officer and line officer. He had just returned from Germany, where he had been military attaché, and had recently been appointed colonel and soon would get command of the 1st Regiment. But this behavior of the Kwantung Army was only an exaggeration of the savagery of most of the Japanese Army. Tojo was trained in this tradition. And when approached by various officials to give opinions on treatment of foreigners who fell under the Army's control, Tojo obliquely sanctioned Army brutality by remarks such as "Everyone in Japan must work to eat."

He certainly sanctioned the mistreatment of Western foreigners, which was Imperial Army policy, intended to humiliate these people before Asian audiences. In Singapore, Hong Kong, and Rangoon,

POWs were paraded and reviled for the benefit of the native population. When many protests were forthcoming through neutral embassies, Tojo and others of his government simply denied that any cruelty was occurring. All during the war there was not a single admission of wrong-doing.

The murders at Balikpapan were repeated at Blora after the demolition by the Dutch of the oil fields at Tjepu. Here only the men were massacred; all the white women were raped repeatedly in front of the military commander, but then sent off to detention camps.

Between December 1941 and April 1942, the postwar war crimes prosecution showed, such massacres had occurred at 26 places under control of the Japanese Army.

In February 1942, after the fall of Singapore, General Yamashita established the Malayan occupation administration by giving each of four Army generals command of a sector of Malaya, each with forces of his own, and each a law unto himself. Yamashita, following the Army policy established in China, ordered his subordinate generals to assemble all ethnic Chinese in Singapore and ascertain their sentiments. Employees of the old British government, Communists, Kuomintang adherents, and anti-Japanese Chinese were to be killed out of hand. The first action was taken on February 16, 1942 by Lieutenant Hisamatsu of the *Kempeitai*, who set up operations in the Tonjong Pagar Police Station in Singapore. Selected assembled Chinese civilians were "interrogated," which meant that their names were asked, and then they were driven to the Tonjong wharf and beheaded. Motor launches came from Singapore Harbor bringing civilians who were pushed overboard and shot as they tried to swim. Most of these were dock laborers from the naval base. Between February 17 and 24, 700 male Chinese were executed, most of them by decapitation with samurai swords by latter-day samurai. The massacres were carried out by soldiers of the *Kempeitai*, Tojo's old military police organization. Throughout Japan, as already noted, the *Kempeitai* were notorious for their cruelty and disregard of rights or life. The fact that Tojo had been *Kempeitai* chief in Manchukuo spoke for itself. These policemen had textbooks on torture, and the force maintained a school where the fine arts of interrogation and prisoner treatment were taught.

Was Tojo aware of these killings? He never admitted it, but it is inconceivable that he could not have known. As war minister he could hardly have been unaware of the developments in Singapore. He had had to act against General Nishimura, commander of the Imperial Guard Division, when General Yamashita preferred charges against that subordinate for excesses. Most of the massacres of civilians were carried out by the *Kempeitai*, and that organization was directly responsible to the office of the war minister, not to the Imperial General Headquarters.

So Tojo's guilt is obvious, although in the end he tried to hide it. During the trials he would admit only that the Japanese Army's concept of the appropriate treatment of war prisoners and interned populations differed significantly from that of the forces of other nations.

As additional evidence, he had made the trip to the area about the time these massacres were occurring. Infamous all over the Singapore region, these were the so-called Chinese Massacres in which, a Japanese officer later testified, at least 5000 Chinese were killed.

These tortures and mistreatment were not confined to the hysterical period of postconquest, but continued as matters of policy throughout the new Japanese empire.

After the conquest of Malaya, a Malay-Indian magistrate at Kuala Trengganu was continued in office as a part of the Japanese plan to use natives in administrative posts. But then the magistrate was accused of spying for the British. Now he was tortured. One night he was left tied to the leg of a table, and the next morning he was kicked until he was unconscious. When he recovered he was buried in the ground up to his neck. Then a Japanese officer put his sword against the man's neck and kept it there for some time. Each moment the magistrate expected death. On the third day he was put into a gasoline drum with forty gallons of oily water. The lid was placed on the drum and soon the sun's rays heated the whole until he could not breathe. He managed to rock the drum violently and shake the lid off, but was left in the drum all day.

The object of this torture was to secure a confession. One *Kempeitai* handbook offered this instruction in the techniques of the art and science:

Methods of procedure
(a) Torture.
   This includes kicking, beating, and anything connected with physical suffering. This method is only to be used when everything else has failed as it is the most clumsy. Change the interrogating officer after using torture and good results can be obtained if the new officer questions in a sympathetic manner.

(b) Threats.

(1) Hints of future physical discomforts, for example: torture, murder, starvation, solitary confinement, deprivation of sleep.

(2) Hints of future mental discomforts, for example: not to be allowed to send letters, not to be given the same treatment as others and (for prisoners of war) to be kept back last in the event of an exchange of prisoners.

By the end of 1942 the Emperor was having some doubts about Tojo's leadership of the government, and it was apparent in other elements of Japanese society that the criticism of and resistance to Tojo were growing. He knew very well that his only base of support lay in the Army, and as much as he wanted to deal with General Sugiyama, his major rival for power, he was not yet prepared to do so. And so the Army continued its rampage through Southeast Asia and China, undoing virtually all that the Minister of Greater East Asia was trying to accomplish. It was apparent in the ministry that there were many people who really believed in the cooperative effort that the Sphere was supposed to be. But they could not control the Army, and neither did Tojo dare risk an open confrontation with the military power-brokers.

Whatever the reason, Tojo did not interfere at all in any of his capacities with the military's ultimate management of the captured territories, and this is why the Sphere remained a hollow shell. As the war grew harder, Tojo turned his eyes away from most sources of possible confrontation with his fellow generals, until that day when he would be ready to assume total control.

For that reason, the prisoners on the Bangkok-Rangoon railroad suffered inordinately. So many complaints were made by British, Australian, and other governments about the dreadful conditions on the railroad that even Tojo finally had to step in as war minister. In the one exception to his accustomed role, he ordered an investigation of conditions at one camp where hundreds had died. General Terauchi offered no assistance whatever, but this was to be expected since he was one of Tojo's principal rivals within the *Gumbatsu*. The investigation should have caused heads to roll in high places, but the only result was the trial and minor punishment of one company commander for ill treatment of prisoners.

And so the Army continued to have its way. In February 1943, as the Allies were just taking in the consequences of the Japanese evacuation of Guadalcanal, which had caught them quite by surprise, Tojo spoke to the House of Representatives of the Diet, to discuss Japanese military preparation and operations of the future.

It was apparent to Japan of course that the Guadalcanal battle had ended in failure, no matter how the military tried to disguise the matter in terms of "regrouping" and change of emphasis. Already Tojo was getting complaints from the outer fringes of the Sphere because of the almost total emphasis on the military. He answered that even if the war ended in Japanese victory it would take time to create the progressive partnership the other members of the Greater East Asia Coprosperity sphere wanted. Meanwhile security must be maintained.

"To guard this so that it cannot be attacked from any point, I am not considering the reduction of Japanese military operation which will form our kernel, even in postwar time. Consequently I believe that there should be no hesitation in wartime management brought about by dreams of the past or by anticipation that there will be an immediate reduction in armaments if the war should end in the near future. The military preparations of Japan, which are the pivot of Greater East Asia, will absolutely not be reduced."

By the winter of 1943 events had wrought many changes in Japanese war plans. The days of easy victory had ended, and with defeats the Army became more obdurate, harder to deal with. In the beginning, Army policy had been to humiliate the proud enemies. In Rangoon, for example, the Japanese had not only paraded British war prisoners through the streets, but forced them to sweep the streets clean, a task reserved for the most lowly coolies in Burmese society. When that picture appeared in London, the British Foreign Office protested through neutral nations to its Japanese counterpart. These protests were known (there were many such, as previously noted), and they were discussed in the ministries, but, as noted, the protests were ignored or replied to with a lie denying any mistreatment.

After the resignation of Foreign Minister Togo, the Japanese foreign office foundered for a while. The man Tojo chose to replace Togo, Masayuki Tani, proved to be anathema to the bureaucrats in the ministry and so his function was impaired. Finally, early in 1943, Tani resigned, and Tojo appointed Mamoru Shigemitsu, a former ambassador to Moscow, to the job. To Shigemitsu, then, came the unpleasant task of telling the lies. For example, by 1943 the desperate situation of the Allied POWs working on the Bangkok-Rangoon railway was well-known in London, but when the British government complained about starvation and mistreatment, they had this reply from Tokyo: "The Government, by exercising great vigilance as to the health and hygiene of prisoners of war, and taking added measures such as monthly medical examinations of each prisoner of war camp, has enabled sickness to be treated in the first stage."

In truth, the POWs had no medical attention at all; thousands of them were ill and dying from beriberi, cholera, malaria, and dysentery.

At the same time the Allied prisoners were being treated in this traditional manner by the Japanese Army, the whole Greater East Asia Co-prosperity Sphere had virtually collapsed before it got properly founded. Army obduracy was the reason.

It is doubtful if Prime Minister Tojo even knew that the concept of a Pan-Asian alliance had failed. He certainly gave that enterprise every attention, and from Tokyo the activities that manifested its well-being in the various countries seemed to be real.

In the first week of November 1943, the Greater East Asia Co-prosperity Sphere held its initial meeting in Tokyo, an event that by reading the Japanese newspapers one would believe to have been of enormous economic and political importance. First, Prime Minister Tojo greeted the delegates and outlined the reason for the conference. It was in response to a Japanese invitation to various nations to develop policies aimed at winning the Greater East Asia war and building the New Order there. So on that day were assembled the most presentable representatives of that new order that Tokyo could produce. There were delegates from China, Thailand, Manchukuo, the Philippines, and Burma. And there was one representative for whom the Japanese had great hope although he did not have the support of more than a handful of his countrymen: Subhas Chandra Bose, Commander of the Indian National Army and head of the Free India Provisional Government.

Tojo began with an oral attack on the United States and Britain; the United States, in particular, he claimed, was trying to take over control of the old British empire, "spreading its tentacles to the Pacific and East Asia." And Tojo reopened an old wound that had rankled the Japanese for decades: "While constantly keeping their own territories closed to us, the people of Asia are denying us equality of opportunities. Impeding our trade they sought solely their own prosperity."

Not surprisingly, Tojo then spoke of the need for common effort to bring all the nations of the region common prosperity: "The nations of Greater East Asia, while mutually recognizing their autonomy and independence, must, as a whole, establish among themselves relations of brotherly amity. Such relations cannot be created if one country should utilize another as a means to an end. I believe they come into being only when there is mutual respect for one another's autonomy and independence—when all countries are willing to accept the principle of 'live and let live' and give expression to their real selves.''

And Tojo then wound up his address: "Japan is grateful to the nations of Greater East Asia for the whole-hearted cooperation which they are rendering in this war. Japan is firmly determined by cooperating with them and by strengthening her collaboration with her allies in Europe, to carry on with indefeatable spirit and with conviction in sure victory in this war, the intensity of which is expected to mount from day to day. Japan, by overcoming all difficulties, will do her full share to complete the construction of Greater East Asia and contribute to the establishment of world peace which is the common mission of us all.''

Then the other representatives spoke up announcing their great pleasure at being in Tokyo, and their gratitude to the Japanese government and Prime Minister Tojo. Encomium followed encomium. Finally all had spoken pledging themselves to the common effort. They then passed a six-part resolution promising mutual cooperation, fraternity and respect for sovereignty, respect for traditions and culture, acceleration of economic development, and cultivation of friendly relations with all races.

As a public relations gesture, the conference seemed to be successful. The Japanese newspapers printed all the stories of the great accomplishments in cooperation in the economic sphere. They made much of the 1943 declarations of "independence" of the Philippines and Burma. Yet no territory occupied by the Japanese Army was independent of that army's control.

And now, as the war worsened, the *Kempeitai* and its naval equivalent, the *Tokeitai*, began to increase the repression of civilian populations in Borneo, Malaya, and other areas. In Borneo the Navy was responsible because the oil supply brought the Japanese fleet to these waters. The longer the war lasted the scarcer fuel became at home. The coming of the fleet also brought renewed security consciousness by the *Tokeitai*, and the fear of espionage, which always dogged the Japanese in conquered territories. They knew how thoroughly they were hated.

By 1943, when the first conference of the Greater East Asia Coprosperity Sphere was held, the concept held by the civilians before the Pacific War had already failed. Japan had gone on the defensive and so there was not the slightest chance that the high hopes for a political and social alliance could be achieved.

14

The War Turns Around

On October 19, 1942 Tomokazu Hori, spokesman for General Tojo's cabinet, warned the Japanese people that the war was entering a new phase: the Americans had established "a second front" by invading Guadalcanal. From that point onward Tojo's task of keeping the Emperor informed of the progress of the war ceased to be a pleasant one. It was true that Admiral Yamamoto's Combined Fleet was winning victories. But these were not matched by Army progress. In China, the war was stagnant. The Japanese held the coastal cities and many towns, but they dared not go into the countryside except in numbers, for fear of guerrillas who swarmed there. Lt. Gen. Naotsugi Sakai, commander of Japanese troops on the Chekiang-Kiangsi front, was killed by a land mine planted by a Communist guerrilla. That was the sort of thing that was happening to the Japanese in China.

The new war situation, Hori said, indicated every sign of protracted strife. "We are facing a stage of real war, which demands the nation's total strength."

Premier Tojo himself echoed the warning in a speech to the Diet on December 28. He informed the legislators that the fighting "has resolved itself into a persistent tug-of-war. Close observation of the situation reveals that moves of the utmost strategic importance are lurking everywhere, giving the impression that the real war is starting now."

The Japanese war was going very well, he claimed, except on Guadalcanal. Tojo told less than the truth, saying that only "a nominal unit of the Japanese Navy" was fighting. He had to be referring to the small force that had been caught on the island at the beginning by the U.S. Marine invasion, not to the nearly 30,000 Army troops that

Imperial General Headquarters had ultimately committed to the Guadalcanal struggle.

But at this same session of the Diet, Tojo's Navy minister, Admiral Shimada, warned of harder days for the nation to come.

In order to preserve order and keep the war machine wheels turning, Prime Minister Tojo had to invoke totalitarian measures, and he did not hesitate. In December 1942 the Diet passed a special emergency law prohibiting political assemblies without permission from the local police and providing for heavy fines for spreading rumors. This law gave the authorities the power they wanted to control all political activity and keep any anti-war activity from materializing.

Tojo and the government were particularly aware of Communist activity and particularly worried about it. The Japanese had always detested Communism for two reasons: their high regard for private property, and the Emperor system. In 1925 when Communism was spreading and seemed likely to take over China (the Sun Yat-sen government was made up of Kuomintang and Communist officials, and the Communists had completely taken over the Wuhan complex in Central China), the Japanese government passed the first Peace Preservation Law. It banned any action, speech, or writing that advocated abolition of private property or of the imperial regime. That 1925 law had recently been amended to provide death penalties for such activity.

After the tide began to turn against Japan at Guadalcanal there were more complaints about Tojo's leadership. Some said he was trying to build his own power, which he denied in a speech to the Diet. Even some Japanese were comparing him to Hitler and Mussolini and Stalin. Not so, he maintained, he was simply the Emperor's loyal servant.

During the month of January Premier Tojo for the first time was not in evidence; he simply disappeared, which was most unlike him because he had developed a pattern of attending public assemblies, meeting and greeting like a ward politician. The fact was—although the prime minister's office denied it—that he was very sick with some undiagnosed fever, and he would not go to a hospital or even consult a physician. Finally he turned to Chinese medicine; the practitioner who treated him soon had him well.

Speaking to the Diet on February 1, 1943, Tojo expressed complete confidence in the future, but he did cite what he considered to be the single danger that Japan might be defeated from within, and to counter this danger he proposed to act swiftly. For that reason he wanted to reform the administration of departments. That was the only reason he professed; it was not occasioned by a desire for power for himself.

But here Tojo was being less than frank. Eight days later the daybook kept by Tojo's secretaries showed that Imperial General Headquarters released the official announcement of the twin disasters that had overtaken Japan in the South Pacific—the withdrawal of Japanese troops from Guadalcanal and Buna, both constituting stunning defeats. If Tojo had total confidence in the Army, then it must be said that the Emperor's confidence in the Army and in Tojo was waning. In view of the worsening situation the Emperor was beginning to realize that materials he was receiving from Tojo, which he used in preparing his Imperial Rescripts, were not based on fact, but on the hyperbole that now had become the habitual output of Imperial General Headquarters.

On that day of the announcement of the withdrawal from Guadalcanal, the German ambassador, M. H. G. Stahmer, came to pay a formal call. The Germans had given up urging the Japanese to attack the Soviet Union, as they had done in the early months of 1941 and just after Hitler's invasion of Russia. Stahmer was trying to cement badly eroded relationships caused by Hitler's insistence and the Japanese refusal to be drawn into a two-front war. The wisdom of Japan's decision had been confirmed in the fact that Japan already was in a two-front war now, as a consequence of the American invasion of the South Pacific.

Stahmer and Tojo met for an hour; they discussed four matters. First was German-Japanese cooperation, which really had not been amounting to much for the preceding two years. Both men knew very well the state of their alliance in spite of the great show of unity they exhibited this day. Hitler had been primed by von Ribbentrop, his foreign minister, to expect great things of the Tripartite Pact; that was because of then-Foreign Minister Matsuoka's anti-Americanism and his enthusiasm for the "strike north" (against the USSR) faction within the Army. But the thrashing of the Japanese in the Nomonhon incident and then their conclusion that their resources would not stand a two-front war of the sort the Soviets would offer had caused the Japanese to shy away, and the close touch with Germany had not been resumed. So the ambassador and prime minister made much of exploring their areas of common interest, and indicating, without promising, great things for the future. Tojo said that he believed Hitler's strong will would bring ultimate victory to the Germans in Europe. Ambassador Stahmer said that all the indications he had seen showed that Hitler was indeed winning, generally speaking, although there were some areas that seemed a bit uncomfortable at the moment. What he was referring to, although he did not specify, was the German situation in North Africa, which was serious although not yet desperate. The British had captured Tripoli in January, and were approaching Mareth.

The second subject of this Japanese-German meeting was to consider British and American propaganda and how the Tripartite Pact partners could deal with it effectively. Tojo opened by saying that many harmful rumors were coursing the world about Japan and Germany and Italy. The Allies were very good at propaganda, he said, and particularly the divisive sort of rumors that were circulating. Tojo, who was very conscious of rumors because of his own position, reiterated his statements, and asked the German ambassador to in future make sure to check out any stories about Japanese attitudes or movements he could not verify; Stahmer was asked to call Foreign Minister Shigemitsu or Tojo himself at any time for this purpose.

Ambassador Stahmer reminded Tojo that he had served with the German embassy in China and that he was personally aware of the British and American program of trying to separate Germany and Japan. He remembered exchanging views on this subject with Shigemitsu when the latter was ambassador to China. And he promised to follow Tojo's advice about checking rumors with the foreign office or the prime minister's office.

They agreed then that the best way to strengthen their alliance was to ignore all propaganda from abroad and rely instead on their own communications, one Axis government with the other.

The third area of discussion was much more sensitive. They called it the European situation, but what they both meant was the German war against the USSR, which had started with Operation Barbarossa, Hitler's invasion of Russia in the summer of 1941. It had not been going so well in the winter and spring of 1942, and then the summer doldrums were followed by the Red Army's autumn offensive. Tojo was first to address the subject of the Soviets. He was very conscious of the old promises made by Foreign Minister Matsuoka and how the Japanese plans had been almost totally reversed since those days. He started talking in a rambling way about the "winding roads of the Soviet situation" but assured the ambassador that Japan would solve the problem, a statement which was supposed to reassure the German that ultimately the Japanese would come to the assistance of their ally with a second front against the Russians.

Having, he thought, disposed of that embarrassing situation, Tojo addressed himself to the North Africa situation where the Germans and Italians were on the defensive. He wondered if the Germans and Italians were about to be defeated. (At that moment it was not true; the untried Americans were having difficulty after having entered the North Africa campaign, and General Rommel was about to launch his Kasserine Pass offensive that would almost knock the Americans out.) But could the Germans and Italians win over the British and the Americans? The Japanese would like to have some reassurances. What were the future prospects?

And to digress, what about Stalingrad? The Japanese had been getting reports from neutral and Allied sources that indicated the Germans were having a difficult time at Stalingrad. (A difficult time? Field Marshal von Paulus had just on February 2 surrendered the Stalingrad German garrison of 90,000 men to the Soviets, over Hitler's violent objections.) General Tojo ventured to offer the Germans some advice here:

They had been fighting in the Stalingrad sector with too many troops of different nations: Germans, Italians, Bulgarians, and Hungarians. They should consolidate their fronts and stop trying to put together a collective army. And finally Tojo wanted to know, what was the situation of Turkey? He knew that Turkey had so far managed to remain officially neutral, and would not join the Tripartite treaty forces. But was it true that the British and Americans were about to occupy Turkey?

Ambassador Stahmer said there were absolutely no negative reports and if any came in, particularly *very* negative reports, they would be rushed to Tojo's attention. As far as the German prospects were concerned, the ambassador said, if they could hold Poland and the Ukraine and the Caucasus, and the Western countries, especially France, then Germany would win and prosper.

Already, the German noted, the Western Allies were beginning to fall out. Churchill had become Roosevelt's lieutenant, and he did not like the position. Stahmer said it was the German view that Roosevelt was the captain. The Americans and British had different war aims, it seemed, and America's was to build a new imperialism. Also the British and the Soviets were quarreling about Turkey; British leaders wanted to occupy Turkey and they were afraid the Russians would occupy it first, coming through the Bosporus.

The discussion closed on China. Tojo asked if Stahmer had any advice to offer Japan. That question was an indication of the problem that loomed largest in General Tojo's mind. The figurative quicksands of China ate equipment and money as rapidly as it could be supplied. There the fight was endless, and although the victories were constant, the war still continued unabated.

The German ambassador had no advice to offer but much sympathy over the difficulties in which Japan found itself. He could say though that he agreed with the Japanese policy toward China and the government of Chiang Kai-shek. One thing he could see happening was that the people were becoming disgusted with the republican form of government imposed by Chiang. The important thing was how long it would take to rid China of the trappings of this republicanism. So the discussion ended with mutual pledges of goodwill and promises for the future, none of which were destined to be carried out, except in the naval field. The Japanese asked for advice about submarine warfare and the Germans responded by sending several U-boats to the Pacific. None of them operated very well in these tricky waters, and the German skippers soon learned that the Japanese boats were concentrating on warships and not on commerce raiding. The Japanese never did learn in this regard, and thus their submarine force was never as effective as it could have been.

In passing, Tojo and Ambassador Stahmer had mentioned the Casablanca Conference, but they were not familiar with the fact that there the U.S. and Britain promised more aid to Chiang Kai-shek's China. The Americans were to build a new road through Assam province of India, called the Ledo Road. It would connect with the China Road at Myitkyina, Burma, just as soon as Myitkyina was captured from the Japanese. This was necessary to replace the Burma Road, which had fallen into Japanese hands.

As the new Japanese empire began to decay so soon, Tojo came in for much criticism from the Imperial palace advisors, from some members of the Diet, and from members of the elder statesman's society, the *Genro*, a group of senior councillors. Most of these people had been around so long that they had little fear of Tojo or the Army, and it was true that Tojo hesitated to arrest them or bother them because they had so much importance to the Throne.

Tojo maintained his control of the government very effectively with two police arms. First was the *Kempeitai*, the national military police, whose chief, as noted, was not responsible to Imperial General Headquarters, but to the war minister, a portfolio that Tojo had kept. He had appointed Maj. Gen. Hakujiro Kato as chief of staff of the *Kempeitai*, so he kept control thus. He also had appointed his former deputy from Manchuria days, Col. Ryoji Shikata, as chief of Tokyo military police. These agencies and one other, the *Tokubetsu Koto Keisatsu*, the Special Higher Police, were set to watching over dissidents and anyone who might be suspected of action the Army did not like. In the period when Admiral Yamamoto was accused of excessive concern for the British and Americans, just before the war, he had been given a military police guard that he did not want and was constantly evading. Supposedly the guard was for his safety. Actually it had been supplied so Tojo and his intimates could keep track of Yamamoto's activities.

In the spring of 1943 Tojo made the next attempt to increase his powers. The passage of the special Wartime Administration Law gave him the power to issue directives to the economic ministries covering war production. So he alone could decide if Japan was to produce more ships, more planes, or more guns.

The spring of 1943 was supposed to bring a great new Japanese drive in the South Pacific, opening with an air campaign conducted in late March and early April by Admiral Yamamoto. Thereafter ground and naval forces were to move in and clear out the Americans, first from New Guinea, which was the Army goal, and then from the Solomon Islands.

But instead of victories, the spring brought more disasters. First was the battle of the Bismarck Sea in March, in which the American Fifth Air Force without naval support virtually wiped out an important convoy and its destroyer escorts attempting to reinforce New Guinea. This was followed by American gains in the Southern Solomons and Japanese difficulties in the Aleutians, which were growing ever harder for the Navy to resupply.

General Tojo was still sounding the "need for unity" note and putting the best face possible on the string of defeats Japan was suffering. He had several meetings with the Navy minister about the problem of shipping, which was one that the Army and Navy had not given much attention during the planning stages. They had not counted on the strengthened effectiveness of the American submarines, which were operating now in the south, around the oil fields, and even in Japanese home waters. In spite of the sources of oil that the Japanese had captured, they could not get as much benefit from them as they had hoped because too many tankers were being sunk.

That spring, too, Tojo decided to make a military inspection in the south, to see for himself how the war was going and to check on the progress of his Greater East Asia co-prosperity efforts. He went to Nagasaki naval air base on May 3, and stayed overnight at the Ueno

Inn. Next day the weather was bad so he took the naval air station commander's car and toured the installations nearby. He finally left by naval aircraft on May 5, and arrived at Manila that same day where he put up at the Manila Hotel. He toured the air base and the ground forces base, and the next day, with the commander of the military forces on Taiwan, he went to Taihoku. Two days on Taiwan and he was back in Tokyo.

The week of May 13 was full of bad news from the Aleutians. The Japanese had suffered in the battle of the Komandorski Islands, and Tojo was briefed on that by his Navy minister. Worse, he was told that the Navy and Army had combined to pull all their troops out of the Aleutians.

Tojo had received the news late, because under the peculiar Japanese system of power established by the Emperor Meiji and his councillors more than half a century earlier the Navy and Army operations departments really didn't have to consult with the premier at all. The civil government, which General Tojo represented as prime minister, had one avenue of access to the Emperor. But both the chief of staff of the Army (Sugiyama) and the chief of staff of the Navy (Nagano) had separate access to the Emperor whenever they wanted it, as did Navy Minister Shimada and General Tojo as Army minister. The chiefs of staff of the two services did not have to consult with the Army and Navy ministries except on matters such as budget. The Army and Navy were totally separate from the civil government except for this factor, and this is why they were able to maintain control of Japan.

As prime minister, General Tojo fretted under this system and increased his efforts to gain more control. These efforts were stoutly resisted by the Navy, who felt that Tojo had no business being both prime minister and war minister. (They did not know that he also aspired to be munitions minister and chief of the Army general staff, as well.) His major supporter in the Navy was Admiral Shimada, the Navy minister, who was not well-respected within the naval organization. (The younger officers referred to Shimada as *Yurufun*, which in English means Droopy Drawers.) When a newspaper photo appeared showing Shimada standing behind Tojo, the Navy took umbrage and complained to the newspaper, fearing talk about Shimada as the "tea servant" of General Tojo.

But the real difficulty between Army and Navy arose from two issues: air forces and ships. Under the Japanese system, the Army had its own transportation corps—cargo and troop ships manned by Army men—and they did not expect to have to rely on the Navy for anything but surface escort and air escort service and air cover during operations offshore. The Navy was given all responsibility for protection of areas that were basically naval in nature. The Philippines, for example, was regarded as dual territory but the Navy was responsible for air protection. The Army planes were being saved for Army operations at some point against enemy ground forces. In the South Pacific the naval air forces had the whole job, with the Army air forces again saved to support Army ground operations in places such as Dutch New Guinea, though not British New Guinea.

Moreover, in Tojo's relationships with the services the Army was very jealous of its position; the relationship between Tojo and Sugiyama, which had never been close, was growing ever more distant. By this summer of 1943 the Japanese drive everywhere was stopped, and in some places like New Guinea and the Solomons it was being reversed. Meanwhile the China albatross around Japan's neck continued to grow and weigh down the nation. Tojo was not at all comfortable about the way matters were going in China. To him China was always the clue to everything. If the Japanese could eliminate Chiang Kai-shek and get the Chinese government at Nanking into total power they could begin to progress with the operations of the Greater East Asia Co-prosperity Sphere. So Tojo still spent as much time as he could on that idea, although the succession of disasters in the military field was taking much of his time and planning effort.

Late in May Premier Tojo announced new drastic economic measures designed to conserve the country's resources. The biggest problem was oil, of course, because of the American submarine sinkings of tankers. But more ships bearing tin, raw rubber, and many other industrial supplies were being sunk. Only the Manchuria and North China resources seemed relatively secure these days; supplies coming from the south could not be counted upon with much assurance. "Heavy battles are in progress and others must be expected," Tojo said in a national radio address. "The time has come for the Japanese people to adapt themselves to the present war situation. A determined battlefront will be established at home and measures taken to ensure an epoch-making increase in war output." The Japanese people heard, and responded. Their resilience was remarkable, especially since they had been on a war footing for six years, and on a total war footing for nearly four years.

The new mobilization measures provided for what was essentially a seven-day week. The age limit for war work, set at 60, was removed. Women began to take on duties such as traffic direction and bus conducting and driving and streetcar operation. Women joined the street cleaning services. High school students were partially mobilized to do war work. The next move that summer would be to close down the geisha houses and entertainment districts of Tokyo, Kyoto, and other cities.

By midsummer 1943 the Japanese defense line ended at Rabaul. Everything south and west of Rabaul was expendable. The dream of expansion was still there, but all the responsible leaders seemed to know that it was now impossible to attain. Reality was catching up with the Japanese, the same reality that made Admiral Yamamoto ask what would happen after the second six months of the war began and the process of attrition was felt. Tojo clung to one dream: if he could solve the China dilemma all else would fall into place, he said. That is why he would ask a person like the German ambassador for advice about China, for Tojo did not know where to turn.

15

"The enemy will grow hasty . . ."

The opposition to Tojo's continuation in power had begun to swell at the end of 1942. By then it was apparent to anyone who had information about the state of affairs in the South Pacific that the string of Japanese victories had ended and that a real war had begun. Prince Konoye had said from the beginning that the people would remain uncomplaining about the war only as long as it brought one victory after another. Konoye had been proved wrong but he was still convinced that revolution and the emergence of Communism were the great dangers facing Japan. In December 1942 he met with Prince Higashikuni, who had been considered for the prime ministry when Tojo was chosen; the prince had been rejected because he was a member of the royal family. Konoye tried to convince Higashikuni that it was time for Tojo to be ousted. Higashikuni was noncommittal. He did not fear the reds under the bed as much as Konoye did, which was reasonable, for the Communists and their sympathizers were deep underground, largely buried in the universities. There was no chance for them to emerge in the political climate established by the secret police.

Just after it became apparent that the Japanese position on Guadalcanal was impossible, and Admiral Yamamoto had objected to wasting any more naval power there, Konoye conspired again to get rid of Tojo. He met with generals Junzaburo Mazaki and Binshiro Obata at the house of Shigeru Yoshida, an opponent of the war who had been ambassador to Britain. Another important figure at the meeting was Seihin Ikeda, the former managing director of the great Mitsui combine, which had supported the *Kodo Ha*, or Imperial Way, forces in the struggle within the Army.

Konoye pointed out that the Army had turned into a monster,

adopting the *Koda Ha* principles but using them to subjugate all the opposition and create a force of unthinking puppets. The only thing that could retrieve the situation, he pointed out, was to bring back all those generals of the *Koda Ha* faction who had been summarily retired when the *Tosei Ha* faction took over the Army. Only these *Koda Ha* could be trusted to seek the will of the people.

They agreed that Tojo's power should be abrogated. Their candidate for prime minister was Gen. Kazushige Ugaki. It was true that Ugaki was 74 years old, but he was very vigorous and he was the most trusted man in the Army. Only he could control that service, and prevent the factionalization that was becoming more apparent every day.

After that meeting, Prince Konoye went to the Marquis Kido, lord keeper of the privy seal, to discuss the matter. He knew that by this move the Emperor would learn of the growing opposition to Tojo. But at this point Hirohito was not ready to take any action. Because of the conflict between Tojo and General Sugiyama the Army situation was very explosive and no one knew what might occur.

The Japanese disaster at Guadalcanal was followed by one misadventure after another. In February 1943 the Americans seized the Russell Islands, an action that was a forerunner to their advance up the Solomons chain. In March came the battle of the Bismarck Sea, in which the large Japanese convoy from Rabaul destined for Lae, New Guinea, was more than decimated, and after which the Imperial Army and Imperial Navy never again tried to resupply New Guinea by convoy. So much shipping had been lost in the Guadalcanal and New Guinea campaigns that the Army was demanding more shipping, which Tojo could not supply. But it was not only in the specific military theaters that ships were being lost by the score. The American submarines, having solved frustrating torpedo problems, were creating havoc in the whole Japanese supply system. The hampering of the nation's ability to conduct overseas commerce was a problem for which the Japanese government was totally unprepared. To meet it the government had to inaugurate several wholly new programs: construction of special long-range aircraft suitable for anti-submarine patrols from the shore, and the construction of small vessels suitable for convoy escort and anti-submarine warfare. These were just beginning to be produced.

General Tojo had not paid much attention to the traditional responsibilities of the prime minister to the Imperial Palace. He did report faithfully to the Emperor on developments in the war, as he was told some of the details, by the Army and by his Navy minister. Often the information was erroneous, and from time to time Hirohito grew impatient with the prime minister's tales. Moreover, Tojo had no great respect for court tradition, and he tended to ignore the *jushin*, or council of senior statesmen. Tojo's sycophant, General Sato, through whom he controlled the Military Affairs Bureau of the Army, said that Tojo regarded the *jushin* as a bunch of doddering old gentlemen who had no influence. It was easy to say so because the *jushin* had no specific responsibilities. It was a sort of private club, made up mostly of former prime ministers. Prince Konoye was a member, as were Admiral Yonai, General Abe, Koki Hirota, and Baron Wakatsuki—the prime minister who had been in power at the time of the Kwantung Army's seizure of Manchuria. But by ignoring the *jushin,* General Tojo deprived himself of potential allies; when he began to pay attention to them in the summer of 1943 it was very late and a number of the senior statesmen had already formed unfavorable opinions of the Tojo government.

On July 23, 1943 Tojo invited the *jushin* to the meeting of the cabinet in what was obviously a move to secure support. First he gave a summary of the internal and external matters that seemed most important, and then he introduced the deputy chief of the Imperial General Staff, General Okada, who summarized the military situation, noting that matters were moving very rapidly on a number of fronts. This was certainly true, the Japanese having been driven from Guadalcanal, New Georgia, and Vella Lavella islands by the Americans and Australians, and on New Guinea General MacArthur was moving north, too. The Japanese did not yet perceive the full scope and import of the Allied plan, but it was to surround the big base at Rabaul—not attack it as General MacArthur had wanted to do—and then let it wither on the vine. Thus the 100,000 Japanese troops centered there for operations all around the South Pacific would be cut off, and while they would have plenty of supply to sit out the war, they would have nowhere to go.

As far as the Imperial Navy was concerned, its major fighting elements were divided among Truk, the Singapore area, and Japan. In April Admiral Yamamoto had fallen, a victim of a concentrated attack by American fighter planes sent out on a special mission. The effort was based on the breaking of the Japanese naval code, telling the American high command where Yamamoto would be on the day in question, and when he would be at the chosen intercept location.

Yamamoto gone, the Navy was having serious difficulty pulling itself together, for there was no single clear head that had a naval policy that might slow the American enemy. That part of the Navy based in Japan was suffering from a serious fuel shortage, and the bases overseas were suffering from all sorts of shortages, most of them engendered by the growing want of merchant ships. Admiral Koga, who had replaced Yamamoto as commander of the Combined Fleet, was waiting for the opportunity to stage the one big battle that was supposed to mend Japan's naval fortunes and win the war. This naval plan was no plan at all, but a holdover of the Yamamoto policy, which, in view of the increasing American production of navy ships and planes, Yamamoto would have changed to a more sensible scheme of attrition had he remained alive.

Tojo had made several trips around the battle zones and the occupied territories this summer, and he was finding matters very serious indeed: corruption was rife in Manchukuo and in China, where the Army held its conquests in an iron grip. In Burma the people had become disillusioned with Japanese promises that brought them nothing, but Burmese resources continued to be demanded for the Japanese military machine. The Thai ally was firmly in the Japanese grip too, and all the promises made of economic assistance turned out to be false. The Philippines was encouraged to believe that it was independent, but anybody with any powers of observation knew that this was not true. The Filipino people shuddered under the arrogance of the Japanese military, as bad here as anywhere. But, of course, General Tojo had not seen any of this, and it is doubtful if he would have recognized what was wrong if he had seen it. Tojo was a very limited man.

There also were some positive aspects of the Greater East Asia Coprosperity Sphere—elements outside the Army circle of control. The Greater East Asia Ministry had many servants in the field and they tried, for the purposes of the military machine and for the future, to instill confidence in Japan, particularly in the hearts of the youth. They had many programs aimed at the betterment of those whom they considered to be the promising future leaders of these countries; some of these were brought to Japan for education. That was the prospect for the future, but the present was dismal indeed in the summer of 1943.

Also looking to the future, at the July cabinet meeting to which the *jushin* were invited, General Okada spoke of the various elements within the Army who had some differing views about where events could and should lead. The greatest single concern addressed was the shortage of troops at the front line, a problem that no one could have foreseen. (What he did not say was that the reason it was difficult to get adequate numbers of troops to outlying parts of the empire was the shortage of transportation and the hesitance of both Army and Navy to commit convoys to troop movement because of the enormous losses, such as those suffered in the battle of the Bismarck Sea.)

The next biggest problem, he said, was the shortage of aircraft, both bombers for the Army and especially fighter planes for carriers and Navy land-based air forces. The struggle with the Americans and the Australians was consuming fighter planes by the hundreds. At Wewak one American air raid had destroyed about fifty fighters on the ground, caught in the same wingtip-to-wingtip fashion in which the Japanese had caught the American planes in the Philippines at the opening of the war.

The third matter to which General Okada addressed himself was the situation within the Greater East Asia Co-prosperity Sphere. Although most people (the Army said) favored the Japanese cause, not all of them did. These populations had to be encouraged to unite in their support of the Japanese war effort as if it were their own; they were all in this war together.

After the general had finished, an admiral offered brief remarks but he did not go into details such as the plans to use the Japanese submarine service to supply the South Pacific garrisons that had been cut off by the Allied tactic of island-hopping. The general merely had hinted at this problem in his talk.

Now General Tojo took the floor. He spoke of some growing doubts in the country about the progress of the war. As for himself, Tojo said, he was perfectly confident that Japan would emerge victorious. True, she was suffering some reverses, but this had always been the nature of war, moving like the waves, billowing up and down. Just before the Pearl Harbor attack, Tojo had said that Japan might have to expect a long war, although he had hoped it would be a short one. Now he knew it was going to be a very long war. One particularly positive factor: the early victories had accrued to Japan an enormous pool of resources. Her war potential was enormous, and one hundred million people were as one person in their determination to win. The people of Japan were supporting the war, and so were the people of the Greater East Asia Sphere.

Possibly this period of defensive action would not be without profit. The enemy was tending to grow impatient and act hastily, Tojo said.

At the front line there were not enough soldiers, it was true, the premier admitted. It was not planned that way but was the result of inadvertence. And he agreed with Okada that mastery of the air was the first principle and that the Japanese had not yet achieved it. Digressing, Tojo said, "As to the Greater East Asia nations being foreign nations, that they are not, and their viewpoint is the same as ours. However, as for the way we treat these people it must be as equals."

Then Minister of State Suzuki spoke up. He had no portfolio but served as the chief planner for the cabinet. About the manufacturers who were building military aircraft, were they really doing their best? he inquired. They must be persuaded to exert every effort. Then he mentioned a related matter: Japan was very short of light metals (such as aluminum) needed to build airplanes. Could not the aircraft manufacturers begin using some strong light woods instead?

The senior member of the *jushin*, Baron Reijiro Wakatsuki, spoke up then. What about the offshore islands? he asked (Nanto shoto, Nansei shoto, Saipan, and Tinian). The Japanese inhabitants in no small numbers did not feel safe there. And in the southern region where the immense resources were used to feed the Japanese war machine, the civilians were feeling very insecure.

General Tojo then offered a rejoinder about the vigor with which the outer lands were being resupplied.

At this free-wheeling, seemingly little-structured conference, Minister Suzuki then raised the problem of moving the resources from the south to feed the Japanese war machine. Success depended on shipping, and there had been a great shortage of cargo vessels—something that was not being rectified.

Baron Wakatsuki then called for a vigorous step forward to be taken to solve the China problem.

Prime Minister Tojo replied that Japan and China previously had had points of difference, but since the British and American influence had been swept from China, the Chinese government was now cooperating with Japan. Foreign Minister Shigemitsu added that they had some difficulties with old treaties, and that now he wanted to revise the treaty with the Nanking government.

Baron Wakatsuki spoke again. The Japanese were considering a movement by the Thai government to incorporate the Shan state entirely into Thailand. The problem was how the Burmese would take that, since the Shan territory was traditionally partly in Burma and partly in Thailand. The baron wanted to know what effect this would have on Japanese relations with Burma.

Tojo replied that it was important to both the Thai and Japan to have the Shan territory incorporated into Thailand, because the Shan region was the scene of most of the Japanese troop activity in the area at that time. The premier reported that he had already told Burmese President Ba Maw that Thai forces were stationed in the Shan region, and Ba Maw did not offer any disagreement.

Also, the Thai had lost territory to Malaya and Indochina—lands they now wanted to get back. But, Tojo wondered aloud, would the Thai people want to take the military casualties that would be caused by trying to take them by force?

Koki Hirota, one of the members of the *jushin* and a former prime minister, then spoke. "According to dispatches the Americans are asking the Soviet Union to let them station American troops in the Soviet Far East. If that is so, cannot we demand that the Soviets allow us to base troops on Soviet territory?"

Tojo said that as far as he knew no such plan was under consideration, and that while it was important to Japan to better relations with the Soviet Union, American relations with the Soviets were not such as to cause any worry at the moment.

Foreign Minister Shigemitsu then gave a sketchy account of his frustrating negotiations with the USSR. And that was the end of the meeting.

The *jushin* were not impressed. As Baron Wakatsuki put it, they never learned anything more from Tojo and his cabinet than they could read in the daily newspapers.

By autumn, General Tojo had become aware of a wave of domestic disapproval of his government's policies. The defeats of the Japanese forces in the South Pacific were continuing, and the newspapers were running articles about the difficulties the Japanese were having everywhere. The articles were framed to display Japanese heroics, of course, but between the lines was truth, such as the statement made by a Japanese pilot that he had never encountered an air force as powerful as the American. The manner in which such articles were written allowed them to be passed by the censors, and the Japanese people began to have glimpses of a war that was being lost. There was a rumor of a plot to assassinate Tojo. And there was rumor of a new cabinet to be appointed by the Emperor, with Prince Higashikuni as the prime minister, and Gen. Kanji Ishiwara, an old foe of Tojo's, as Army minister. Ishiwara previously had stood up to Tojo several times and called on him to resign for his incompetence.

On August 8, Adm. Keisuke Okada, who had been prime minister at the time of the 2-26-36 rebellion, sent an emissary to persuade Marquis Kido that Tojo had to be replaced. Kido did not commit himself but he did say that he would bring any signs of open rebellion to the attention of the Emperor.

What constituted rebellion? asked Admiral Okada.

A unanimous vote of censure of Tojo by the *jushin*, replied Lord Kido. So Admiral Okada set up a confrontation with the prime minister and the *jushin* at the Peers Club. Tojo came, but not alone. He brought along Navy Minister Shimada, Foreign Minister Shigemitsu, and Finance Minister Kaya. The *jushin* began asking him about his military failures. Tojo retorted by questioning their lack of a sufficiently positive attitude to the war. So, as it turned out, the *jushin* lost heart and allowed Tojo to lecture to them about their want of optimism. The whole point of the meeting was lost in the confusion.

Tojo had nothing to fear from the left, which was not active at all during the war years. The *Kempeitai* and the other special police kept the Communists and left Socialists on the run. But Tojo did fear the very conservative right wing of the Japanese spectrum—their patriotism was unassailable. But many of them did not feel that Tojo was doing a good job of running the government. The word "arrogance" was often heard in their discussions of the premier.

It was hard to oppose the government openly but there were subtle ways. For example, it was quite patriotic to distribute leaflets urging greater participation in the war. So one group handed out pamphlets that read "American planes should be destroyed! British planes should be destroyed!" (*Beikoku no hikoki o yattsukero! Eikoku no hikoki o yattsukero!*) But the Japanese characters for Tojo's first name—Hideki—and those for "British planes" were the same. And besides there were virtually no British planes in the Pacific. There were Australian and New Zealand, but not British at that point except in India and Ceylon. So anyone with a whit of sense who saw the leaflet read: "American planes should be destroyed. And Hideki (Tojo) should be destroyed."

On September 6, 1943, Takeo Mitamura was arrested. He and Seigo Nakano had been trying for a long time to get Tojo fired. They had gone to Prince Higashikuni with stories of the autocracy of the Tojo government. They had asked Prince Takamatsu to try to use influence on Tojo. But Tojo was impervious to suggestion or argument, a characteristic that had been instilled into him in his years of Army training.

Because of the growing unrest, Tojo began clamping down on dissent rather more. A month later his police arrested more than a hundred members of right-wing organizations who were speaking out against the government. These detainees included members of Col. Kingoro Hashimoto's *Sekiseikai*, which was really an anti-government political party at this time. Hashimoto was famous in Japan (and infamous in the West) as the man who had tried at least twice to stage an Army rebellion against the civil government in the early 1930s. More important, he had ordered the firing on the British gunboats in the Yangtze River at the time of the Japanese capture of Nanking—the day the American gunboat *Panay* was also sunk. Hashimoto had been a member of the Cherry Blossom Society and was one of the most ardent advocates of Army dictatorship. He himself was not arrested, only because he claimed immunity as a member of the Diet. Essentially on that basis Nakano and Mitamura were freed, too. A judge refused to extend their arrest on the eve of an emergency session of the Diet because the Constitution guaranteed members freedom from arrest unless with the consent of the Diet members.

Still, even though there were constitutional guarantees, the police had their ways of harrying people. Nakano was arrested again the next day and detained for hours, and then taken home by military policemen who stayed in his house. These *Kempeitai* obviously were acting on the orders of Tojo, who, as war minister, controlled them.

That night Nakano committed ritual suicide with a sword, whether to embarrass Tojo or from sheer desperation was never known. But the suicide did embarrass Tojo greatly. When asked to comment, the premier said grimly, "He was a traitor," but offered no proof. An alternate explanation was that Nakano had been receiving secret money donations from General Sugiyama's slush funds in the continuing struggle for power between Sugiyama and Tojo, and that the *Kempeitai* threatened to expose this connection. It was known that with no visible means of doing so Nakano had amassed a considerable fortune.

The scandal of Nakano's death was enormous. Tojo's assistants asked the Nakano family to limit the funeral to relatives in the hope of avoiding a political demonstration, but the heirs defied Tojo and the procession became an anti-Tojo spectacle with more than 20,000 people journeying to Oyama cemetery to show their opposition to the government. The editor of *Asahi Shimbun*, one of the most prestigious of Japanese newspapers, presided over the ceremony.

In response, Tojo now tried to stage various events to bolster his position. On October 21 he reviewed an enormous parade of mobilized

students at the Meiji Shrine Gardens. Two weeks later he opened the
Greater East Asia Conference with flourish, as if it were a meaningful
meeting instead of the conquered saluting their conqueror. Not many
people were fooled. The conference labored like a lion and came up
with food for a mouse, a proclamation in support of the Japanese war
aims.

But then Tojo was given an unexpected lift from a foreign quarter.
When Franklin Roosevelt, Winston Churchill, and Chiang Kai-shek
met at the Cairo Conference, the American president and the British
prime minister issued a proclamation announcing that they would never
quit fighting until Japan surrendered unconditionally. Such a capitulation was repugnant to the Japanese, who feared that the destruction of
the Imperial System would be an enemy's first action. The people
refused to entertain such a prospect, and Tojo was the beneficiary of
an outburst of patriotism.

16

The Thrust for Power

In the summer of 1943, Tojo was beset by criticism from high places for his conduct of the war. In a way this was unfair criticism, because General Sugiyama and the leaders of the *Gumbatsu* did not consult Tojo on operations, and he often did not know what was being done. The whole Guadalcanal fiasco, for example, was a result of inattention on the part of the Imperial General Headquarters to the real nature of the American enemy. There had been a period, in August and September of 1942, when a determined Japanese Army thrust, to accompany the naval victories that Admiral Yamamoto was winning, could have forced the American marines to evacuate the island. But IGHQ played the game of too little and too late for too long.

Tojo's series of trips around the conquered territories in the spring and summer of 1943 was occasioned by his growing suspicion that the truth about Japanese military and naval operations was being concealed from him and from Admiral Shimada, his Navy minister.

On his return, Tojo had to face a growing barrage of criticism. Prince Takamatsu, the younger brother of the Emperor and a naval officer with the general staff, urged the Emperor to replace the Navy minister with someone that service considered to be independent of Tojo and more competent. Hirohito grew annoyed with his young brother, who was only a commander in the Navy at that time, and told him to stop meddling in affairs of state. He would not, he said, "listen to the prattling of an irresponsible prince."

The arguments were telling nonetheless. The failing Japanese fortunes in the war weighed heavily on Hirohito; he lost weight and he became so nervous that several times he had to leave Tokyo and take refuge from the cares of state at the summer palace at Hayama. But

Hirohito was not yet ready to admit that his own choice to control the Army, Tojo, had failed.

Major General Prince Kaya, cousin of the Empress and a nephew of Prince Higashikuni, was another in the Imperial circle who profoundly disrespected Tojo; he had held this feeling since 1942 when he blamed Tojo for failing to provide the ships necessary for the defense of Guadalcanal and the Japanese bases in New Guinea. By the summer of 1943 Tojo was grimly aware of the ferment around the Imperial Palace, although he kept quiet on the subject.

One of the results of Tojo's inspection tour of the battle areas was his decision to establish a Munitions Ministry. And who would be the new munitions minister? Hideki Tojo, of course. Tojo had arrived at the conclusion that if anything was going to be done he would have do it himself. The new portfolio would help him press for the necessary increase of war materials, and it would help him put a stop to the interservice rivalry that was making it difficult for aircraft manufacturers to produce at a satisfactory level. Theoretically the interservice rivalry question had been settled at the end of 1942, when the Army finally agreed to help the Navy air forces defend the Solomons and to participate in the offshore battles around New Guinea. But, in fact, virtually nothing had changed. The Army did send a few aircraft on joint missions, but most of them got lost because the Army air forces had neither the training nor the skill to carry out aerial navigation over water.

As the war situation became more serious the tangle grew worse. The Munitions Ministry was unable to stop the rivalry between the two service air forces. In the matter of shipping, the Army continued to make demands on the civilian economy that were impossible to meet. And the great store of war materials the Japanese boasted of having acquired with the early captures in 1941 and 1942 were proving to be illusory in part, because of the shortage of shipping.

In connection with the meeting of the principal nations of the Co-prosperity Sphere in Tokyo in November, the Japanese government put on an enormous drive to convince people in Japan and the satellite territories that the "cooperative" international enterprise had substance. Burma, Indonesia, the Philippines, Manchukuo, and Nanking China all were "independent." Subhas Chandra Bose, the head of the Free India committee, was treated as though he were also a head of state. During the first week of November, Tojo was busy preparing for and then attending and supervising the meetings. He entertained the distinguished visitors with Imperial receptions and state dinners. Finally, at the end of the week he took most of them to Haneda Airfield and saw them off on their journeys home aboard Japanese military aircraft.

School children were mobilized for one of the occasions and a mass meeting just outside the Imperial Palace drew a crowd of 100,000. But the meetings and the ceremonies hid the reality: Japan was running short of manpower and that autumn of 1943 all male students above the age of 20 were ordered to report for induction into the service by December 1.

Several of the Greater East Asia dignitaries stayed on for more talks. Ba Maw of Burma was one, for Tojo felt the need to somehow try to retrieve the relations with Burma that had worsened to a condition bordering on armed insurrection in that country.

Another who stayed over was President Laurel of the Philippines. The Japanese had promised the Filipinos total independence within the year, and there were many discussions of the future state of relations. Tokyo panoply aside, in the Philippines as well as in Burma, the Japanese did not dare to go out into the countryside alone. The southern islands, in particular, were swarming with guerrilla fighters, some of them American, but a great many of them Filipinos.

But on November 12th Ba Maw and Laurel left, and Tojo turned to Japan's only really independent ally in Asia, the Thai government, and to Subhas Chandra Bose, for whom Tojo had great hopes.

The Provisional Indian Government had been organized on October 21, a few weeks before Bose came to Tokyo. Its fortunes were guided by the Burma Area Army that had just been organized to relieve the 15th Army for some of the preparations against India.

In Tokyo Bose and Tojo talked about coming military operations. The 15th Army would move against a corner of India, and once it was captured, Bose would move his Provisional Indian Government there, and set up shop on Indian soil. He confidently believed that millions of Indians would flock to his banner and he convinced Tojo that this could be so.

Tojo then began planning for a dual offensive on the Asian mainland early in 1944: against Imphal in India, and towards Chungking in China. The 15th Army in Burma was asked for an operational plan. When one staff officer suggested that the plan would fail he was abruptly removed from his position and sent to line duty. This operation was too important to Tojo to allow it to be undercut by logic. If only Japan could invade India, here was an army ready to fight shoulder to shoulder with the Imperial forces. But the problem was that the resources and the men in Southeast Asia were in short supply and the unsettled condition in Burma did not help. Yet Bose, who met privately with Tojo on November 13, was eager for the Japanese to move. He pointed out that the British were deeply involved in the European war and there could not be a more promising occasion to bring off a successful breakaway by India. Bose pledged to the Japanese the continued use of the Andaman and Nicobar islands, which they needed for air bases, subject to their ultimate return to an independent India. He pledged the support of the Indian independence movement and Indian Independence Army, but what he really wanted was Japanese action to "liberate" India from the British yoke. Tojo wanted it, too.

The war continued to worsen for Japan. The Americans had bypassed several islands and on November 1 had landed in the middle of Bougainville, the largest of the Solomons, at Empress Augusta Bay. Their intent was not immediately clear and Imperial General Headquarters did not at first take it very seriously.

A few days later the Japanese assembled a large force of surface warships, intent on smashing the American invasion forces off the beaches. This reaction fleet was a little slow, however, and an American carrier task force intervened and hit the assembly area at Rabaul before the ships could get started, causing so much damage to the Japanese cruisers that the whole operation had to be given up.

On November 23 an American force of very great size—the largest yet—invaded the Gilbert Islands. The fighting on Betio was fierce, but brief; the Japanese had only 5000 troops on the island and although they fought to the death, it did not take long to kill them, given the American resources. Tojo held the Army general staff responsible for what had happened in the Gilberts, and for that matter, for what happened previously at Guadalcanal.

Now the American objective became clear. The Americans were fighting a blocking action on Bougainville and obviously had no intention of going south on the island to engage the Japanese division there. Instead, they were protecting the Empress Augusta Bay area, to build airfields there from which they could assault Rabaul and put that base out of commission, thus removing the heart of the whole Japanese southern Pacific operation.

At the end of December General Terauchi of the Southern Army submitted a plan for Operation U, the Imphal campaign. General Sugiyama expressed some doubts:

Although there is a very high probability that British-Indian forces will land on the shores of Southern Burma, is Operation U a desirable measure to counter this opportunity?

When the Imphal plains are captured the area to be defended becomes seriously enlarged. Will this create a consequent necessity to increase the military forces involved?

Since the Japanese Army air force is weak, are ground operations feasible?

Is there any uneasiness regarding rear logistics?''

General Terauchi replied that he had confidence. If the operation was successful it would result in a saving of military forces in the area. The defenses of Burma would then be stabilized.

As 1943 ended, Tojo's spokesman summed up the Pacific war to that date. Noting the second anniversary of the attack on Pearl Harbor, Tojo had predicted victory for Japan in 1944, but had also warned that it would not be an easy one. Tojo hinted that it might not be long before the Allies struck at the core of the Inner Empire.

In the first year, he said, Japan had secured an enormous territory and resources to fight this war. In the second year she had launched the political offensive with the establishment and perfection of the Greater East Asia Co-prosperity Sphere. Now in the coming third year, Japan would launch several new offensives, smashing the enemy and bolstering the unity of the Sphere.

But the people of Japan must realize, Tojo said, that the fighting was reaching "the decisive stage."

The unrest in Tokyo was becoming more apparent every week. Tojo badly needed a victory to ward off his detractors. His hope was that Japanese moves in China and Burma would take off the pressure in the Pacific. He pressed, and on January 7, 1944, the Imperial General Headquarters issued instructions: "The Commander in Chief, Southern Army will break the enemy on his front at the opportune time and will capture and secure strategic areas near Imphal, and in Northeastern India for the defense of Burma."

But that month there was bad news from the China front, where Tojo had also wanted to move this winter. In the Hukawng Valley, along the northern border of Burma, the Chinese First Army was attacking Lt. Gen. Chinichi Tanaka's 18th Division and was advancing south to the Kamaing district, across the Patkai mountain range from Imphal. Farther northeast, in the Yunnan province region of China, ten divisions of Chinese troops crossed the Upper Salween River, and moved against the Japanese 56th Division of Lt. Gen. Yuzo Matsuyama.

On the south Burma coast in the Akyab region two divisions of British and Indian troops did indeed launch the attacks IGHQ had feared, but were pushed back by a counteroffensive launched by Lt. Gen. Tadashi Hanaya.

The struggle between Tojo and Imperial General Headquarters continued. It seemed that General Sugiyama was winning when both he and Count Terauchi were made field marshals by the Emperor, while General Tojo was not promoted. By the end of 1943 the increasing sea attacks on Japan's shipping were becoming so numerous and so telling that Tojo had to address himself to the shortages they were causing in almost every area. He pointed out that the closer the Allies came to Japan the longer their lines of communication would become, and predicted that ultimately this would mean disaster for the Allies and victory for Japan.

Once again, in a speech to the Diet, he talked about air power. Mastery of the air, he said, would be the decisive factor in victory on the ground and at sea. Therefore he announced a new effort to increase production of aircraft, particularly of fighter planes.

But the same old problems dogged the government. Army and Navy were constantly quarreling about allotments of materials and weapons. The Army wanted at least half the airplanes produced, but the Navy was entrusted with the defense of virtually all the remaining areas outside China, Manchukuo, and the homeland. It was in Navy territory that the vicious air battles were being fought, and the Navy needed more aircraft than the Army, but because of the system the Army was getting planes and then hiding them away for future use, while the Navy went short.

But in the first days of 1944 the Emperor saw fit to call in Field Marshal Sugiyama and Navy Chief of Staff Nagano and reprimand them for obstructionism in the war effort, and for overstating the Army victories, which Sugiyama had been doing for a long time.

Tojo now was talking about resolving the Pacific war problem by winning on the Asian mainland. The war against China must be carried to Chiang Kai-shek's doorstep in Chungking. India must be attacked through Burma. The plans for this attack against the Imphal-Kohima area were already in progress. Just a foothold in India would provide a base for Bose and his Indian Liberation Army. That force could not then be ignored by the British, and it was expected to draw thousands if not millions of Indian sympathizers, despite the outright rejection of Japanese overtures by Mohandas Gandhi, the leader of the Indian Congress Party.

The continuing British pressure in the Akyab region of southern Burma still was causing much trouble for the Japanese command. Besides, the Chinese had launched that attack in the Salween valley, and although it was not being pursued very hard, it did offer a potential threat.

The American navy had turned the sea war around in recent months. The assault on the Gilbert Islands in November had been a mighty display of combined sea and air power. The American carrier force in the Pacific now numbered six heavy and four light carriers, plus a number of small or "escort" carriers, whose strength was yet really untried, and there were more carriers of all categories coming along soon.

Then in December the Americans had struck the Marshall Islands and wrecked many Japanese air facilities and aircraft. It was an indication that the Marshalls must be on the list for invasion. When the American fleet hit those islands again in January Admiral Koga told Tokyo to be aware that soon the attack on the land would come.

Then on the last day of January 1944 the Americans landed in the Marshalls, and the story of previous successful invasions was repeated. After some hard fighting the Japanese garrisons of the island of Kwajalein and all the others of the atoll were overcome by the Americans. When Field Marshal Sugiyama misrepresented the Army situation to the Emperor, Hirohito became annoyed and called in both the marshal and the Navy minister for serious discussions. He did not summon Tojo, which was significant. General Tojo understood where the blame was being laid, and he decided that he would transfer Sugiyama to other duties. He could do this because, as noted, he was not only prime minister but Army minister. Yet he could not have done it without the concurrence of the Emperor. In fact, Hirohito was thoroughly disgusted with both Army and Navy high commands and ready for a change. On February 19 Tojo called a staff meeting at Imperial Headquarters and dropped the bombshell: Marshal Sugiyama was being transferred to the very important duty of air inspector for the Army. His job as chief of the Imperial General Headquarters would be taken by General, Prime Minister, War Minister Tojo.

On this same day, with Tojo's concurrence, Admiral Shimada, the Navy minister, fired Admiral Nagano, the chief of staff of the Navy, and took over that position for himself. So the country now faced the fact that with the assistance of Yurufun (Droopy Drawers) Shimada, Tojo had taken supreme power over the war effort. Truly, he now was the Imperial warlord. From this point on, no matter what happened, Tojo would bear the full responsibility.

The defense of Japan entered a new stage. Admiral Koga flew to Japan to consult with Shimada and Tojo. They agreed that the Combined Fleet was a thing of the past, and that the Navy now had to concentrate its defenses. Yet there was not enough fuel in Japan for the Navy to concentrate the ships of the fleet in the home islands. There was not enough fuel in the Marianas for the Navy to concentrate there. So the fleet would be split up, part of it to go to the Palau Islands, and part of it to stay in the Singapore area, and from now on it would be called the Mobile Fleet. The other admirals argued that Japan was building more ships, but Koga told them to be practical. The only ship on the ways that had any possibility of being completed soon was the supercarrier *Nagano*, and Koga was not quite sure what he was going to do with a single supercarrier. Japanese strategy had to be changed. Henceforth air defense would concentrate on the "unsinkable carriers," the outer islands on the fringes of the Japanese Imperial core.

In these discussions in February, all, including Tojo, agreed that Saipan was the key to the new defense. They had known about the B-29 Superfortress for a long time. They knew it was in production, and that it was supposed to have twice as big a bomb load as the B-17 and to be able to travel twice as far. Looking to the possible bases for such aircraft, the Japanese settled on China and the Marianas Islands. They sent military expeditions in to clean up central China and prevent the Americans from using those airfields. So the Americans would have to use airfields very far west in Szechuan province and in Shansi. These were so remote that the B-29s would have difficulty getting to Manchuria, let alone Japan. But Saipan—that was something else again. Now Tojo was dictating to his generals and admirals: the enemy could not be allowed to capture Saipan!

In February the Americans seized the Green Islands 120 miles southeast of Rabaul. Marching up New Guinea, Bougainville, and the Green Islands, the Americans were ringing Rabaul. So what would come next? An attack against Rabaul? Imperial General Headquarters did not tell General Imamura, the area commander, that he was on his own. The defense line of the new Japanese empire no longer included Rabaul.

Nor did it include Truk, once called the Gibraltar of the Pacific. On February 17 and 18, the American carrier fleet attacked Truk and destroyed its utility as a naval base. They shot down many aircraft but found only a few minor ships in the harbor. Admiral Koga had already dispersed the remnants of the Combined Fleet, now called the Mobile Fleet, as noted. The destruction of Truk was kept secret by IGHQ, but the truth began to leak out.

More serious was the continuing American invasion of the Marshall Islands, another fortress group that the Japanese had controlled since the Versailles Treaty at the conclusion of World War I awarded them the mandate over this previously Imperial German possession. On February 22 the Americans began taking the islands after Kwajalein: Engebi, Eniwetok and Parry. It was very bad news indeed; at this point Tojo still was counting on a combined drive in Burma and China to ease the war situation in the Pacific and turn defeat to victory. Egged on by Subhas Chandra Bose, with promises of assistance from the Indian side, he ordered Gen. Renya Mutaguchi to use the 15th Army to assault India.

Operations against Imphal began. Lt. Gen. Genzo Yanagida's 33rd Division advanced from the south into the Chin Hills that separate Burma and India, and occupied those hills by March 1. On March 8 he marched toward Imphal with a small striking force. A week later the 15th Division under Lt. Gen. Masabumi Yamauchi and the 31st Division under Lt. Gen. Kotoku Sato started the siege of Imphal and the neighboring town of Kohima, to take and protect the bastion wanted by Subhas Chandra Bose. The bulk of Bose's Indian National Army participated in the fighting toward Imphal. The 5th Air Division covered the beginning of operations, particularly the crossing of the Chindwin River. The Japanese had local air superiority at the time, but the 5th did not have the strength to continue and so air cover was withdrawn. By March 20 the British 17th and 32nd divisions had been thrown back in the Imphal and Kohima areas. The advance was proving to be successful. It seemed as though Tojo might have the victory he needed.

And Tojo needed it more than ever. At the closing session of the Diet in March, Tojo warned that the war situation never had been more dangerous to Japan that it was at this moment. And by now the opposition to him had begun to crystallize.

Tojo gave a party to celebrate the session and honor the retiring members of the 84th session of the Diet. It was held at the prime minister's official residence and there the opposition manifested itself. During the addresses, the Speaker of the House of Representatives, Tadahiko Okada, bluntly suggested that Prime Minister Tojo resign.

Many Diet members applauded. Tojo turned very pale but he controlled his face and said nothing.

Deposed Commander-in-Chief Sugiyama sent a note to the Emperor warning that if Tojo were allowed to be prime minister, war minister and chief of staff, Japan was on her way to a new shogunate. And that was not all. Tojo also controlled the munitions ministry and, through his toady, the Navy ministry and the Navy Operations. The entire government had been concentrated in the hands of one man.

Having failed to shame General Tojo into resignation, Admiral Okada decided to use his Navy connections, rather than his parliamentary connections, to force the premier out of office. As a first step he began a campaign of attrition against Admiral Shimada, now Navy minister and Navy chief of staff, pointing out Shimada's dependence on Tojo and his inability to act in the best interests of his service.

Meanwhile the dissatisfaction with Tojo had reached the Imperial Palace, and was fermenting there. The opposition was greatly increased when Tojo usurped the position of chief of staff to go with his portfolio as war minister; it had been traditional for these two positions to be quite separate. This move by Tojo created new enmities, and it even began to have negative consequences for the Emperor, because it was recognized that the Throne would have to have acceded in Tojo's power grab. The logic presented by Tojo to the Emperor was that in this crucial period it was essential that all the reins of power be held in one set of hands, so that optimal use of Japan's slender defense resources would be assured. There was no room for any mistakes.

Hirohito had accepted that explanation but many people around him had not. Several of the Imperial princes called Tojo's failings to Hirohito's attention. His brother Prince Chichibu (whom some in the court had already begun to think of as an apt successor to Hirohito) was among them. In retirement from the military service and suffering from tuberculosis, Chichibu still had the strength and forcefulness to complain to the Emperor about the unprecedented seizure of power. He suggested that Tojo might even have ambitions to usurp the throne, though that was never true. Tojo did not realize that what he was doing was shutting out virtually all honest advice.

Chichibu roused himself from his sickbed to carry on his own campaign against General Tojo. He first wrote a letter to the head of the personnel section of the Army ministry, expressing his anxiety as a retired major general about Tojo's usurpation of powers. Then, in April he sent his aide to see Vice Chief of Staff Jun Ushiroku. The aide, Maj. Katsuyuki Shizuma, had been given a number of questions to pose to the Imperial General Staff:

1. Why had the Army violated the long-standing rule that the functions of Army minister and chief of staff could not be held by the same person?

2. Was it possible for one man to fill the distinctly different responsibilities of these two posts?

3. If there was disagreement between the cabinet and the general staff, which course would Tojo recommend to the Emperor?

4. If the war reached a point at which it would be necessary to decide whether to quit or to continue, would Tojo react in his capacity of prime minister, representing all the people, or as chief of staff, representing the Army?

General Ushiroku replied that there had been no intention to destroy the rules and that Tojo had taken this action strictly as an emergency measure. But Ushiroku did not give any clues as to how long Tojo intended to hold these extraordinary and really unconstitutional powers. Therefore the major went away with his questions essentially unanswered, and Prince Chichibu was not at all satisfied by the encounter. To him it looked as though Tojo was indeed making preparations to become shogun, or to unseat the Emperor as supreme commander of the armed forces.

The prince worried over the matter and in mid-May he again dispatched Major Shizuma to get answers to the last two questions he'd asked earlier. He knew, of course, that the Imperial Army generals as a bloc were unrelentingly committed to the prosecution of the war to victory, for Japan had never lost a war. But Prince Chichibu also knew that this war was not going the right way.

Still, Major Shizuma did not get the answers to the questions. But after the major's visit General Ushiroku went to Chichibu's villa in Gotemba to assure the prince that nothing would be done to undermine the Emperor. Nevertheless, within the royal family the displeasure with Tojo continued to grow. Prince Takamatsu, now a captain with the Imperial General Naval Staff, had previously reported to Emperor Hirohito that the Navy, instead of working steadily for peace, had been preparing for war all the time after 1934. What he said then was true, but it involved only part of the Navy, the "fleet" faction as opposed to the "treaty" faction. True, there were virtually no members of the treaty faction on active duty now, but in the background were men such as Admiral Yonai, one of the *jushin*, and Admiral

Okada, the speaker of the house in the Diet. Although on that service's retired list, they retained considerable influence among naval officers.

For two and a half years the Navy had fretted under Tojo's control of the government and the military. Admiral Shimada, now both Navy minister and Navy chief of staff, had done the same thing to his service that Tojo had done to the Army. Many naval officers wanted the admiral removed from office altogether, but no one dared approach Tojo with criticism of his favorites. So the contest was waged via more concrete issues; the current continuing struggle was for aircraft. Prince Takamatsu was trying to fight that battle for the Navy. In February he had asked for the support of the Marquis Kido, Hirohito's principal advisor, to change the ratio of Navy and Army planes since the Navy was almost entirely entrusted with the fighting in the Pacific and the Americans were making mincemeat of their air fleets. The Army, its eyes on China and Burma, refused to concede anything, and Tojo supported the Army.

Like a calm pond after a stone is thrown into the middle, the circle of discontent began to widen in Tokyo. Prince Konoye, who had supported Tojo in the beginning, joined those who now wanted him ousted. Konoye spoke to his son-in-law, Morasada Hosokawa, who was Prince Takamatsu's private secretary. This was not the first time. Hosokawa had been in touch with the prince on this subject as early as 1943, warning that Tojo seemed to be growing ever less competent. But now Konoye felt that the situation was getting completely out of hand.

17

Tojo's Last Chance

In the spring of 1944 the winds of negative opinion about General Tojo's management of wartime Japan began to reach gale proportion. Much of the criticism came from within the royal establishment and from people close to the Imperial Palace. They, more than others, were able to voice and share their opinions without much fear of the dreaded *Kempeitai*, who by now seemed to be ubiquitous in Japan, seeing everything, hearing everything, and reporting everything to Tojo.

Prince Takamatsu, the Emperor's young brother, was the member of the royal family most voluble against Tojo, much more than Prince Chichibu, whose illness kept him out of the capital most of the time. As early as the summer of 1943, Takamatsu had been coming to the palace to report on one defeat after another and to urge the replacement of Admiral Shimada if not of Tojo. Hirohito, as we have seen, was inclined to be brusque with his younger brother.

But in this the Emperor was wrong. Takamatsu's objections to Tojo and Shimada were Navy objections and they represented the views of many of the senior officers, who resented the military system that gave the Army superior position in budget matters. As the war worsened in the Pacific this resentment increased in the matter of aircraft. The Navy had the responsibility for fighting the air defense war against the Allies. The Army air force was still responsible only for air activity to support Army operations, and in the spring of 1944, the only offensive Army operations were occurring in Burma and China. Still the Army continued to get half the total production of the aircraft industry, planes which the Army sequestered to save for future army operations, while the Navy went so short of aircraft as to affect the attrition of fighting in the South and Central Pacific.

Takamatsu was joined by a much more important figure of the royal family, Prince Higashikuni, who was the uncle of both the Emperor and the Empress. He had been considered by the men around the Emperor for the post of prime minister when it went to Tojo, but the idea had been rejected because of the danger to the Imperial line of having an Imperial prince in charge of what might become a war (and had).

Prince Higashikuni had really opposed the war. Three weeks after the Pearl Harbor attack Higashikuni had suggested to the Emperor that Japan make peace, but at that time Hirohito was overwhelmed with the succession of Japanese victories and would not listen.

Higashikuni had considerable influence in Japan and was commander of the Home Defense. But such was the power of the Army over all Japan in this period that Higashikuni went unheard. In the spring of 1942 he had reported to the Emperor that the Army handling of the Doolittle raid and raiders had created a strong negative reaction abroad. For doing so he had been reprimanded by General Sugiyama, the chief of staff of the Army and head of the *Gumbatsu*, for interfering in the relationship between the Army and the Emperor. Thereafter Higashikuni had refrained from making public reports, but he frequented the palace and discussed the war often with Hirohito. Since 1942 he had been urging the Emperor to force a peace with China on the Army.

Early in April 1944, Prince Konoye became so disenchanted with Tojo's management of the war that he asked Higashikuni to help him get Tojo ousted from the premiership.

Because Prince Higashikuni was a professional soldier, his views had strong impact on the Emperor even though Hirohito was not yet prepared to accept them. Another whose opinion Hirohito valued was Maj. Gen. Prince Kaya, Higashikuni's nephew and a cousin to the Empress. Prince Kaya had been trying to get Tojo turned out after the fall of Guadalcanal, for he blamed the prime minister for not supplying the ships that would have made the resupply of Guadalcanal possible. This was actually not a very fair criticism, because the Americans by the end of 1942 had achieved air superiority at Guadalcanal and the Japanese ships that did get down there usually were sunk. The situation had grown so desperate at that time that any resupply that was managed was carried out by destroyers, which could fight their way down and back. But Kaya continued to share the operational Army leaders' distaste for Tojo, and in the spring of 1944 the prince was convinced that the war was lost and should be abandoned.

But that brought into play the most important factor that played into the hands of the military leaders who wanted to fight to the death. Roosevelt and Churchill had used the words "unconditional surrender" in their demand. Were that to be accepted the whole Imperial future would be put into the hands of the Allies.

Prince Kaya suggested to Higashikuni that three royal family generals—Kaya, Higashikuni, and Asaka—meet with Hirohito and suggest as a group that he dismiss Tojo and appoint Admiral Prince Fushimi to command the armed forces.

Others around the Emperor kept talking about the war and the need to bring it to an end. In 1943 the Marquis Sanjonishi had suggested that Tojo was incompetent, which Hirohito did not then believe.

But by the spring of 1944, the Emperor was having serious doubts. Many people who came to see him told him that Japan was losing the war. Nobuhiko Ushiba, counselor of the Japanese embassy in Berlin, came back to say that the Axis was losing the war everywhere. The industrial leader Koichiro Ishihara said the same, as did Professor Hiraizumi of Tokyo Imperial University.

With all this swirling about him, the Emperor, by the spring of 1944, was suffering from a nervous disorder brought about by his failing confidence and the frequent arguments with others in the royal family, particularly Higashikuni and Takamatsu. More than ever he escaped to Hayama, the summer palace, to get away from the war and the cares of state. He lost weight and he had difficulty sleeping.

After the American capture of the Marshall Islands, General Tojo knew that the American drive across the Pacific was virtually unstoppable. He had placed his hopes on the Asian continent, where the Japanese were on the offensive, in India and in China. That operation had now virtually failed.

Did Tojo ever read the operational plan presented to Imperial General Headquarters for the Imphal operation? If so, his permission to let the operation go forward would prove him a complete failure as strategist, for the logistics of the plan were laughable:

Officers and men should carry maximum provisions.
(It was well known that men laden down with supplies could not fight properly.)
Elephants and oxen should be used for hauling stores and equipment.
(A great idea in the time of Genghis Khan, but not in the twentieth century.)
The oxen should be eaten when provisions run out.

(So then who hauled the equipment?)
Personnel should be prepared to eat grass.
(They did.)
The advance along the road to Imphal from Kohima should be made in
two weeks after the commencement of operations.
(Even a fully mechanized army could move only half that fast.)
The road should be repaired after its capture, in order to convey supplies
at once by motor vehicles.
(Allied air attacks made the road worse and worse as each day went by.)

The tragedy was that all this had been foreseen by Lt. Gen. Nobu-
yoshi Obata, the chief of staff of the 15th Army; he had said the plan
was *bakamono*—a fool's enterprise. As a consequence, he was transferred out of the command immediately, and sent to Manchuria, where
he enjoyed a distinguished career in the waning days of the war.

At first the Imphal operation had gone smoothly. Tojo had great
hopes for this "Operation U" to establish the New Indian government
on Indian soil. But almost immediately after the capture of Kohima the
troubles had begun. First was the problem of logistics. The Japanese
had to resupply Burma by sea, and British and American submarines
were making that extremely difficult. Inside Burma the road system
was being blasted by British and American bombers; the supply
caravans coming from the south were hit heavily from the air, and
about half the supplies never reached the front. The defenders were
getting their resupply by air drop from British and American aircraft.
But the Japanese had no transport planes in Burma and not enough
bombers to convert for supply missions. So the Japanese soldiers
began to go hungry. The monsoon rains began in May, which made
troop movement very difficult, and the whole operation bogged down
from lack of supply and lack of proper equipment. On May 15, General
Mutaguchi, commander of the 15th Army, removed Lt. Gen. Masabumi Yamauchi as commander of the 15th Division and Lt. Gen.
Genzo Yanagida of the 33rd Division, but it made no difference. It was
not the generals but the whole Imphal operation that was wrong. Those
staff officers who had been cashiered for suggesting that the operation
would fail had been quite right from the beginning. But one of the
Japanese Army's principal failures had always been an unreasonable
optimism. It adhered to the foolish belief that a Japanese soldier was
worth at least three of those of any other nation because of the Bushido
spirit. The failure was sickness, hunger, lack of ammunition, lack of
weapons, and failure to command the air—precisely the factors that
had caused the Americans to lose the campaign on Bataan.

The British, whose force began with only two divisions and then increased to almost four, soon captured the Kohima-Imphal road, and began to press against the Japanese 31st Division. They were led by tanks, which the Japanese could not stop because they had no anti-tank guns. After the capture of the Imphal-Kohima road on June 23 the British were supplied on the ground, which added immeasurably to their fighting ability.

General Mutaguchi ordered a final "do or die" offensive to capture Imphal, and concentrated his force on the northeast part of the Imphal Plain. He had pulled the 31st Division out of Kohima, and this unit and the 15th Division led the fighting.

The high command promised supplies, but the supplies did not come. Gen. Kotoku Sato, commander of the 31st Division, became furious with 15th Army command: "The tactical ability of the 15th Army staff lies below that of cadets," he wired General Mutaguchi. Then he began to retreat rather than see his division destroyed by hunger and sickness. Mutaguchi began to question what the division was doing, and General Sato cut the communications wires. Soon General Sato was relieved as commander of the division and ordered sent to Rangoon for court-martial, but in the division and in the 15th Army many officers agreed with Sato. The Army in Burma had begun to fall apart.

General Mutaguchi knew very well that Operation U could not succeed now. Too much time had elapsed and the monsoon season had begun. He was afraid to tell this to General Tojo. With virtually nothing being done then to stop the destruction of his forces, the operations continued to sap their strength until July 4, 1944, when Tojo finally called off Operation U. On July 8 Mutaguchi ordered the retreat to begin.

This too was a disaster. The retreating Japanese troops had no air cover. They were harried from the air by British and American planes, and outflanked by paratroops. From the sides guerillas attacked them, and in pursuit was a British armored column. The retreat was another Japanese defeat, costing thousands of lives.

In the meantime the Japanese troops of the 18th Division assigned by the 33rd Army to cover the Salween area and prevent the Chinese advance there failed to stop the enemy. The Chinese reached Kamaing on June 16. East of Kamaing an American column of irregulars, called Merrill's Marauders, was slogging through the jungle to outflank the Japanese. The Americans reached Mytkyina on the upper reaches of the Irrawaddy River, on May 17. Now the Japanese were cut off on one side by the Americans, and on the other side by the Chinese.

The 49th Division had just arrived in Burma that spring and so Tojo ordered them forward to help the besieged 18th Division. But again, he did not count on the difficulty of travel and supply in a Burma whose roads and railroads had been wrecked by Allied bombing. Lt. Gen. Saburo Takehara tried to bring his division up, as ordered, but the roads stopped them. At the same time they came under attack by an irregular British force, which had been landed behind the Japanese lines weeks earlier and had captured much of Central Burma. The Chindits, as they were called, whittled away at the 49th, and that division's combat effectiveness was cut in half.

So a significant part of Tojo's plan for success on the Asian mainland had miscarried. But the most important continental objective to Tojo was to win the China war, and the first step of the new initiative would be to establish a corridor all along the east coast, from Manchuria down to Malaya. After that, supplies could be moved easily (theoretically) by truck and train from one end of the Greater East Asia Sphere to the other. In brief, the plan envisaged a phased drive south from Beijing to Canton, wiping out the American airfields in central and southeast China, and establishing a solid line of communications along the coast.

In April Lt. Gen. Eitarro Uchiyama led four divisions of the 12th Army and part of the 5th Army from North China. Their mission was to capture and secure the Beijing-Hanchou railroad south of the Yellow River. Then they would move to Hunan and Kwangsi, driving the Chinese from the Wuhan district on the Yangtze while a bit later the 23rd Army would strike north from Guangdong. The Chinese airfields used by the Americans at Guilin and Liujou would be captured as the 23rd cleared out the rail lines running to Guangdong.

On April 18 the Japanese began moving and by May 9 had linked the northern and central China areas as they had never done before.

On May 27 the 12th Army began to move on the Hunan-Kwangsi area, and the 23rd moved. Changsha was captured and then Hengyang Airfield, the forward base of the American 14th Air Force, which had for so long caused so much trouble for the Japanese forces in south China.

These operations were going very well that summer, and General Tojo was much heartened by them, when events in the Pacific seized his attention.

18

The Fall of Saipan (and Tojo)

As the Japanese could easily see, the American advance in the Pacific was proceeding along two lines. One was General MacArthur's march up the New Guinea shore, with the expectation of jumping off from there and attacking the Philippines at some later date. The second line of advance was across the Central Pacific by the American naval forces. Already they had taken the Gilbert Islands and the Marshalls. Truk, the great naval base, had been evacuated as useless with this turn of events, and Rabaul, the base of operations for the South Pacific, had been bypassed.

In the summer of 1944 Tojo then was expecting an attack in either area. In fact he got attacks in both.

In a matter of weeks, Army Chief of Staff Tojo and Navy Chief of Staff Shimada managed to confuse the Army and Navy field commands completely. From China, Burma, and the South Pacific, regional army commanders complained that Imperial General Headquarters no longer had an overall plan for the war, but kept improvising and issuing unclear and sometimes conflicting orders. Gen. Korechika Anami, commander of the Second Area Army, was ordered to pull back in the face of the Allied advance on New Guinea, but Tojo kept changing his mind as to where that army should center its activity. On May 2 he told Anami that Biak was expendable, but finally on May 9 he ordered Anami to hold the area near Sorong and Halmahera, and to secure the inner portion of Geelvink Bay, Biak Island, and Manokwari.

"IGHQ is in a whirl," said Anami. The reason for the switch was that the Navy had changed its mind. Admiral Shimada was trying to figure out where he would stage the "decisive battle" in which the Navy would go all out to try to destroy the striking power of the American fleet. At that moment Shimada believed it would be at Biak.

But then when the question of use of the Army and Navy air forces for defense was brought up, Shimada decided that the Navy air force must be kept intact, not split half for the Marianas and half for the New Guinea area. Biak would just have to be sacrificed if necessary.

All well and good, but when the Americans attacked Biak on May 27 Shimada and Tojo changed their minds and Shimada diverted nearly 500 planes from the Marianas area to New Guinea. It was a bad guess, because the Americans brought their fleet up to the Marianas and that is where the decisive battle of the A-Go Operation was fought. Those 500 pilots diverted to New Guinea sat and cooled their heels and caught malaria while their fellows were fighting and losing in the Marianas. The Navy plan of using its carriers and airfields for shuttle attacks looked good on paper, but now the Americans could mount an attack of more than 1000 aircraft, and they soon had what the Japanese called "mastery of the air." The absence of those 500 Japanese planes had something to do with the failure, but the actual naval battle did not work out at all as any of the Japanese had expected. The Imperial forces got the edge initially by finding and attacking the American fleet before it came into range for the Americans to attack the Japanese launching sites. But the Japanese aircraft were simply overwhelmed by the fighter planes from the American carriers, and no significant damage was done to the American ships, while American submarines sank two of Admiral Ozawa's carriers and the American carrier planes did more damage when they finally were close enough to attack. The result was the effective end of the Japanese carrier force as a fighting unit, and the retirement of its remnants toward Japan after losing the battle, leaving the Army forces in the Marianas without naval support.

By this time the Imperial Palace was the center of a storm of intrigue with many people advocating an end to the war one way or another. Lord Keeper of the Privy Seal Kido had decided during the winter that Japan should try to make peace, using the Soviet Union as its intermediary since the USSR was allied with the Americans in the war against Hitler. But Kido knew that he must move almost silently because the Army would do anything it could to stop such a plan.

Prince Konoye too had decided that the war was lost and he went to Marquis Kido asking for his intercession to persuade the Emperor to fire Premier Tojo and appoint an Imperial prince to take over. Kido said that if the war reached a point where it was necessary to stop it, he would ask the Emperor to demand Tojo's resignation. Where they disagreed was whether that point had been reached yet.

In his view that the point had been reached, Prince Konoye was supported by Gen. Koji Sakai of the Army general staff and Rear Adm. Sokichi Takagi of the Navy general staff. If Japan did not stop the war soon, they advised, their resources would be completely used up and the country would become ungovernable, subject to what many people feared, a Communist revolution. As the American planes were beginning their preliminary assault on Saipan early in July, Prince Konoye wrote to Kido saying the day had arrived and suggesting that Kido name Prince Takamatsu to the Emperor as the person who should be made prime minister, with the task of negotiating peace with the Allies.

Kido replied that the situation was indeed serious but he said he wanted Tojo to resign of his own will, as previous prime ministers had done in the face of failure.

At the foreign office, Foreign Minister Shigemitsu was waiting. Earlier he had suggested to the Throne that a special emissary be sent to Moscow to treat with the Russians, but the Army had got wind of the notion and had strenuously objected to that proposal. The spectre of surrender—*unconditional surrender*—haunted the military for several reasons. One was the self-serving realization that all the military men then would be out of jobs, the Imperial Army disbanded. For those above such mundane considerations there was another reason, almost always invoked in any discussion of ending the war without victory. That was the fate of the Emperor. The Army asserted that the Emperor would be deposed by victorious Allies, and also that the Japanese would all become slaves to the West under the unconditional surrender provisions. This argument was very effective with the Japanese people.

The Emperor had supported the Shigemitsu proposal, but in view of the Army ruckus, Hirohito backed down and did not insist on the action, so nothing had been done.

The actual Allied landings on Saipan began on June 15. Because the Japanese had no air support the Americans managed to land three divisions on that first day, and from that point on the fighting was ferocious. Starting with the airfields in the south, the Americans seized one point after another. They were assisted always by repeated air attacks from fighter planes and bombers, with no interference from the Japanese, for every one of the defenders' planes was gone by that time.

General Tojo reported faithfully to the Palace. On June 25 the Emperor summoned a body that had never before met to make an important decision: the *Gensui-in*, the Board of Field Marshals and

Fleet Admirals. To the meeting came Field Marshal Sugiyama, former Army chief of staff; Fleet Admiral Nagano, former chief of staff of the Navy; and the Imperial princes, Fleet Admiral Fushimi and Field Marshal Nashimoto. General Tojo and Admiral Shimada attended ex officio by invitation. The board recommended setting up a new line of defense in the Pacific, writing off the Marianas, and also the unification of the Army and Navy air forces under one command. But so confused was the situation, and so ingrained the antipathy between Army and Navy, that the second recommendation was never carried out.

By the first of July the Japanese defenses were crumbling. On July 1 Chief of Staff Tojo had a message from Saipan that told the story: "The officers and men have not eaten for three days."

By this time Emperor Hirohito was thoroughly convinced that the war had to be ended. He told Marquis Kido that he was ready to order the troops home. He would assume responsibility for the war and the surrender. But when Prime Minister Tojo heard of this plan he objected strenuously.

Again the Emperor hesitated.

Because of his irresolution, plots and conspiracies began to arise around the Palace. One suggested the removal of the Emperor by regicide. Another intended his transfer to Manchuria.

The Army had its own plan: the replacement of Hirohito by an Imperial prince who would agree with the Army policy of continuing to fight—to the death of the whole nation, if necessary.

On July 8 Prince Konoye met with Prince Higashikuni and they agreed that Hirohito should abdicate. Crown Prince Akihito, who was still a child, should succeed to the throne, and Prince Takamatsu should be appointed regent. Then Takamatsu should appoint Higashi-kuni as prime minister with the task of terminating the war and negotiating peace.

This matter was discussed at the palace with the Emperor and Takamatsu, and Higashikuni told Takamatsu that the resignation of Hirohito would be a good idea. It would be received favorably by the Allies, who seemed to blame both Hirohito and Tojo for the war. It would serve as a symbol of peace.

Hirohito considered the idea. But he said he did not believe it was constitutional for him to abdicate: there was no provision for it in the modern constitution, and the practice had been so common during the shogunate that the reason for its noninclusion in the new constitution must have been deliberate. Hirohito was always conscious of the effect of his every action, and just as he had refrained from using power to prevent the war or to stop it, he now hesitated to quit in the middle.

He was, however, ready to change the cabinet.

When Tojo heard this, which he did within a few hours, he stubbornly refused to quit. He said his reasoning was the same as that of the Emperor. But that could not have been true, because in mid-June Tojo had told the Marquis Kido that he was willing to step down as prime minister if they could find someone to replace him. At that point Higashikuni had interceded and told Tojo that his responsibility was to resolve the war he had created and get the country out of the mess that he had made.

The battle for Saipan continued. On July 11, Lt. Gen. Yoshitsugu Saito, commander of the Saipan defenses, sent a message to Tojo: "I have issued the following order: On the 7th—the day after tomorrow—we will advance to attack the American forces and will all die an honorable death. Each man will kill ten Americans."

Then radio communication with the Saipan defense force ceased.

On July 12 Tojo asked the Emperor to issue a proclamation on the fall of Saipan that would encourage the people, and to call for national unity in time of crisis.

Hirohito refused to issue any statement. And when Tojo said he wanted to change his cabinet to strengthen it, the Emperor said that shuffling the cabinet at this stage was not going to solve any problems. Tojo told Marquis Kido that he intended to stay in office. Kido relayed that to the Emperor, who did not like the idea. With Tojo's record of usurping power, he now feared that the prime minister would take some action that would jeopardize the powers or rights of the Throne.

On July 14 Tojo came again to the palace in his capacity of chief of staff of the Army. Hirohito was very cold. He mentioned the growing opposition to Admiral Shimada in the naval officer corps and requested that Tojo appoint a new Navy minister. That day Tojo asked Shimada to resign and the admiral did so. Tojo also resigned his own post as Army chief of staff. Gen. Yoshijiro Umezu took that post, and Field Marshal Sugiyama came back, as Army inspector general of military education. Adm. Naokuni Nomura was appointed Navy minister. Tojo also asked Admiral Yonai to join his cabinet, but Yonai refused, saying the Navy minister post had already been filled and that was the only one he would accept.

Tojo was struggling to stay in power, but Prince Konoye wanted him out. The Marquis Kido agreed that if the *jushin* agreed that Tojo should resign, then Kido would take that recommendation to the Emperor. So

Konoye arranged a meeting of the *jushin* that very evening. The criticism of Tojo was general, and so Kido was told that the *jushin* wanted the resignation. He told the Emperor. A few minutes later Prince Higashikuni and Prince Asaka arrived at the palace for an audience, and both of them recommended that Tojo should be dismissed. The Emperor agreed.

So on July 18, General Tojo was given all this information by Kido and he resigned as prime minister, as war minister, and as munitions minister—and all his cabinet resigned.

Was this the end? Not quite.

19

End of the Line

Even as Premier Tojo resigned, in that summer of 1944, a plot had been formed to eliminate him by assassination. The leader of the plot was Maj. Tomoshige Tsunoda of the Imperial General Staff, who had been a soldier in China under the command of Prince Mikasa, the Emperor's youngest brother.

Tsunoda's first step had been to put out a pamphlet in July; it called for Tojo's resignation, the establishment of a new cabinet under Prince Higashikuni, and immediate peace talks with the Allies through the intervention of Moscow. What was unusual about this plot was that several civilian members of the plot belonged to the East Asia League, which long had been regarded as a ''right wing'' organization. Most of the young officers at Imperial General Headquarters had quite an opposite view, that the Army should fight on until the end, no matter where it took the nation. But when Prince Mikasa turned his copy of the leaflet over to the *Kempeitai*, the plot collapsed, and a thorough investigation began.

As noted, Tojo tried desperately to stay in power. Before the resignation he invited Admiral Yonai to enter his cabinet as a minister of state, thinking that this move would improve his position and particularly with the anti-war element who wanted a quick resolution of the war. Tojo then asked Minister of State Nobusuke Kishi, his deputy in the Munitions Ministry, to resign to make room for Yonai, since the number of ministers without portfolio was limited by the Constitution. To Tojo's surprise Kishi turned him down. It was a harsh blow to the prime minister's ego, for it meant that he could not manipulate his own cabinet and that he must either cause the resignation of the whole cabinet or acknowledge himself as a mere figurehead. It was the most humiliating event yet of Tojo's military and political career, and finally proved to him that his resignation, which he knew was desired by the Imperial Palace, was inevitable.

What Tojo did not know was that a disastrous report that he had never seen had been circulating among the *jushin* and others around the Imperial Palace. This report had been made by Admiral Tagaki. At the end of 1943 he had been asked to make a survey of the war situation and he had done so, predicting the fall of the Marshall Islands, the collapse of the Imphal campaign, and the attack on the Marianas, which then would enable the B-29 bombers to attack Japan.

Tagaki had completed his survey in February 1944, and the results were so depressing that he would not even pass them on to Admiral Shimada, because he knew of the extremely close relationship of Shimada and Tojo. He feared that if Tojo learned of his recommendations—that Japan withdraw from all the Philippines, and Burma, and from all the overseas territories except the Ryukyus (Okinawa) and Taiwan—the premier would ignore the recommendations, although perhaps taking some extreme measures of reprisal against Tagaki and those who had participated in the survey.

Tojo was very well aware of the undercurrents swirling around him because he was using the *Kempeitai* more and more to maintain control of Japan. He used them so much that Emperor Hirohito confided to a friend that the reason for Tojo's fall was that he had too many *Kempeitai* around, and other powerful individuals as well as those around the palace began to resent what was obviously interference in their affairs. For example, Colonel Matsutani, a member of the Army General Staff, and an associate of Major Tsunoda's, had tried a more moderate approach to Tojo some weeks before. He and a number of other young officers of like mind, who were well aware of the developments in the South Pacific, had concluded that Japan should get out of the war as quickly as possible. The colonel had access to Army Chief of Staff Tojo in those last days and Matsutani raised the issue with him. The interview was stormy, with Tojo denying all that Matsutani claimed—and a few hours later Matsutani was posted to the China front.

By this time, on the eve of his resignation from the prime ministership, Tojo saw political enemies everywhere. Admiral Tagaki had not shown his report to Admiral Shimada, lest Tojo see it, but he had shown it to Admiral Yonai, who had then shown it to Admiral Okada, another member of the *jushin*. Okada had been so upset by the findings that he had gone to Tojo without telling Yonai, and Tojo in turn had erupted in rage and refused to discuss the situation with Okada. He had accused the *jushin* of trying to overthrow him. In a sense this was true, and ultimately the distrust of Tojo everywhere in the places of power had forced his resignation.

He made another attempt to intimidate the cabinet and the people around the Throne. From the office of the war minister came a paper addressed to the cabinet officials by name, accusing each of the former prime ministers of the *jushin* of conspiracy to oust Premier Tojo. The War Ministry proposed to release this draft to the press and wanted the concurrence of the cabinet. The implication was very clear that the war minister's power of using the *Kempeitai* to investigate subversive activity was about to be invoked, perhaps against members of the cabinet who sympathized with the *jushin*. But the cabinet, led on this issue by Foreign Minister Shigemitsu, took no action on the paper.

In another mistake in his desire to retain power, Tojo's employment of the *Kempeitai* was reckless. For example, Toshikazu Kase, a foreign office official, was in touch with former foreign minister Togo and others, particularly the *jushin*, who were showing great concern about the direction of the war. "I knew my phone was tapped," said Kase. "I received frequent visits from police agents who with artificial smiles invited my comment on the futility of continuing the war or upon the brutality of the misgovernment of General Tojo. Many others walked into such traps and were subsequently taken to jail."

Having finally asked the *jushin* for advice and having been told that he should resign, Tojo had done so, but even on July 18 he hoped to retain power. The resignation was tendered privately and no hint of it appeared in the press. The Emperor was concerned about the nation's morale, so he was not eager to authorize a premature announcement, and anything that might happen before a strong cabinet could be put together was considered premature at this stage of the war.

Now came a game of musical chairs that might have been funny had it not been so serious to Japan. After Tojo's resignation was received and immediately accepted by the Emperor, on the morning of July 18, within a matter of a few hours, the *jushin* were convened by Marquis Kido, Lord Keeper of the Privy Seal, on the urging of the Emperor. Nine people attended that meeting in the Imperial Palace: the seven *jushin*, the Marquis Kido, and the president of the Privy Council, the Baron Yoshimichi Hara.

The problem now was to find a successor to Tojo as prime minister. No one wanted the office, given the war situation. The Emperor had already indicated the parameters of the job, to fight the war but also to bring it to an end.

In times past, men had competed vigorously for the premiership, but not now. At this meeting each representative of the different segments of Japanese society urged others to take on the task, but rejected the post for himself or his own close associates.

At this point, General Abe was the only Army man among the *jushin*, and he suggested that the new prime minister should come from the Navy. Admiral Yonai was his candidate. But Yonai said that the candidate should be a civilian who could bring the Army and Navy into that state of unification recommended earlier by the council of field marshals and fleet admirals.

. Not possible, said Baron Wakatsuki, who had bitter memories of the Mukden Incident and the Kwantung Army's refusal to take orders from a civilian cabinet. The prime minister must be a military man. His candidate was Gen. Kazushige Ugaki, who had served four times as war minister, and had been named prime minister-designate after the collapse of the Hirota cabinet in 1937. Ugaki had been frustrated then by the Army clique, who had first warned him not to take the job and had then refused to give him a war minister, thus making it impossible for him to form a cabinet. But Ugaki's friends knew that he did not want the thankless task.

Koki Hirota, who had styled himself as "the ordinary man" and had always felt out of place among the *jushin* (who were almost all noblemen), proposed that one of the Imperial princes be nominated. Baron Hara, who was not a former prime minister but essentially one of the *jushin* because of his post with the Privy Council, suggested that all the former prime ministers form a collective cabinet, thus leaving himself out of the sphere of responsibility.

Finally, Prince Konoye, who had been so close to the Army for so long in his own tenure as prime minister three times, agreed with Baron Wakatsuki that only an Army man could control the Army. Gradually all the others came around to that position. But they did agree to right the wrong committed by the Army in its arrogance in 1937, when it had virtually forced Prime Minister Hirota to change the rules regarding the war minister, to make the holder of that office an active-duty Army officer, not retired, thus putting the whole government into the hands of the Army. This in itself was a signal achievement. It was recognition of what had gone wrong, and the *jushin's* insistence that the prime minister might be a retired general snatched the power of destruction from the hands of the Army. By this time the *Gumbatsu*, or Army clique, had collapsed into powerless segments. Field Marshal Sugiyama had been deposed by Tojo. Field Marshal

Terauchi had been exiled to the Southern Army Command, where he was out of the political scene. Tojo was disgraced. Gen. Akira Muto, once chief of the powerful Military Affairs Bureau and one of the oligarchy, had been relegated to command of the 14th Area Army on Taiwan.

Admiral Yonai nevertheless suggested Terauchi, who had recently transferred his headquarters from Singapore to Manila to be closer to the fighting fronts. But the others were not sure that the Army could spare the field marshal. Marquis Kido suggested that two alternative names be put forward, and so they were: Gen. Kuniaki Koiso, the governor general of Korea, and Field Marshal Shun'roku Hata, commander of the Japanese Expeditionary Army in China.

That very afternoon, those three names were commended to the Emperor, and feeling the need to move quickly in this hour of crisis, Hirohito considered them immediately. He summoned General Tojo to the Imperial Palace for advice. Tojo, seeing in the summons a sign that all was not lost, hastened to the Palace. When given the names, he took this last opportunity to stick the knife into his rival, Count Terauchi. The field marshal, Tojo said with the confidence of sure knowledge, really could not be spared from the task of directing the southern armies. No one else had the experience to do the job.

The Emperor then decided to nominate General Koiso, and summoned him to Tokyo.

The way seemed clear to the solution of the crisis, but Prince Konoye then had second thoughts. Perhaps a general would not be satisfactory to the Army, and the inner circle should not take the chance of failure at this moment. So he suggested that Koiso be nominated as a figurehead, but that the actual government be in the hands of joint Army-Navy "co-premiers," and that Admiral Yonai be the Navy representative. He took this up with the Marquis Kido, who concurred and then called the *jushin* to see if they agreed. They did, and Yonai consented to serve, provided he was given the specific task of Navy minister, which meant he would not have any interference from the remnants of the fleet faction. There was a precedent for a joint cabinet under the Meiji Constitution; in 1898 Japan had been ruled by a joint Army-Navy government.

By now it was July 19. General Koiso had hurried down to Tokyo from Seoul, not knowing quite what was required of him. Soon he found himself in the anteroom of the Imperial reception hall, waiting with Admiral Yonai. Together they were received by the Emperor, who explained the situation for Koiso's benefit. Then Hirohito asked them to form a joint government for the good of the nation.

Now they needed a war minister. Tojo still had hopes of retaining power. As war minister still, until the appointment of a new one, he controlled the *Kempeitai*, and he used them unmercifully to secure support for his reappointment to the post of war minister. But it was not so easy now. He had disposed of Field Marshal Terauchi, but General Umezu, the new Army chief of staff, wanted no part of Tojo. Field Marshal Sugiyama, who was also called in by Umezu to help in the decision, had his own hatred for Tojo. And because he was retiring war minister, Tojo had to be consulted. When he proposed that he retain the post, he was quickly put down by the other two, with an assist from General Koiso, who did not want Tojo either. So Tojo's last attempt at holding a vestige of power failed ignominiously, and to make the matter more humiliating, Field Marshal Sugiyama was chosen to be the new war minister, which removed Tojo's control of the *Kempeitai* and all else.

Could Tojo at this point have attempted a coup d'etat, while he still had the vestige of power and control of the police organizations? The new cabinet was not yet appointed, and so Tojo was still titularly prime minister, and as far as press and public were concerned nothing was yet known.

But Tojo's Army support had withered, dried up by his seizure of the office of chief of staff, thus destroying the *Gumbatsu* unified control of the Army, and dividing it into factions as it had been in the 1930s. Indeed, when Emperor Hirohito appointed Koiso and Yonai to take over the government he warned them of two problems. First, they must observe the constitution. (This was a rebuke for Tojo, who had violated the constitution by seizing the control of Army operations when serving as war minister.) The second caveat was against provoking the Soviet Union. There was hope in the Palace that the USSR yet could be utilized as a channel to reach the Western Allied leadership and settle the war. Moreover, there was such a reaction against the Army clique, which represented the control faction of the Army in the 1930s, that Hirohito feared a return to power of the *Kodo Ha*, and a new struggle for power within the Army.

So in brief, there was no chance for Tojo to stage a coup d'etat. Sugiyama immediately assumed control of the *Kempeitai*, which removed Tojo's last bit of personal authority. In an army that had been noted for the violence of its politics Tojo passed out like a lamb.

All these negotiations had been conducted secretly, most of them in the Imperial Palace, and the people of Japan were unaware of the dramatic changes. The major reason for the veil of secrecy was the general understanding within the government that, if not immediately, then very soon, the fall of Saipan must be announced as the breach of the Inner Empire by the Allies. It would come as an enormous shock and the government must be prepared to withstand it.

On the morning of July 19, speaking as prime minister, which he would be for a few more hours, Tojo announced the fall of Saipan to a shocked Japan.

"Our Empire has entered the most difficult state in its entire history," he told the radio audience of Japan. "But these developments have also provided us with the opportunity to smash the enemy and win the war. The time for decisive battle has arrived."

The premier then left the studios of Radio Tokyo for the last time. He went to the prime minister's office in the Diet building and cleaned out his desk. Then Tojo went to the official residence and collected his personal belongings. After all hope had been lost, he had informed his wife Katsuko only on the night of July 18 that he was being forced out of office. She had prepared to return to their house in the suburbs. They traveled across Tokyo by staff car to his private residence for the last time. He was now just another unemployed general of the Imperial Army with no authority and nothing to do but work in his garden. When they tuned in the radio that afternoon, they heard the news that Japan had a new government.

"Using all means available, the present cabinet was not able to achieve its objective," said the Radio Tokyo announcer in typical indirect style. "The government has finally decided on a complete reconstitution in order to prosecute the total war."

Mrs. Tojo was querulous about Tojo's future.

"You are going to quit, but will that end your responsibility?" she asked.

"I am not evading my responsibilities," he replied. "I have done everything I can, but even if I wanted to carry on, conditions have made it impossible. There is no help for it."

The next day, July 20, he learned that his name had been put on the retired list, and he had no further connection with the Army except to draw his pension.

Personally, Tojo was at that moment a very lucky man. The Tsunoda assassination conspiracy had been primed for July 20. On that day they were going to deliver a bomb loaded with potassium cyanide to the prime minister's office. But when the day arrived there was no further need.

Two weeks after the event, Emperor Hirohito gave a banquet for former premier Tojo and the members of his cabinet, and made a point of praising them for their service to the country. But it was a charade. Tojo was not invited to join the *jushin*, the first prime minister ever so rejected by the Emperor.

20

The War Nears Its End

Retired General Hideki Tojo now had cause to regret the life he had led. He had taken no time for recreation and very little for family, devoting himself at every step to his career. Now, suddenly, he was cast adrift, with nothing to do but play the role of householder in the almost rural Setagaya suburb of Tokyo. He had no hobbies, and he had no friends. He was not consulted by the government and he had no place in the *jushin*. Suddenly, from being the most important public figure in Japan next to the Emperor (who was not regarded as a figure at all, but as a god), he was the least important—a non-person.

He had seven children. Hidetake, his eldest son, was employed in a war industry in Manchukuo. His second son, Teruo, was working in the Mitsubishi company. The third son, Toshio, was in officer training at the military academy.

Daughter Mitsue, the eldest, had not married but had elected to remain with her parents, as Japanese girls sometimes did, and take the responsibility for their care in their declining years. Daughters Sachie and Kimie were still children, and daughter Makie had married an Army officer who was stationed with his unit in Tokyo. The household consisted of Tojo, Ketsuko, the four girls, and the child of daughter Makie.

The garden was large by Tokyo standards, dominated by two big pine trees, but most of the flowers and shrubs had been taken up and replaced by food plants. The family kept chickens for eggs. Tojo gardened, mostly raising vegetables to supplement the ever more slender supply of food in Tokyo, and he did some writing. Occasionally one of his secretaries or a former colleague would visit the house, but not often. He had absolutely no contact with the Army or the govern-

ment, and most of his information came from reading between the lines
of the newspapers.

In the autumn of 1944 there was some brightness for Tojo emanating
from China, where the Japanese Army was making good its promise to
clear out a coastal corridor that would end at the Indochina border and
link the southern territories with Manchuria, but the deterioration of
both the roads and the trucks as well as the shortage of fuel made the
victories more illusory than consequential.

One by one the products of Japan's early triumphs vanished that
summer and autumn of 1944. The fall of Saipan was followed swiftly
by the American capture of Tinian, and a few weeks later of Guam.
After that the Americans began bringing in the B-29 bombers, which
were still, that summer and fall, hitting Kyushu and Manchuria from
the fields in West China, although they did not have the range to reach
the Kanto plain of Honshu, the industrial center of Japan. But everyone who knew anything about the war knew now that the bombers
would come to Japan's cities too soon.

The Koiso government began immediately to dismember the apparatus of governance imposed by the Army in the Konoye cabinet
period. The Liaison Conference was abolished and so was Imperial
General Headquarters as a supreme war council. Instead Koiso and
Yonai invented the Supreme Council for the Direction of the War,
which broadened the base, but functioned as a small war cabinet. It
consisted of the prime minister, foreign minister, two service ministers, and two chiefs of staff. Since all these officials were military men,
it was still a military government. The great difference was that the
Imperial Army had lost control of the government, for the first time
since 1937.

To rebuild the public support for the government that Tojo had
allowed to erode over the preceding three years, the Koiso cabinet
appointed thirteen distinguished citizens from outside the government
to act as advisors. As the newspapers said in editorials, the purpose
was to bring the government closer to the people. However Japan still
was run by a military oligarchy, although the characters and their
orientation had changed. Koiso had been a *Kodo Ha* man at the time
of the 1936 Army insurrection, and his appointments favored friends
of that period. Among them were the notorious Col. Kingoro Hashimoto, who came to exercise a controlling influence in the Young Men's

Corps, which was supposed to incite Japanese youth to even greater efforts in the war than they were giving.

General Koiso was in his own way trying to establish control over the government for his clique, but he was not totally successful, one reason being that as a retired officer he could not assume the role of war minister and thus could not personally control the *Kempeitai*. War Minister Sugiyama had been around too long in too many capacities to let the prime minister have complete control of the government, particularly since they came from opposite ends of the Army spectrum.

In this struggle for power the people won a small victory. The restrictions on freedom of expression began to dissipate. Only two months after Tojo's fall, two members of the Diet attacked the regulations against free speech and publication that Tojo had carefully orchestrated.

They were not arrested, as they would have been under the Tojo government. The regulations remained, but a noticeable slackening in their application was observed, and the newspapers began to sneak into their pages clearer glimpses of the deteriorating war situation.

To all appearances, Koiso ran the cabinet singlehandedly, and remained as firm a supporter of the prosecution of the war to the end as Tojo had ever been. But in private Koiso and Yonai were trying to arrange for a negotiated peace, and their chosen instrument was the Soviet Union. They wanted to send one of the former foreign ministers who had known Stalin well, such as Koki Hirota or Yosuke Matsuoka, to see the Soviet premier personally and secure his assistance in getting in touch with the Western Allies. But this was the fall of 1944, and the Soviets and the Western Allies were rolling up victory after victory over the German armies. It was apparent that the end of the war in Europe could not be far off. After that, Stalin had plans to enter the war against Japan, as he had been urged to do by the Americans and British. The Japanese had waited until it was too late to secure any help from the Russians, and nothing came of Koiso's efforts.

For the preceding two years Tojo had lavished an enormous amount of personal attention on Burma, regarded as one of the jewels in the Greater East Asia Co-prosperity Sphere. But what Prime Minister Tojo had done politically for the Burmese relationship had been undone by War Minister Tojo's Japanese Army with its imperial policies that earned hate and resentment from the Burmese citizenry. After the Imphal campaign failed that summer, the Burma front began to fall apart. In late September the British attacked in the Akyab area and extended their front. By October they had killed 60,000 Japanese troops and the Burma army was in shambles. The British 14th Army advancing on Mandalay, the river and rail center of central Burma, discovered thousands of corpses of Japanese soldiers who had committed suicide in despair. Just as many died of starvation and disease. At the height of the Imphal operation the Japanese had 330,000 troops in Burma. In the retreat only 70,000 survived.

October 1944 came and Tojo listened on the radio as Prime Minister Koiso made the sort of speech Tojo had made so many times, describing the war situation in broad terms and urging the people of Japan to greater efforts for their own salvation. In the third week of October came the stunning news of the American invasion of Leyte Island in the Philippines. Tojo had expected that, the plans for the "great decisive battle" involving all of Japan's available naval forces and all the air and land forces available in the Philippines. He did not learn, and would not know for many weeks, that the Japanese had suffered a disastrous naval defeat in the battles around Leyte, in the Sulu Sea, at Surigao Strait, off Samar Island, and off Cape Engano. He soon learned of a new military element, the *tokubetsu tokkotai*—Special Attack Units or Kamikazes—the suicide plane attacks that had replaced normal air operations. Tojo had been aware of the development of Kamikaze units in both the Army and Navy air forces, but on a purely experimental level. In October the suicide plane became the major Japanese weapon in the skies and at sea.

In November 1944, Tojo learned from an acquaintance still on active service that the Americans had established the B-29s on the Marianas Islands airfields and were bombing Iwo Jima. On November 24 came the first B-29 air raid on Tokyo from the Marianas. When Tojo read about it in the newspapers the next day, what he read was the story of the heroic exploit of one Army fighter pilot, who had bravely crashed his plane into the bomber, shearing off its right horizontal stabilizer and sending it plummeting into the sea.

So the day had come, as predicted by Admiral Yamamoto to Tojo years before, when the Americans would be bombing Japan and making matchsticks of her cities.

The war marched on. From the newspapers Tojo learned of the "heroic defense" at Lingayen Gulf on Luzon Island in January 1945, which meant that the Americans had landed on Luzon. Then he learned of the annihilation of thousands of the enemy at Manila, which meant the Americans had captured the Philippine capital.

On February 16, for Tojo it was worse. That day the Americans landed at Iwo Jima, and the same day 1500 American carrier-based aircraft assaulted the Tokyo and Yokohama areas, bombing and strafing for nine continuous hours. The American fleet had moved to within three hundred miles of the Japanese coast.

At this point the air of desperation that permeated Tokyo brought a change to Tojo's life. He had left the government in disgrace, a pariah, but the events of the preceding six months had blurred the images of the past. The Emperor, beset by would-be advisors from all sides, was trying desperately to find the best course for the nation. Tojo was recalled to service by being belatedly admitted to the society of the *jushin*, albeit reluctantly. This call was an indication that the Meiji Constitution structure of the Japanese government remained essentially unchanged. That constitution had so far survived the Army assault through the *Gumbatsu* and the Tojo assault. Still, Japan, which was a repressive state (as it always had been), had not become a fascist state with total power in the hands of a person or a party. The courts still functioned and protected the people against many of the excesses of the government. The bringing of Tojo into the *jushin* should have been a matter of form; he had been a prime minister. Now at last he was to be a member of the council of elders, no matter how inimical the Emperor and those around him now were to Tojo's way of thinking or his advice.

So as not to arouse the suspicions of the Army, where the *Gumbatsu* had reasserted control under the war ministry of Field Marshal Sugiyama, the Emperor and Marquis Kido had decided that the members of the *jushin* would not be assembled as a group, but would be consulted privately. So one by one, beginning in January 1945, they had been brought to the palace for audiences in the guise that they were simply paying their New Year's respects.

Tojo was received last of all. He, alone among the *jushin*, was confident of victory, seeming to be unable to comprehend all that had happened in recent weeks. He told the Emperor that the world was not as dark as it seemed. He predicted a falling out of the Russians and Western Allies after the collapse of Germany. He was confident that the Kwantung Army and the Korean Army could hold off the Russians in the north. He was so ignorant of the true state of naval affairs that he said that the remnants of the Imperial Navy were strong enough to protect Japanese communications lanes with China. There was no worry about China.

At home he was confident of the ability of the Japanese Army to protect their native islands from invasion. Food was short, but the people were not starving. The air raids on Japan, he said, were not nearly as serious as those inflicted on Germany by the Allies.

His advice was that Japan should hold out. For the first time he admitted that total victory probably was not possible, but a negotiated peace on favorable terms still was possible if the Emperor would be steadfast.

Twelve days after Tojo minimized the effect of American air raids on Japan, the B-29s staged the first fire raid on Tokyo. A firestorm was produced, with flames raging through the capital, burning everything before them. Whole districts were completely razed, and the Sumida River was so full of corpses it looked as if it were blocked by a log jam. The bodies rolled up on the beach in tiers. Tokyo already had become a ghost city—millions had fled—but this night enormous numbers were killed, whether one hundred thousand or two hundred thousand no one will ever know. That is because most of whatever records were made eventually were burned, and so many people already had fled Tokyo, some to be killed elsewhere, that reliable statistics could not exist.

Tojo always had held that settlement of the China conflict was the key to ending the Pacific war, and in this General Koiso agreed with Tojo, at least as regards the ultimate aim, if not the conditions. Koiso wanted to make peace with Chiang Kai-shek, which should then start the ball rolling with the other Allies. In mid-March an envoy named Miao Pin arrived from Chungking to talk peace, based on Japan's total withdrawal of troops from China. This Tojo never would have agreed to, but Koiso wanted to do it. Prince Higashikuni supported the idea, too, but it faltered because the Army was obdurate. It would give up nothing, and Foreign Minister Shigemitsu objected to "selling out" the Wang Ching-wei regime of Nanking. So the China peace plan failed, much to Koiso's chagrin.

Koiso now began struggling for power with War Minister Sugiyama, the premier demanding that he be restored to the active list of generals so he could be his own war minister, but the *Gumbatsu* was too strong for him and he failed. So Koiso resigned and thus the whole cabinet fell with him.

In this new crisis, on April 4, Tojo was called with the other *jushin* to an emergency meeting at the Palace. Prince Konoye suggested that the issue of peace be settled first. Tojo argued that the war must be prosecuted to the end. The Marquis Kido let it be known that the

Palace was losing confidence in the Army. He did not want a cabinet dominated by the military, but Tojo fought for a military cabinet.

A quarrel developed in the meeting, with Tojo warning that the Army would not permit any cabinet that it could not control. Kido retorted that the people were pretty sick of the Army. Kido wanted the premiership to go to Admiral Suzuki, a retired admiral who had had no use for the Army since they tried to assassinate him in 1936. Tojo campaigned for General Hata, who would perpetuate military dominance.

Tojo went too far and suggested that if the Emperor appointed a prime minister the Army did not like, the Army would refuse to serve. Admiral Okada, another who had nearly been killed by the Army in 1936, asked if Tojo meant that the Army would not defend the nation unless it could control it. Tojo had no answer to that. Kido said that the question was not whether the Army would cooperate with the cabinet but how much longer the people of Japan would tolerate the Army.

Tojo was finally silenced by a delayed realization of the enormity of what he had said, and everyone else at the meeting was shaken by a similar realization that what he had said about the Army probably was true. Still, the others ignored Tojo and proceeded after much discussion to persuade Admiral Suzuki to accept the post of prime minister. It was a choice welcomed by the Emperor because it meant getting rid of Army control, after having tried and failed with the Koiso-Yonai combination. That government fell because Koiso had tried to dominate it.

So Admiral Suzuki took office, with the general understanding, although no explicit instructions were given by the Emperor, that Suzuki was to end the war.

The Army could have done at this point what it had done before: prevent the formation of a government by withholding a war minister. But the words of Marshal Kido had not gone unnoticed at Army headquarters; they were a warning that the Emperor was growing dissatisfied with the Army. With problems enough, the Army was not ready for a confrontation with the Emperor, so no objection was offered even when the *Gumbatsu* realized that for the first time since the outbreak of war the Suzuki cabinet represented a break from Army control. As his war minister, Suzuki chose Gen. Korechika Anami, an old friend from the 1920s when both had served at the Imperial Palace. The Army made three demands, however, in accepting Anami. First, the cabinet would prosecute the war. Second, the cabinet would prepare for the final battle, which meant fighting in Japan itself. And third, the cabinet would work out a formula for cooperation between Army and Navy.

The anti-war advocates, whose political strength now was about equal to that of the pro-war forces, still were not ready for a confrontation any more than was the Army, so Suzuki acceded to the Army demands, at least theoretically. But Admiral Yonai, an anti-war man, remained as Navy minister. Shigenori Togo, who wanted to end the war, was foreign minister. Four of the ministers were admirals, only two were generals, and three others in the cabinet had played important roles in the 1936 incident as targeted victims when the Army had tried and failed to seize power. They had not forgotten the Army and its ways.

There was some irony in the appointment of Togo as foreign minister. He had been offered the post and had declined when Suzuki indicated that he believed the war might drag on for a while. Only when Suzuki indicated that Togo would be free to pursue a peace plan, would he accept, and then he became not only foreign minister but also minister of Greater East Asia. That overturned the decision of Tojo, made in 1942, that the Greater East Asia ministry should be controlled by the Army, not by the foreign office.

As for Tojo, the formation of the Suzuki cabinet was a complete rejection of all that he stood for; the argument with Kido showed the complete rejection of Tojo and his ideas by the Throne.

Tojo was bitter and after formation of the new cabinet he told a newspaperman that now all was lost for Japan:

"This is our Badoglio Cabinet," he said, referring to the Italian government formed after the overthrow of Mussolini in Italy—the cabinet that signed an armistice with the Allies. But nobody was listening seriously to Tojo anymore, not even his own Army colleagues, who had grown to distrust him even though their aims were the same.

So in the spring of 1945, Tojo sank back into anonymity as the war and peace forces of Japan battled for supremacy in the Imperial councils. Ultimately, when the peace forces won and Emperor Hirohito defied the Army to force the surrender of Japan, no one bothered to ask Tojo what he thought of that development.

21

Ordeal

In the summer of 1945 the B-29s struck Tokyo repeatedly, always with firebombs now, and in one of the raids Tojo's little studio house was destroyed by the flames. Thereafter he urged Katsuko and the children to leave the capital for a safer place. A little wistfully he said he could not go himself:

"I have to remain here. The Emperor may call on me."

How forlorn a hope. There was no one the Emperor was less likely to call upon in that summer of 1945, for Tojo represented the war party, and peace was in the air. Yet even now the Army was resisting the trend with every fiber. The Emperor had been systematically excluded from open participation in the Imperial Conferences since the late 1930s when he took the Marquis Kido's advice that it would be unseemly for him to speak. But now Hirohito insisted on a change, and no one could resist him. He could convene special sessions of the Imperial Conference, and attend if he wished. Through the Marquis Kido he could make his views known.

On June 6 the Supreme Council, which was the now capsulized War Cabinet, considered new proposals by the Army to continue the war. The Army's supporting documents were full of statistics all of which showed the virtual impossibility of persevering, but the Army was insistent. Willpower would win the war, said the generals. There must be no surrender, said the *Gumbatsu*.

In that environment of determined patriotism no one at the meeting dared say no, and so the next day at an Imperial Conference the announcement was made that the Army plan had been accepted: all Japan was prepared to fight to the death. But hours later at another Supreme Council meeting Foreign Minister Togo pointed out that Japan's chances of negotiating a peace of any sort were reduced every day. And so on June 8, for the first time since the war began, the findings of the Imperial Conference included caveat, as well as the usual army braggadocio about fighting to win to the end: "It behooves us to seize any opportunity that may occur of conducting the war under more favorable circumstances. Suitable measures should be devised that can actually be pursued, for instance in China and Russia." For "conducting the war under more favorable circumstances" read: finding a way to end the war.

The cause of the peace-seekers in the cabinet was set back alarmingly on July 26 when the Allies released the findings of their Potsdam Conference. They called for the unconditional surrender of all the Japanese armed forces. "The alternative for Japan," the communiqué threatened, "is prompt and utter destruction."

The Japanese generals rejoiced, but in such an atmosphere the Emperor had no time or thought for General Tojo, who represented precisely the "fight to the death" point of view.

After the first atomic bomb was dropped on Hiroshima, a captured American pilot (who knew nothing about the subject) suggested that Tokyo might be next on the atomic list. Tojo believed that. Now the war had come to be a matter of survival, he told his wife. "Our ancestors must have lived in caves at one time. So can we." He was prepared to live underground for months, and come out during the daylight hours to dig sweet potatoes and forage for food.

"That way we will win," he said.

The family had a friend in the Tokyo suburb of Ome, in the mountain country to the north, and so they packed up their belongings, sent some ahead, and prepared to close the Tokyo house. But before they could move they were overtaken by events. The second atomic bomb was dropped on Nagasaki, and the Soviets entered the war and began rolling through Manchuria and Korea. They encountered Kwantung and Korean armies that had both been depleted for months by transfer of their troops to the southern fighting zones and to Taiwan.

As the Tojo family prepared to move north, suddenly General Tojo was summoned to the Imperial Palace. The Imperial Conference had met on the night of August 9, after the second atomic bomb had been dropped on Nagasaki. At that conference, for the first time the civilians and military men who opposed the war had spoken out. Yet when the conference deadlocked on the subject of war or surrender, Emperor Hirohito then decided that Japan would capitulate. The Army men pleaded with him, on hands and knees, but his mind was made up. After the decision was taken and the conference ended, Hirohito called the *jushin* together as a courtesy to inform them, not to seek their advice.

General Tojo wanted to argue but was cut off with the reminder that one did not question an Imperial decision. So he listened and went home.

That was the last contact General Tojo had with the Japanese government, and it might have been his last appearance as a public person had matters worked out a little differently.

In the next few days events began to move with great rapidity, although Tojo knew nothing more about them than he had been told at the last meeting of the *jushin*. On August 13 the word of the coming surrender had permeated Imperial Army Headquarters and a group of young officers, including Tojo's son-in-law Maj. Hidemasa Koga, decided to stop the Emperor from surrendering. Koga was an important link in the plot because he was an officer of the Imperial Guards Division which protected the Emperor, and thus had access to the Imperial Palace. That day he appeared briefly at the Tojo house and saw Tojo's wife for the last time. He did not see the general, who was busy with a guest. Then Koga rushed off on his motorcycle to busy himself with the details of the plot.

When Tojo emerged from his study he discovered that his son-in-law had been at the house and had spoken to daughter Makie about going to Kyushu with the child. Koga had made sure that she had locks of his hair and nail clippings, from which Tojo knew that Koga was up to something that might end in his death. He got a car and went to the war office at Ichigaya. There he discovered what was happening. He found Major Koga and spent hours talking to him, getting him to promise that he would remain cool, although the plot was thickening every hour. When Tojo arrived at home long after dark that evening, he told his wife and daughter that Koga had made such promises.

But all Tojo's talk was to no avail, for the other young officers, red-faced and inside white with rage, were shouting for action. That meant anything up to and including the deposition of Emperor Hirohito and his replacement on the throne by one of his brothers or another prince.

The rebels seized the palace, and announced that they had the Emperor a prisoner within. But they could not find what they sought, the recording of the radio broadcast the Emperor had made to announce the surrender of Japan.

The palace guard division was summoned, and the rebellion petered out in the small hours of August 15. Major Koga, with many others, committed suicide after having indulged in an orgy of bloodletting that included another search for Admiral Suzuki, whom members of their faction had failed to murder in 1936 and now failed to murder again.

At noon on August 15 word was received at the Tojo house of Koga's death by suicide; the message arrived shortly after they had listened to the surrender broadcast. Tojo, who knew what had been coming, seemed unmoved. He told his daughter to prepare herself to receive the body of her husband, and that afternoon, as Koga's friends arrived in twos and threes, Tojo talked to some of them. Several wanted to do something to make a final stand in the war, but he counselled them to abide by the Emperor's wishes and "eat stones" as the Army now had to do.

Now came the suicides, some of them prompted by grief at the turn of events, such as that of General Anami, the new war minister; some, such as that of Field Marshal Sugiyama, prompted by the expectation of being tried and executed by the enemy for war crimes. Those indictments would include the killing of the Doolittle fliers and thousands of the prisoners of war from Malaya and the Dutch East Indies. General Shirokura, who had run the *Kempeitai* for Tojo for so long, killed himself apparently to avoid the punishment he was certain to receive for his many crimes.

General Tojo knew, of course, that he was at the top of the Allied list for some sort of retribution, although he did not know quite what it would be. He continued to work in his garden and to wait. There was nothing else to do but commit suicide, and he was not inclined to do that, at least not until he could see how the wind would blow. He did take the precaution of having his neighbor, Dr. Suzuki, show him the location of his heart, which indicated that he would use a pistol rather than a traditional samurai short sword to commit *seppuku* should the time arrive. On one of the occasions when he discussed the possibilities with his wife he spoke like a samurai of old: "My life does not matter," he said. "A military man must always be prepared to die."

One reason that Tojo hung onto life was a sense of obligation. Sometimes he would talk about the war and he would say that he took the complete responsibility for it. Of course it was not quite true. As one Japanese businessman said later, "We were all in it together," and that was indeed true—all, from Emperor Hirohito, who made no real move to stop the Army's drive to war after the rebellion of 1936. But the Emperor's sin, if it was one, was to fail to act, not in any action he took. Tojo and the other generals acted; the matters of treatment of enemy civilian populations and war prisoners lay at their doors.

Tojo's real commitment was to divert trouble from the Emperor if

he could do so. At one point he proposed to issue a statement
acknowledging his responsibility for the war. This came about in
connection with an interview with General Shimomura, who had
assumed the job of minister of war after General Anami committed
suicide in the wake of the failed August rebellion against the Emperor.
When Shimomura asked Tojo what his intentions for the future were,
Tojo replied that he would make a statement of responsibility for Gen.
Douglas MacArthur, the Supreme Commander of Allied Forces. But,
he said, he did not want to go into the dock and be judged by his
enemies in "victor's justice."

There was talk that the government ought to get Tojo out of Tokyo
and into some isolated place where he would not arouse any attention.
Incredibly, some believed that thus the Allies might forget about the
question of overall responsibility for the war. There was also the
possibility of Tojo's assassination for permitting the defeat of Japan,
and he received such threats from time to time.

Tojo's first contact with the Americans came when the press de-
scended on him a few days after the occupation began. The press
arrived and Tojo emerged from the garden, where he had been working
in the sun, wearing shorts and a shirt. They met in the garden and sat
in ceramic chairs. Tojo offered the reporters cigarettes and chain-
smoked himself all during the interview.

The Allied reporters fired questions, but Tojo fielded them by asserting that he was nothing but a defeated general who had now become a
simple farmer. He knew nothing about politics or current affairs. He
believed that Japan's war had been a just war, he said, but he did not
expect them to believe that.

He stated then that he accepted responsibility for the war. When the
reporters asked if that meant he was a war criminal he replied that
whether or not one was a war criminal depended on whether one was
a winner or a loser.

Eventually the reporters went away. But Tojo knew that he had not
seen the end of the Allied interest. He made his will. He asked that his
funeral be held in his native Kyushu. He wrote his political will, too,
accepting responsibility for the war, and particularly for the defeat of
Japan.

Then he waited.

He had not long to wait.

The next day the family had just finished luncheon and Tojo had
retired to his study when a half-dozen American vehicles full of
military policemen surrounded the house. Tojo heard the commotion

and was told what was happening. He guessed that the Americans had come for him.

He opened the window and asked if anyone spoke Japanese. One man stepped forward and they began to talk. Why were they there? Tojo asked. They had come to take him, they said. Did they have a warrant for his arrest?

Yes, they said.

Tojo closed the window, and recalling his conversation with General Shimomura, he decided that the time for action had come. From the desk drawer he extracted a pistol, and he aimed at his heart and fired.

Scarcely had the reverberation died when the military policemen were in the house. They broke down the door to the study. On the desk was a letter in Japanese: Tojo's final statement. In it he apologized to the Emperor for not winning the war, and for the casualties caused, but he stood firm in his belief in the Greater East Asia Co-prosperity Sphere and the need to throw the white man out of Asia, which was what his war was all about. (See Appendix C.)

They found Tojo in his chair, bleeding. A Japanese doctor was called from next door. He said the case was hopeless (because he knew that was what Tojo wanted). But the Americans wanted victor's justice. An American army doctor arrived and administered a transfusion of American blood. Tojo was rushed to an American army hospital, where it was discovered that Tojo's aim had been a little off. He had missed his heart by a fraction of an inch. The American medical treatment saved him, and he was prepared by his enemies to face trial and the inevitable execution that he fully expected.

22

The Last Battle

So General Tojo recovered from the wound so near his heart, and after he was pronounced fit to leave the American military hospital he was imprisoned first at Omori, which had been a Japanese prison camp for Allied prisoners of war, and then at Sugamo Prison, one of the few buildings still standing in the heart of Tokyo.

His last battle was to be fought against his enemies, on Japanese soil, as he had wished.

Neither in Tojo's mind, nor in that of any thinking person, could there have been any doubt as to the outcome. The Japanese had attacked first, and they had lost the war. Some person had to become the symbol against whom the enemies of Japan could vent their rage. In the Western public mind that symbol had long been the Japanese Emperor. But General MacArthur had decided that the Emperor, as symbol of a system that was bowing to MacArthur's new order, was more valuable to the Allied cause than would be an Emperor on trial.

When Tojo was transferred to Sugamo Prison on December 8, 1945, he found himself surrounded by old associates. Since the surrender the Allies had been rounding up people they had tabbed as war criminals. These included the Marquis Kido; General Araki, the proponent of the Imperial Way; generals Doihara and Itagaki from the Mukden days; General Matsui, in charge of the China force at the time of the Rape of Nanking; General Umezu; Yosuke Matsuoka; and a number of others, including Koki Hiroka. As noted, Field Marshal Sugiyama had committed suicide. So had Prince Konoye; Adm. Takejiro Ohnishi, the originator of the Kamikazes; and Adm. Matome Ugaki, in charge of the air defenses of the home islands, who had sent hundreds of young men to their deaths at Okinawa in their suicide planes. But these officers along with many others had committed suicide for reasons of honor and to avoid that victor's justice. Prince Konoye, for example, killed himself on the night before he was scheduled to report to Sugamo Prison.

At Sugamo Prison one of the guards was Sgt. Sohei Yamate, a Hawaii-born Nisei who had served through most of the war in the U.S. Army in the China-Burma-India theater as interpreter and interrogator of Japanese POWs.

Here is Sergeant Yamate's story:

It was in early October of 1945, that I was assigned to Sugamo Prison along with a fellow named Okamoto. During an interview with Lt. George Sonoda, the assignment officer, we were questioned primarily on our experiences in China and about the Japanese POWs we had encountered. The POWs were mostly stragglers from the Chikian Battle. Okamoto and I were picked to go to Sugamo Prison, as a result of the interviews.

The prison was near the Ikebukuro Train Station. It was the only large building left standing in the area. The surroundings were bleak and except for an occasional smokestack here and there, the area had been completely devastated. Our incendiary bombs had done a good job.

Sugamo Prison, being intact, with some housekeeping, was readied for occupancy. Our quarters were right there in the prison grounds, probably the former guards' billet. Later, we moved outside the prison into newly constructed quonset huts.

Since the prison was ready for "guests," the war criminals were quickly brought in. Our job was to escort the prisoners through the gate into the courtyard and on to the processing room. In this room we did fingerprinting and recorded the routine information: name, address, next of kin, general medical condition, et cetera. After us, the medical group under Dr. Lloyd Edwards took over, followed by a delousing treatment. The prisoners were physically very clean but we couldn't take any chances. The cells were assigned according to their status on the upcoming trials. The top echelon had individual cells.

Our work was easy but with only Okamoto and I on duty we could not goof off or go on leave to see the country. In late December, replacements came from the States and they all outranked us, so we were still stuck.

At first the prisoners had been instructed to report to Sugamo Prison by a certain date, and to our surprise, they all reported as scheduled. One day, we were told that Prince Konoye was coming in the next day. That night the prince committed suicide. After that incident, the other war criminals were no longer notified as to their reporting dates. The military authorities quietly picked them up and brought them in.

The ambassador to Italy, Shiratori, was brought in, and I believe he was one of the people involved in the Germany, Italy, and Japan pact. The ambassador to Germany, Oshima, was also in Sugamo. Of all the war criminals, he was the most arrogant. I heard later that some of our boys assigned to General Eisenhower's headquarters tapped in on his line in Germany and obtained some valuable information.

The Marquis Kido, one of the closest persons to the Emperor, was brought in. I had heard about him, and after the processing asked him some questions concerning the Emperor. I got the impression that the Emperor was very much aware of what was going on in the war. The Marquis had kept him fully informed. He told us that Japan had sent diplomats to Russia in the spring of 1945 to have the Russians help Japan negotiate for peace. He said the Russians would not acknowledge the diplomats so they knew that Russia was involved with the Allies.

Anyway, here was the Marquis in Sugamo. I thought maybe the Emperor might be coming in. We knew about General MacArthur's decree that the Emperor was to keep his throne. The rumor mill worked overtime saying that the Emperor might be coming in to Sugamo. I would have enjoyed processing the "Big One."

When General Homma arrived at Sugamo Prison, I was surprised at his height. He was about 6 feet tall, and was personally greeted ty the prison commander, Colonel Hardy. I was told by the colonel that he and the general had known each other before the war. The general had attended Oxford University and spoke fluent English. Talking to the general was easy, he was very amiable. General Homma was held responsible for the Bataan Death March and all the actions of his men. He was taken from Sugamo to the Philippines, found guilty, and sentenced to death by hanging.

General Hideki Tojo came to the prison with some fanfare. The press and the photographers were there. He had recovered from a botched job of trying to commit suicide. He had used a .32-calibre pistol and missed his heart. As he was brought to the gate I met him and escorted him in to the processing room. He was only 5 feet tall. I saw his wound and I also saw a beaten man. He did as he was told.

His wife and children came to visit him. The colonel instructed me to sit in on the visitation and to carefully check that no contraband was passed on. There was some fear of suicide attempts. I asked that no physical contact take place. We sat at a long table with several chairs. General Tojo sat on one end, his wife and children on the other end, I sat in the middle. They could say anything. There were no restrictions on the number of visits. If there were any, I was not aware of them.

I still remember telling the general not to commit suicide because the colonel would hold me responsible. This was a private matter between Tojo and myself. He remarked to me on several occasions, "Don't worry,

Sergeant, I won't commit suicide." Tojo also commented that he would take full responsibility for the war. The upcoming war crimes trial, he declared, was one of victor over loser.

I remember not being too impressed or awed by the former status of each war criminal nor who they were. I have always believed that a human being was no better or worse than me. We had won the war and they were our prisoners.

The "Class A War Criminal suspects" were officially called "suspects," giving lip-service to the Anglo-Saxon adage of innocence presumed by law. That presumption was not made by their jailers and others. The prisoners were interrogated several times as the prosecution built its case.

Books have been written about the war crimes trials, and they seem scarcely germane here. Tojo knew that his enemies were going to convict him of war crimes and kill him. He expected such a death ever since he had failed in his suicide attempt and he was ready for it. He did engage in argument from time to time with the chief prosecutor Joseph Keenan, but he knew very well that it was useless. His conviction was preordained by the system.

As to the treatment of Allied civilians and prisoners of war, which was a major factor in his indictment, he said that the Japanese and the rest of the world had different views on the subject. This was true. The Japanese had never signed the Geneva Convention on treatment of POWs, although the government, at the outset of war, had indicated it intended to abide by that convention. It had not. Who was to blame? As head of the government, Tojo was the first selected. He denied knowing anything about mistreatment, which had to be a lie. But it was a lie very common in Japan in those days, as the enthusiastic superpatriots of the past suddenly realized that the time had come to pay for their excesses.

One reason for the trial, which was held openly so the Japanese public could attend, was to exhibit to the Japanese those excesses of their leaders. But in this the war crimes trials failed. The Japanese soon lost interest in the proceedings. They, too, knew how the trials would end so there was no suspense; meanwhile the problem of daily living, of securing food and fuel, was very real.

A spark of interest was kindled on December 28, 1947, when General Tojo took the witness stand. His testimony strung out over four days. He took full responsibility for the war, but he claimed the war was forced on Japan by British and American encirclement.

The Allied case was laid out: brutal surprise attack; unjust war; mistreatment of prisoners, such as the Doolittle fliers; mistreatment of civilians; and after-battle atrocities. Tojo took all or partial responsibility for it all. After the one slip noted earlier, he tried to absolve the Emperor of responsibility, saying that Hirohito "had no free choice in the governmental structure," which was true. Still, as noted from time to time, Hirohito had kicked over the traces, but always over the pleading figures of advisors such as Prince Saionji and the Marquis Kido, whose behavior in court now was less than admirable as he tried to absolve himself of guilt. For among all Hirohito's advisors Kido was the one who kept telling him he must not disturb matters by making his own views known, and he must not interfere with the processes by which the military junta—the *Gumbatsu*—manipulated the Japanese government.

In the end Tojo did have his say about the proceedings: "Never at any time did I conceive that the waging of this war would or could be challenged by the victors as an international crime, or that regularly constituted officials of the vanquished nations would be charged individually as criminals under any recognized international law or under alleged violations of treaties between nations. I feel that I did no wrong. I feel that I did what was right and true."

Of course it made no difference, as Tojo knew it would not. The court proceedings ended in April 1948. Seven months elapsed, during which Tojo and the others remained in prison. Some died, such as Yosuke Matsuoka and Admiral Nagano. Several of the others were sentenced to life imprisonment, and others to lesser prison terms. But generals Tojo, Doihara, Itagaki, Kimura, Muto, Yamashita, Homma, and Matsui, and former prime minister Koki Hirota, the only civilian so sentenced, were all to die by hanging.

The verdict on Tojo was rendered on November 11, 1948:

Tojo became Chief of Staff of the Kwantung Army in June 1937, and thereafter was associated with the conspirators in principle in almost all of their activities. He planned and prepared for an attack on the USSR; he recommended a further onset in China in order to free the Japanese Army from anxiety about its rear in the projected attack on the USSR; he helped organize Manchuria as a base for the attack. Never at any time thereafter did he abandon the intention to launch such an attack if a favorable chance should occur.

He became Minister of War in July 1940, and thereafter his history is largely the history of the successive steps by which the conspirators planned and waged wars of aggression against Japan's neighbors, for he was the principal in the making of plans and the waging of wars. He advocated and furthered the aims of the conspiracy with ability, resolution, and persistency.

He became Prime Minister in October 1941, and continued in office until July 1944. As war minister and prime minister he consistently supported the policy of conquering the National Government of China, of developing the resources of China on Japan's behalf, and of retaining Japanese troops in China to safeguard for Japan the results of December 7, 1941 [Pearl Harbor]. His attitude was that Japan must secure terms which would preserve for her the fruits of her aggression against China, and which would conduce to the establishment of Japan's domination of East Asia and the Southern areas.

All his influence was thrown into support of that policy. The importance of the leading part he played in securing the decision to go to war in support of that policy cannot be overestimated. He bears the major responsibility for Japan's criminal attacks on her neighbors. In this trial he defended all these attacks with hardihood, alleging that they were legitimate measures of self-defense. We have dealt with that plea. It is wholly unfounded.

Then the court announced the victor's penalty on the vanquished for his crimes. The penalty was death by hanging—to a Japanese a particularly unpleasant form of execution.

After that it was a question of waiting while Tojo's associates exhausted their pleas.

Epilogue

Many months after the execution of Tojo and the other six major war criminals at that Christmastime, 1948, in a little park very near the site of Sugamo Prison, admirers of Tojo and the others who had been executed placed a marker to commemorate their lives and death. The inescapable inference is that this was a political act of defiance of the American victors. It was chiseled into the back of a huge boulder, in one corner of the park, with the inscription on the inside of the boulder, not to be seen from the concrete walkway. One really had to know that the memorial marker was there to find it. Everyone in Japan soon knew. A few years after the event Sugamo Prison was torn down and on the site was erected the 60-story skyscraper known as Sunshine 60. Today that huge building towers over the little park where General Tojo is commemorated.

There is another marker, too, a joint memorial to the seven who were executed, erected atop Sanganesan Hill at Hazu in Aichi Prefecture by right-wing sympathizers who still believed in the mission of Japan to liberate Asia from the white man and to lead Asians to greater gory. The inscription reads "The Tomb of Seven Martyrs." It was written by Dr. Ichiro Kiyose, in 1960 the President of the House of Councillors of the Diet, and at the time of the war crimes trials a member of the Japanese defense counsel staff.

As for Tojo's last will and testament to the people of Japan, it was taken from him by his American jailers, who wanted no political repercussions from the executions. Tojo had spent his last two weeks of his life writing this testament. Because he correctly expected the document to be impounded by the Americans, he spent many hours dictating his thoughts to Buddhist Priest Hanayama, who later made that version public through the newspapers. But the publication caused

223

no stir, for there was nothing in Tojo's political testament that he had not said before: the warning against the danger of Communism, praise for the Emperor and defense of the Imperial Way, criticism of the Americans for letting Communism envelop China, criticism of the Americans for staging the war crimes trials, prediction that America and the USSR would soon be at war with each other, and criticism of the disarmament of Japan under the new constitution.

The Tojo testament disappeared into the maw of the American occupation bureaucracy, and there was lost or misplaced, for in 1991 the American National Archives conducted a search, in my behalf, for the document, to no avail. No trace of it was to be found.

By that time no one in Japan cared, with the exception of a small minority of members of various right-wing superpatriotic organizations that still existed, although their activities were limited and their influence on Japanese affairs was nil.

The Socialists and others in Japan still worry lest the right-wing once more become ascendant, with all its old hopes of revivifying the Imperial Way and the concept of "Great Japan." But to the vast majority of Japanese people this is all a myth, as is the history of the 1930s and first half of the 1940s, a myth that has no relationship to a modern Japan, where the concepts of disarmament and peace are very strong, and the name of Hideki Tojo is anything but a household word. Indeed it is scarcely recognized by three new generations of Japanese.

Appendix A

The following Imperial Rescript, issued on December 8, 1941, was reprinted on the eighth day of each month until September 1945, in every newspaper in Japan, to remind the people of Japan of the reasons for their war.

IMPERIAL RESCRIPT

We, by grace of heaven, Emperor of Japan, seated on the Throne of a line unbroken for ages eternal, enjoin upon ye, Our loyal and brave subjects:

We hereby declare War on the United States of America and the British Empire. The men and officers of Our Army and Navy shall do their utmost in prosecuting the war. Our public servants of various departments shall perform faithfully and diligently their respective duties; the entire nation with a united will shall mobilize their total strength so that nothing will miscarry in the attainment of Our war aims.

To insure the stability of East Asia and to contribute to world peace is the far-sighted policy which was formulated by Our Great Illustrious Imperial Grandsire and Our Great Imperial Sire succeeding Him, and which We lay constantly to heart. To cultivate friendship among nations and to enjoy prosperity in common with all nations, has always been the guiding principle of Our Empire's foreign policy. It has been truly unavoidable and far from Our wishes that Our Empire has been brought to cross swords with America and Britain. More than four years have passed since China, failing to comprehend the true intentions of Our Empire, and recklessly courting trouble, disturbed the peace of East Asia and compelled Our Empire to take up arms. Although there has been reestablished the National Government of China, with which Japan had effected neighborly intercourse and cooperation, the regime which has survived at Chungking, relying upon American and British protection, still continues its fratricidal opposition. Eager for the realization of their inordinate ambition to dominate the Orient, both America and Britain, giving support to the Chungking regime, have aggravated the disturbances in East Asia. Moreover these two Powers, inducing other countries to follow suit, increased military preparations on all sides of Our Empire to challenge Us. They have obstructed by every means Our peaceful commerce and finally resorted to a direct severance of economic relations, menacing gravely the existence of Our Empire. Patiently have We waited and long have We endured, in the hope that Our government might retrieve the situation in peace. But Our adversaries, showing not the least spirit of conciliation, have unduly delayed a settlement; and in the meantime they have intensified the economic and political pressure to compel thereby Our Empire to submission. This trend of affairs, would, if left unchecked, not only nullify Our Emperor's efforts of many years for the sake of the stabilization of East Asia, but also endanger the very existence of Our nation. The situation being such as it is, Our Empire, for its existence and self-defense, has no other recourse but to appeal to arms and to crush every obstacle in its path.

The hallowed spirits of Our Imperial Ancestors guarding Us from above, We rely upon the loyalty and courage of Our subjects in Our confident expectation that the task bequeathed by Our forefathers will be carried forward and that the sources of evil will be speedily eradicated and an enduring peace immutably established in East Asia, preserving thereby the glory of Our Empire.

Hirohito
(Imperial Seal)

The 8th day of the 12th month
of the 16th year of Showa.

Appendix B

The Imperial Rescript granted by Emperor Hirohito on August 14, 1945, officially ending the war for Japan by surrender:

To Our good and loyal subjects

After pondering deeply the general conditions of the world and the actual conditions obtaining in Our Empire today, We have decided to effect a settlement of the present situation by resorting to an extraordinary measure.

We have ordered Our Government to communicate to the Government of the United States, Great Britain, China and the Soviet Union that Our Empire accepts the provisions of their Joint Declaration.

To strive for the common prosperity and happiness of all nations as well as the security and well-being of Our subjects is the solemn obligation which has been handed down by Our Imperial Ancestors and which We lay close to heart. Indeed, We declared war on America and Britain out of Our sincere desire to assure Japan's self-preservation and the stabilization of East Asia, it being far from Our thought either to infringe upon the sovereignty of other nations or to embark upon territorial aggrandizement. But now the war has lasted for nearly four years. Despite the best that has been done by everyone—the gallant fighting of military and naval forces, the diligence and assiduity of Our servants of the State and the devoted service of Our one hundred million people, the war situation has developed not necessarily to Japan's advantage, while the general trends of the world have all turned against her interest. Moreover the enemy has begun to employ a new and most cruel bomb, the power of which to do damage is indeed incalculable, taking the toll of many innocent lives. Should We continue to fight it would not only result in the ultimate collapse and obliteration of the Japanese nation, but also it would lead to the total extinction of human civilization. Such being the case how are We to save the millions of Our subjects or to atone Ourselves before the hallowed spirits of Our Imperial Ancestors? This is the reason why We have ordered the acceptance of the Joint Declaration of the Powers.

We cannot but express the deepest sense of regret to our Allied nations of East Asia, who have consistently cooperated with the Empire towards the emancipation of East Asia. The thought of those officers and men, as well as others, who have fallen on the fields of battle, those who died at their posts of duty, or those who met with untimely death and all their bereaved families pains Our heart night and day. The welfare of the wounded and the war sufferers and those who have lost their home and livelihood are the objects of Our profound solicitude. The hardships and suffering to which Our nation is to be subjected hereafter will certainly be great. We are keenly aware of the inmost feelings of all ye, Our subjects. However, it is according to the dictate of time and fate that We have resolved to pave the way for a grand peace for all the generations to come by enduring the unendurable and suffering what is insufferable.

Having been able to safeguard and maintain the structure of the Imperial State, We are always with ye, Our good and loyal subjects, relying upon your sincerity and integrity. Beware most strictly of any outbursts of emotion which may engender needless complications or any fraternal contention and strife which may create confusion, lead ye astray and cause ye to lose the confidence of the world. Let the entire nation continue as one family from generation to generation, ever firm in its faith of the imperishableness of its divine land and mindful of its heavy burden of responsibilities, and the long road before it. Unite your total strength to be devoted to the construction for the future. Cultivate the ways of rectitude, foster nobility of spirit, and work with resolution so as ye may enhance the innate glory of the Imperial State and keep pace with the progress of the world.

Imperial Sign (Manual)
Imperial Seal

The 14th day of the 8th month
of the 20th year of Showa.

Appendix C

TRANSLATION OF FINAL STATEMENT OF
HIDEKI TOJO

1. I express my deepest apologies to the boundless Imperial benevolence.

I fervently hope for the safety of the Imperial Household and for national prosperity.

2. The Greater East Asia War, as circumstances have now developed, has come to an inglorious conclusion. Since I cannot bear the knowledge that I have caused his Majesty deep anxiety and have piled up a countless number of the bodies of his faithful subjects, and further, that I have dishonored our glorious history by failing to attain the objectives of the war, and since I feel my deep responsibility as a bearer of public trust at the time of the opening of the war, I have determined to take my life in expiation. I feel also that in this way I may pay my debt to the officers and men who died in many battles, and their families.

3. I, who have received special favors from the Emperor, feel that I can in no way atone for the injury sustained by the national dignity in being subjected to the disgrace of control by enemy nations. This will have a detrimental effect on the national soul. I feel that the future will determine the right course for the Empire. I do not believe that it will be determined by the victory. Beyond the surrender demands, Japan must find her own way.

4. Although we have been defeated in war, I for one believe in the rightness, in the light of all history, of the concept of the Greater East Asia War. The spiritual vitality of our divine state can never be taken from us. I believe that as long as the Imperial Household exists in its solemn glory, it will be nourished by the unflagging loyalty of the people, and our Imperial Nation will return to prosperity.

5. Since, despite the numerous difficulties that beset the future course of the Empire, the efforts of our millions of people during this period will surely preserve the national policy, both in name and in fact, I do not abandon my

hope that the eternal glory of the Empire will be accomplished. Looking toward the Imperial Palace from afar, I pray for the health and long life of His Imperial Majesty and I am determined to devote the life of my spirit to the protection of the welfare and prosperity of the nation.

10 September 1945   His Excellency the Former Prime Minister
                                Army General; Court Rank—Junior Grade,
                                Second Class; Order of Merit, First Class;
                                Order of the Golden Kite, Second Class.
                                        Tojo Hideki

Postscript: I feel a deep gratitude to the peoples of Greater East Asia who have given their fullest cooperation in the task of freeing Greater East Asia, and I regret that we were not able, because of the final result of the war, to attain our objectives. I will not abandon my prayers for their lasting well-being.

Notes and Acknowledgments

As so many times before I am indebted to my friend Seiichi Soeda of the Japan Foreign Press Center for paving the way for me to see people and to acquire research materials for this book. The Tojo family is very sensitive to outside probings into their personal affairs, and although Mr. Soeda tried diligently he was unable to get Tojo's surviving son to agree to an interview. I am indebted, too, to Kenji Koyama of the Japanese Defense Agency War History Room for the opportunity to peruse his files for materials about Tojo in the Manchuria period and earlier, when Tojo was not yet a general and not yet the focus of much attention outside the ranks of the Army. Adm. Zenshiro Hoshino, who knew Tojo through associations at the Imperial Palace, discussed that general with me, and Tojo's department in the last days of World War II when peace was on the Emperor's mind and the Army was stoutly resisting any course but a battle to the death.

Librarians at the Diet's National Library, the library of International House of Japan, the Library of Congress, the library of the Foreign Correspondents Club of Japan, and of the Japan Foreign Press Center all lent me books or gave me access to them. I am indebted to Hiroko Hattori of Tokyo for editing and translations and to Olga Grunzit-Hoyt for editing the manuscript.

1. SOLDIER TO POLITICIAN

Tojo's role in Japanese politics and World War II is not very well understood in the West because the old Japanese system under the Meiji Constitution is similarly not understood. During World War II it was easy to characterize Hitler and Mussolini, who were dictators, unalloyed, but the Japanese situation then makes such a characterization not fully apt for Tojo. He was a dictator for only a very short time in 1944; his ascendency here was resisted by all concerned, and ultimately failed—the proof of that his fall from grace and power on July 18, 1944. The rest of the time, from October 18, 1941 until July

231

18, 1944, he was only one of the generals of the *gumbatsu*, the military oligarchy that had seized power in Japan in 1936. True, he rose steadily in that cabal, ruthlessly dispersing his enemies, but even at the end of his tenure he was not in absolute control of the Army or the nation. One of the best studies of Tojo's place in the Japanese scheme of things during the war is Ben-Ami Shillony's *Politics and Culture in Wartime Japan*, Oxford University Press, 1981. As his book's title reflects, he explores the avenues of culture and politics, not the military, and his picture supplements that of the more conventional images of Tojo as the wartime premier and war minister.

2. POLITICIAN-SOLDIER

When General Tojo rose from chief of the *Kempeitai* in the quasi-independent Kwantung Army to chief of staff of that same command, the officers of that force heaved sighs of relief. As head of the police the meticulous Tojo had dossiers on every one of them—reports that ranged from their sexual and drinking habits to their military deportment and political views if any. When Tojo was advanced the Emperor, too, felt relief because for the first time the Kwantung Army was coming under control of Army Headquarters in Tokyo. But what the Emperor did not then know, and soon became apparent, was that the Kwantung Army was not as recalcitrant as it had seemed, and that all along the generals had manipulated that army as a weapon in their struggle for control of Japan. In 1935 and 1936 Emperor Hirohito began to get a glimpse of this manipulation when the Tianjin Garrison and the Kwantung Army apparently whipsawed Tokyo in their drives for more power. Actually all this was orchestrated, and when the "young officers" rebelled in 1936 there was no rebellion in the forces in China. They were carefully held under control.

Hirohito appointed Koki Hirota as prime minister after the February 26, 1936 incident. He enjoined Hirota to safeguard the Japanese nobility, as Hirota biographer Saburo Shiroyama reported. Later the Emperor demanded an enormous sum for the Army and Navy budgets, much to Hirota's distress. It was obvious, then, in 1936 that the Army was in control of Japan.

The Lukouchiao (Marco Polo Bridge) incident has been reported in many books in many ways; I used the Boei official history of the war in China, but also Hsu Longhsuen and Chang Mingkai's *History of the Sino-Japanese War*, published by Chungwu of Taipei in 1971.

For material about Tojo's march into Inner Mongolia (which was scarce) I used *The Japanese Army in North China* by Lincoln Li published by Oxford University Press, Tokyo, in 1975. The Konoye biography and his diary were useful in putting the prince's premiership into perspective.

3. WAR MINISTER

I used the Sugiyama memo and the Konoye diary in the beginning of this chapter—also the Butow and Browne books about Tojo. The *Asahi Shimbun*, the *Mainichi Shimbun*, and the *Japan Times* carried reports of Tojo's activities in the Diet as war minister. The Ike book on the Liaison Conferences was also helpful here.

4. THE ABCD OF PARANOIA

A reading of Joyce Lebra's book on the Greater East Asia Co-prosperity Sphere is a good beginning for a study of the Japanese feeling that they were surrounded by the Western powers who intended to reduce their nation to the sort of colonial possession that China and India had become.

A study of the Versailles Treaty and the discussions that led to it will give some indication of the resentments fostered in China and Japan by the treaty, which must be listed as a cause of the Sino-Japanese and Pacific wars. A study of the U.S. State Department archives for this whole 1940–41 period reveals that the American position vis-à-vis Japan was continually hardening. Secretary Hull, in particular, in the tone of his conversations with the Japanese, could not refrain from letting show the fact that he was privy to the Japanese secret diplomatic messages between their Washington embassy and Tokyo. Also, as noted, Hull's personal antipathy to Foreign Minister Yosuke Matsuoka was impossible to conceal. These were important and generally overlooked mileposts on the road to war.

5. THE DECLINE AND FALL OF PRINCE KONOYE

The story of the Emperor's encounter with General Sugiyama comes from many sources: *Fifty Years of Light and Dark: The Hirohito Era*, by the editors of *Mainichi Shimbun*; the Kido diary; and my own biography of Hirohito published by Praeger in 1992. The reports of the Imperial conferences come from my *Japan's War*, published by McGraw-Hill in 1987. The American diplomatic record tells the story of the failing Japanese-American negotiations. The selection of Tojo to lead the cabinet, as Hirohito told Terasaki years later, was dictated by necessity. It was obvious to the Emperor that only a military man would be accepted by the Army, and Hirohito felt that he could trust Tojo, alone among the generals, to do the Throne's bidding. The choice of Tojo, then, was a desperate last grab for peace.

6. THE RISE OF TOJO

The Butow and Shillony books were important to this chapter. Japanese newspapers of November 17 and 18 were valuable for the reports from the Diet and to reflect the mood of the country. The report of the cabinet decision for war comes from Butow's book.

7. EASY VICTORIES

Much of this material comes from *Tojo Naikaku Sori Daijin Kimitsu Kiroku, Tojo Hideki*, by Takashi Ito, et al. *(Tojo's Secret Diaries),* hereinafter referred to as *Secret Diaries*. In spite of its exciting title, this book is a record of the prime minister's appointments and activities day by day, written by two of Tojo's wartime secretaries. Covering the period from his assumption of office until July 18, 1944, the journal also reports some of his thoughts on public matters, and the texts of many of his interviews with statesmen and military officers, but few of these people are Japanese. The work was published by the University of Tokyo Press in 1991.

8. THE LIMITS OF POWER

Secret Diaries was the major source here for Tojo's activities, supplemented by newspaper reports. Shillony was the source for the material about the Japanese elections. The material about General Nishimura comes from *The Death of a General: The Story of General Tomoyuke Yamashita*, Bantam, New York, 1957. The story of the April 1942 bombing of Japan comes from *The Doolittle Raid* by Russell Glines, Orion Books, New York, 1990. The reports of the treatment of the Doolittle fliers come from Lord Russell's *Knights of Bushido*, published by Cassell of London in 1958.

9. THE IMPERIAL WAY

The material about the Imperial Way comes from my own *The Militarists*, published by Donald Fine in New York in 1985. The information about the treatment of conquered peoples comes from Lord Russell's book and the records of the war crimes prosecution in Tokyo. The story of the prisoners dispatched to Korea is from Lord Russell's book cited above. The material about the Diet and political affairs is from Shillony. Part of the quarrel with Foreign Minister Togo was revealed in the Butow book, another part in the *Secret Diaries*. Tojo's words at Palembang, to the effect that each man must work for his daily bread or rice, were thrown back at him in his war crimes trial. So were Tojo's words about the Japanese ideology about prisoners of war.

10. THE DREAM: UNITED ASIA

Joyce Lebra's book gives an excellent view of the development of Pan-Asianism among the Japanese. The various quotations and accounts of military policy here come from that work. Tojo's speech on Greater East Asia is mentioned in *Secret Diaries*. Konoye's position is related in his speeches, radio addresses, and his diary of those days. Togo's position was made known in his own writings and in the Lebra book. The progress of the Greater East Asia bill in the Diet is related in *Secret Diaries*. From the beginning it was clear that a major quarrel between Tojo and General Sugiyama, his rival for leadership of the *Gumbatsu,* was brewing over their differing positions regarding Greater East Asia. Sugiyama insisted that the captured and allied territories be milked for the benefit of the Imperial Army, and Tojo argued for a truly cooperative system. The Army won the argument because of the unwritten rule that an area commander was supreme in his area. Thus, no matter what actions were taken in Tokyo, the Japanese military commander in Rangoon decided what was going to happen in Burma. For this reason—Burma being a case in point—the indigenous people and government began very soon to turn against the Japanese.

11. TOJO DEALS OUT ONE ENEMY

The material in the beginning of this chapter is from *Secret Diaries*. The question "What is a Marine?" is quoted from the diary of Adm. Matome Ugaki, chief of staff to Admiral Yamamoto. The report on the December 1942 Diet meeting is from *Asahi Shimbun*. The account of the stormy meeting between Tojo and General Tanaka comes from the Shillony book, and the story of the important meeting at the Imperial Palace is from *Secret Diaries*.

12. THE CHANGING DREAM

The Army policy had been enunciated in the early days of the Japanese victories. Adherence to the practice of that policy in the captured territories was increasingly the reason that Tojo could not make the Greater East Asia Co-prosperity Sphere a working organization. Everywhere he turned, as is shown in *Secret Diaries,* he ran into obstructions. Most of them came from the unwilling victims of Japanese economic aggression, who adopted a role of passive resistance. Some came from the stupidities of the Army, as in Burma where Japanese troops in 1943 fired on Burmese National Army troops who would not do their bidding. The accounts of the valiant efforts of some Army idealists in behalf of Pan-Asianism are given in the Lebra book. The study of

General Imamura's success in Indonesia comes from the Japan Self-Defense Force history series volumes on the Southern Region.

13. THE COLLAPSE OF HIGH HOPES

The story of the events at Balikpapan in January 1942 is from Lord Russell's book. The report of the events in Shandong Province in 1928 is from Hsu and Chang, and part from other sources I used in *Japan's War*. The details of mistreatment of native populations come from Lord Russell's book and the official proceedings of the war crimes trials. Tojo's Diet speech of February 1943 was reported in the newspapers. The accounts of the meetings of the Greater East Asia Co-prosperity Sphere members in Tokyo that year fill about thirty pages of *Secret Diaries*. Every major speech of those conferences is quoted in full.

14. THE WAR TURNS AROUND

Tojo's Diet speech of December 28, 1942, was reported in *Asahi Shimbun*. The account of the passage of the special emergency law prohibiting political assemblies is from the daily newspapers of December 1942. It was not long before Tojo was forced to defend himself in the Diet against charges that he was behaving in a dictatorial manner. Tojo's January disappearance from the public scene was not recorded anywhere, not even in *Secret Diaries*. It came to light in Courtney Browne's postwar conversations with Tojo's widow, after his death. He had suffered for more than a month with an undiagnosed fever, and was cured by an Oriental physician practicing Chinese medicine, in which Tojo really believed more than modern military medicine.

The meeting with German Ambassador Stahmer in February is fully described in *Secret Diaries,* as are Tojo's visits to the war fronts, but his impressions are not. It was apparent in the diaries, however, that tension between the Army and the Navy was growing worse, not better.

15. "THE ENEMY WILL GROW HASTY . . ."

The various efforts to get rid of Tojo are detailed in Shillony. The Emperor was growing restless in his discontent, sensing that Tojo was withholding much information from him, a fact that became completely apparent in the Terasaki conversations at the end of the war. The details of Tojo's meeting with the Jushin on July 23, 1943 are given in *Secret Diaries*. The source for the stories of Imperial palace discomfort with the Tojo government are from Shillony, who also tells the story of the Nakano suicide.

16. THE THRUST FOR POWER

The trips around the captured territories are noted in *Secret Diaries*. The adventures of Prince Takamatsu and others are from the Shillony book. The material about Tojo's seizure of power over the Army and munitions ministry is from Shillony and from the Boei series that deals with Imperial Headquarters. The material about the Imphal campaign is from Hayashi and Coox's *Kogun: The Japanese Army in the Pacific War*, and from Lebra's book. Tojo's warnings and the Diet sessions reports come from the Japanese newspapers of the day. The concerns and machinations of the imperial princes are from the Kido diary, Shillony, and Hirohito's conversations with Terasaki.

17. TOJO'S LAST CHANCE

The material about the furore around the Imperial Palace is from the Kido diary and the Shillony book. The Emperor told Terasaki about some of this, including a report from seven professors at Tokyo University, Japan's equivalent to Harvard, all of whom recommended that the war must be stopped or Japan would be destroyed, and "the polity" and the future of the Imperial line endangered. Hirohito was very much taken aback by this dispassionate report that confirmed his worst fears.

The material about the abortive Imphal campaign is from *Kogun* and from the Boei series volume on this subject.

18. THE FALL OF SAIPAN (AND TOJO)

The confusion of the Army and Navy commands by Tojo's interference is noted in *Kogun*, Shillony, the Boei series, Kido, and Hirohito in his conversations with Terasaki. Prince Konoye's behavior was noted in his diary, in the biography of Konoye, and in Kido. Shillony discusses part of it. Until the reports of the Terasaki conversations were revealed in 1991 no outsider really knew the extent of the turmoil within the Imperial Palace in the summer of 1944 and thereafter.

19. END OF THE LINE

The discussion of the plot to assassinate Tojo comes from Shillony. The picture of the confusion in the palace and government is given by Hirohito in the Terasaki conversations. The story of the establishment of the Koiso-Yonai government was told by Hirohito to Terasaki.

20. THE WAR NEARS ITS END

The material about Tojo's personal life after his resignation comes from the Courtney Browne book. Browne interviewed Tojo's widow after the execution and apparently she found him to be a sympathetic person, because she told him a good deal about her husband. The collateral material about the state of the war effort and politics in Japan in 1945 is from Shillony and most of all from the daily newspapers of the period. Tojo's acceptance into the ranks of the Jushin and the consultation by the Emperor is told in the Terasaki notes and in Shillony.

21. ORDEAL

Togo's remarks at the Imperial Conference meeting of June 8, 1945, come from *Japan's Longest Day,* by Soichi Oya, published under the title *Nihon no Ichiban Nagaihi* in Tokyo by Bungei Shunju in 1965. So were the following days' discussions. Another source for the recollection of those parlous times was the Emperor's conversations with Terasaki, several years afterwards. The material about Tojo is from the Courtney Browne biography and the Butow book.

22. THE LAST BATTLE

The account of Tojo and the war crimes trials comes from Browne, Butow, and from Sohei Yamate, who served as one of the guards at Sugamo prison and thus saw Tojo every day. The Japanese newspapers sometimes carried articles on the trials, although not every day, as interest in Japan waned in the weight of the voluminous evidence presented by the prosecutions, much of it highly repetitive.

EPILOGUE

Tojo has never achieved martyr status in Japan, and it is doubtful if he ever expected or wished to do so, unlike Hermann Goering, the principal Nazi defendant in the German war crimes trials. The world has passed World War II by. The Japanese evinced a spate of interest during the 1960s and 1970s when the volume of their own official war history was being published. This interest focused especially on campaigns they knew little or nothing about, such as Midway and the battle of the Coral Sea. There also was a certain revival of interest in 1991, the fiftieth anniversary of the coming of the war, but it has been confined mostly to television documentaries and probably will decline long before 1995, the anniversary of the Japanese surrender.

In the early 1990s the military is very thoroughly submerged in the general scheme of government, and during the Persian Gulf war the Japanese people made it quite plain that this is how they want it to be for the future. In 1992, they queasily accepted the government's decision to join United Nations Peacekeeping operations, dispatching members of the Japanese Defense Forces, who had never left Japan since 1945. But it was certain that these operations would be limited and closely watched, by the Japanese and other Asians. No more *Gumbatsu*. No more warlords. No more Tojos.

Bibliography

Akimoto, Ritsuo. *Senso to Minshu*. Tokyo: Gakuyo Shobo, 1977.

Arakawa, Ikuo and Ikimatsu, Keizo. *Kindai nihon shosoi-shi*. Tokyo: Yuhikaku, 1973.

Akisada, Tsuruzo, *Tojo Hideki*. Tokyo: Keizai Ouraisha, 1967.

Asahi Shimbun, eds. *Taiheiyo Senso e no michi*.Tokyo: Asahi Publishing Co., 1963.

Bisson, T. A., *Japan in China*. New York: Octagon Books, 1973.

Browne, Courtney. *Tojo: The Last Banzai*. New York: Holt, Rinehart and Winston, 1967.

Butow, R.J.C. *Tojo and the Coming of the War*. Princeton: Princeton University Press, 1961.

——————. *Japan's Decision to Surrender*. Stanford: Stanford University Press, 1954.

Byas, Hugh. *Government by Assassination*. New York: Alfred A. Knopf, 1942.

Chichibu no miya ke. *Yasuhito shinno jikki*. Tokyo: Yoshikawa kobunkan, 1972.

Causton, E.E.N. *Militarism and Foreign Policy in Japan*. London: Allen & Unwin, 1936.

Dull, Paul S. and Uemura, Michael. *The Tokyo Trials*. Ann Arbor: The University of Michigan Press, 1957.

Glines, Russell. *The Doolittle Raid*. New York: Orion Books, 1990.

Hani, Goro. *Nihon Gonkoku shugi no fukkatsu*. Tokyo: Gendai Hyoronsha, 1974.

Hattori, Takushiro. *Dai to a senso Zenshi*. Tokyo: Hara shobo, 1965.

Hayashi, Saburo and Coox, Alvin D. *Kogun: The Japanese Army in the Pacific War*. Quantico: The Marine Corps Association, 1959.

241

Higashikuni, Naruhiko. *Higashikuni nikki*. Tokyo: Tokuma shoten, 1968.

Honjo, Shigeru. *Honjo nikki*. Tokyo: Hara Shobo, 1967.

Hoshino, Zenshiro; Ooi, Atsushi; and Suekuni, Masao. *Taiheiyo senso hishi*. Tokyo: Zaidan houjin, nihon kokubo kyokai, 1988.

Ike, Nobutaki. *Japan's Decision for War: Records of the 1941 Policy Conferences*. Stanford: Stanford University Press, 1967.

Ito, Masanori. *Gumbatsu Koboshi*. Tokyo: Bungei Shunju Shuin Sha, 1958.

Ito, Takashi; Hirohata, Tadamitsu; and Katashima, Norio. *Tojo naikaku soridaijin kimitsu kiroka*. Tokyo: University of Tokyo Press, 1991.

Iwabuchi, Tatsuo. *Gumbatsu no keifu*. Tokyo: Chuo Koron Sha, 1948.

Joho, Yoshio. *Tojo Hideki*. Tokyo: Fuyo Shoten, 1974.

Kadoya, Fumio. *Showa jidai*. Tokyo: Gakuyo Shobo, 1973.

Kido, Koichi. *Kido koichi nikki* 2 vols. Tokyo: Tokyo Daigaku Shuppan Kai, 1966.

Kiya, Ikusaburo. *Konoe ko hibun*. Tokyo: Takanoyama Shuppan Sha, 1950.

Konoe, Fumimaro. *Konoye nikki*. Tokyo: Kyodo Tsushin Sha, 1968.

Kuroda, Hidetoshi. *Showa gumbatsu*. Tokyo: Tosho Shuppan Sha, 1979.

Lebra, Joyce, ed. *Japan's Greater East Asia Co-Prosperity Sphere in World War II*. Kuala Lumpur: Oxford University Press, 1976.

Li, Lincoln. *The Japanese Army in North China*. Tokyo: Oxford University Press, 1975.

Longhsuen, Hsu and Mingkai, Chang. *History of the Sino-Japanese War*. Taipei: Chungwu, 1971.

Russell, Lord. *Knights of Bushido*. London: Cassell, 1958.

Sakuda, Kotaro. *Tenno to kido*. Tokyo: Heibon Sha, 1948.

Sato, Kenryo. *Tojo Hideki to taiheiyo senso*. Tokyo: Bungei Shunju Shin Sha, 1960.

Shillony, Ben-Ami. *Politics and Culture in Wartime Japan*. Oxford University Press, 1981.

Index

243